MOON

MARRAKESH & BEYOND

LUCAS PETERS

CONTENTS

1 traditional Moroccan *zellij*—mosaic tiles

2 ornate lamps in the medina

3 A tajine cooks in the busy medina.

4 seeking isolation in traditional Bedouin tents

5 the towering Hassan II Mosque in Casablanca

6 camel near Erg Chigaga

DISCOVER
MARRAKESH & BEYOND

You've never experienced a destination quite like the famed "Red City." For years now, Marrakesh has been one of the world's greatest travel destinations, and for good reason. Unlike other destinations that invite you to *see*, Marrakesh invites you to *do*. Whether you want to relax in one of its many gardens, pools, or hammams; learn to cook the Moroccan way in one of the popular cooking courses; or haggle for the best price in the bustling medieval markets, Marrakesh is a destination that is guaranteed to engage all your senses.

My first time in Marrakesh, back in 2009, I felt like I was transported to another universe. Sights like the Saadian Tombs, Bahia Palace, and the Secret Garden are all wonderful, but the real charm of the city is found just around sunset out on the Jemaa el-Fnaa. As the sky darkens, the entire square lights up with traditional music, snake charmers, acrobats, and more. That this has happened every night for a millennium is a modern marvel.

From Marrakesh, you can easily visit the snow-capped heights of the High Atlas Mountains, enjoy year-round suntanning weather along the Atlantic Coast, or travel deep into the Sahara. Many of the mountain destinations can be done as day trips, including hikes through rustic Amazigh villages that look as though they haven't changed in centuries. Along the Atlantic, you'll find some of Morocco's finest beaches in Essaouira, Taghazoute, and Agadir. In the desert, you can discover the nomadic culture of the Sahara and feel the utter amazement of spending a night out on the great sand sea.

Finally, many travelers will find themselves in Casablanca for a day or two on their way to or from the Red City. Beyond the daily rush of big business, there are a few sights to see, including Morocco's largest mosque, as well as a number of great restaurants.

MY FAVORITE
EXPERIENCES

1 Feeling the real pulse of Marrakesh every night on the carnivalesque wonder that is **Jemaa el-Fnaa,** Marrakesh's liveliest public square (page 40).

2 Chilling like a modern-day *pasha* in one of Marrakesh's brilliantly renovated **riads,** or one of the truly special accommodations that dot the surrounding region (page 87).

3 Wandering through the incredible UNESCO World Heritage site of the **Aït Ben Haddou,** one of the finest examples of the kasbah architecture of the desert region and the setting for countless Hollywood productions (page 215).

4 **Hiking** through the rustic Berber villages and humble homes of the majestic **High Atlas Mountains** to experience the older, more ancient Morocco (page 135).

<<<

5 **Pampering yourself in a hammam,** or traditional Moroccan spa, with options available at all levels, from budget to luxury. This bathing ritual is impossible to skip (page 58).

>>>

6 **Cooking a traditional Moroccan meal** at a cooking class, enabling you to take the tastes of Morocco home with you to share with your friends and family (page 53).

<<<

7 **Catching a wave in Taghazoute,** the self-proclaimed "Surf Capital" of Morocco, a touch of San Diego in Morocco (page 203).

>>>

8 **Camping in the Sahara Desert,** disconnecting all of your devices to connect with the infinite universe far, far away from it all (page 233 and page 238).

>>>

9 Cooling off beneath the **Ouzoud Waterfalls,** Morocco's largest, a great escape when the city is scorching (page 124).

10 **Splurging on a five-star meal** at one of Marrakesh's stellar restaurants. To say this city is a foodie's dream is an understatement (page 75).

11 Sipping a G&T at Casablanca's best gin joint, **Rick's Café**—here's looking at you, kid (page 156).

<<<

EXPLORE
MARRAKESH & BEYOND

BEST OF MARRAKESH

Three days and two nights is just enough time to see the biggest sights in the **old medina,** tour one of Marrakesh's popular **gardens,** and get a feel for life here. More days will give you more flexibility and a more relaxed pace. Prioritize getting a **guided tour** your first full day in Marrakesh. This will allow you to quickly see the major sights and avoid getting lost, though getting lost at some point is inevitable.

Before arrival, it's smart to **reserve accommodations, guides,** and any fine-dining **restaurants** you wish to try.

Make sure to download a **map** of Marrakesh (or have a print one with you, such as the one in this guidebook), marked with your accommodation. This will prove invaluable, whether you are in a taxi or walking through the medina for the first time.

Koutoubia Mosque in Marrakesh with flying pigeons

If You Want	Destination	Why Go	Getting There from Marrakesh	How Long to Stay
Mountain Hikes	Ouirgane Valley (page 101)	fresh mountain air; fantastic accommodations	car (1 hour)	half a day for just hiking; consider spending the night
	Toubkal National Park (page 129)	treks through rustic villages; Morocco's most majestic mountain range	car (1.5 hours)	1 day; 3 days if summitting Mount Toubkal
Waterfalls	Ourika Valley (page 113)	hikes along the popular Setti Fatma waterfalls	car (1.5 hours)	half a day for just hiking; a full day is better
	Ouzoud (page 121)	Morocco's largest and grandest waterfall	car or bus (3 hours)	1 day
Movie glamour	Casablanca (page 145)	art deco city center; bustling urban atmosphere; posh bars and restaurants	car or train (3 hours)	overnight before or after an international flight
	Ouarzazate (page 209)	kasbahs; celebrity spotting	car or bus (5 hours)	2 days
Beach relaxation	Essaouira (page 165)	chill, artsy vibes; charming seaside	car or bus (3 hours)	1 day, or 2 days to allow for a fantastic dinner
	Agadir and Taghazoute (page 191)	beach bumming; surfing	car or bus (3 hours)	1 day, or 2 days to catch some early morning surf and an ocean sunset
Existential wonder	Overnight in the Sahara at Erg Chebi or Erg Chigaga (page 222)	desert camping; stargazing; pondering the vastness of the universe	car or bus (12 hours)	3 days: 1 night in the desert and ideally an extra night in Ouarazate on the way there and back

>DAY 1

- Get your bearings in Marrakesh's maze-like **medina,** starting at the **Koutoubia Mosque**—first under the watchful guidance of Saeed, your guide from **Marrakesh by Locals,** and then, if you dare, on your own.

- Spend time lounging on the terrace of your luxurious **riad.**

- Enjoy an exquisite Moroccan dinner at one of Marrakesh's **world-class restaurants** before diving into the city's **legendary nightlife,** from posh bars to exhilarating nightclubs.

A family explores the colorful Bahia Palace.

>DAY 2

- Explore the **Ville Nouvelle,** the Red City's newer neighborhood. This more relaxed day is full of photo ops. Be sure to **pack your camera.**

- Head into Gueliz to visit the **Majorelle Gardens** and the **Palmeraie,** a palm tree-lined district of Marrakesh's most palatial homes.

- Dive back into the medina for a **camel burger** and to browse the offbeat **Perfume Museum.**

- Head out onto the **Jemaa el-Fnaa**

eating out on the lively Jemaa el-Fnaa

to take in the electric atmosphere of this famous square at night.

>DAY 3

- Get to work cooking your own Moroccan meal at **Faim d'Epices,** sipping on artisan tea or coffee while you learn how to make a traditional Moroccan tajine and salad with Chef Nezha.

- After eating the perfectly spiced tajine of your creation, head back to Marrakesh to spend the

afternoon **bartering in the souks,** challenging your friends to see who can get the best price.

- In the late afternoon, head out from Marrakesh on the **adventure** of your choice: **sunbathing on the coast, exploring the desert,** or **trekking through the mountains.**

ATLANTIC COAST ROAD TRIP: ESSAOUIRA, TAGHAZOUTE, AND AGADIR

With its enviable nearly perfect year-round weather and long stretches of sandy beach, this strip of Morocco is something like paradise. In **Essaouira,** you'll have the chance to see a smaller, trendy **medina** with lots of **art** and **music,** while farther south in **Taghazoute,** you can experience a deeper connection to the **ocean** through **surf** and **yoga,** while some **fine dining** and **sunbathing** takes place in nearby **Agadir.** As with most places in Morocco, you'll want to **reserve accommodations in advance** and make **dinner reservations** in Essaouira and Agadir. Though possible to explore by bus, this is a region best seen from the privacy of **your own four wheels.** Just don't forget to pack your **swimsuit.**

BEST ACCOMMODATIONS

- **Kammy Hostel:** For students, backpackers, and shoe-stringers, there is a lot to like about this hostel, from the clean rooms to the friendly staff. Take advantage of the incredibly cheap price in Marrakesh to splurge elsewhere in your travels (page 87).

- **Riad Boussa:** Charming. Stylish. Cozy. Well-located. Riad Boussa ticks all the boxes, and at its price point, for the quality of service, linens, excellent breakfast, and diligent owner, this is one address in Marrakesh that is guaranteed to please (page 89).

- **Domaine Malika:** Enjoy your mountain escape in this four-star property with lots of windows and local touches that will make your stay in the Ourigane Valley truly memorable (page 111).

a cozy room at Riad Boussa

- **Chill Art Hostel:** Perhaps the best hostel in all of Morocco: spacious and clean, with all the amenities you could want. Chill Art Hostel cares about creating intentional travel communities at a great price (page 187).

- **Munga Guesthouse:** Eco-friendly and stylish, this is Taghazoute's premier place to be for great surf, food, friends, and yoga (page 207).

- **Bivouac Chergui:** If you've made it all the way to Erg Chebbi in the Moroccan Sahara, you'll want to glamp it to the max. Take advantage of the air-conditioned bivouac tents, warm hospitality, music, and bonfires, as well as a light show to beat all light shows put on every night by our good friend, the Universe (page 234).

›DAY 1: MARRAKESH TO ESSAOUIRA

- Start out early from Marrakesh right after breakfast to maximize your time in Essaouira. The **N8** national road connects Essaouira directly with Marrakesh on an easy three-hour drive.

The rocky coast hugs the coastal road.

- After dropping your bags off at the **Chill Art Hostel,** get a sense of the town's hippie vibe with lunch at **Yoo Healthy Food.**

- Spend the afternoon and evening wandering the **medina,** ducking into the odd **art gallery,** and soaking up some rays on the **beach** before heading back to your hostel to make some new friends on the **rooftop terrace.**

the famous blue boats docked in Essaouira

>DAY 2: ESSAOUIRA TO TAGHAZOUTE

- After **breakfast** with your new friends, take a last walk through the medina, maybe picking up a piece of funky art as a **souvenir** of your stay.

- From Essaouira, follow the **N1** national road south down the Atlantic Coast. This is a beautiful 2.5-hour drive. Allow for more time to pull over, take a photo, and explore. Consider packing a **picnic lunch** for the way.

- Check into your accommodations and head out to **Banana Beach** for an afternoon in the sun before tucking in for the night.

>DAY 3: TAGHAZOUTE AND AGADIR

- Wake up early to start your day with a little **sunrise yoga.**

- After breakfast, grab a board and head out for a little **surfing.**

- Pack into the car and head down to **Agadir** for lunch, a short 20-30 minute drive south down the **N1.**

- After lunch, take a walk along the **boardwalk,** relax on the **beach,** and head back to Marrakesh for dinner. From Agadir, Marrakesh is an easy 2.5-hour drive east on the **A7** paid toll autoroute.

the chill beach of Agadir

OUARZAZATE, AÏT BEN HADDOU, AND DESERT CAMPING

It's hard to get all the way to Marrakesh and not be drawn in by the romance of the desert, falling under the spell of the vast Sahara. Visit some of the world's finest **kasbahs,** meet up with some of Morocco's friendliest people, and have the night of your life **tucked in beneath the stars.**

This itinerary is best done with a **car.** You'll want to make sure to **reserve accommodations in advance** if you're planning on staying in one of the **desert camps.** Make sure to **keep an eye on the weather.** The desert is a place for extremes, whether that comes in the form of heat, cold, or sandstorms. Pack accordingly.

>DAY 1: MARRAKESH TO AÏT BEN HADDOU AND OUARZAZATE

- Head over the **Tizi n'Tichka pass** via the **N9** national road from Marrakesh. You'll see signs for the **Kasbah Aït Ben Haddou** turnoff about 20 kilometers (14mi) before Ouarzazate. Turn off the N9 and follow this road for 20 minutes.

- Spend the early afternoon exploring this ancient city, and stay for lunch in one of the kasbah cafés.

- To get to **Ouarzazate,** backtrack to the N9 and follow the sign for Ouarzazate, a short 20-minute

A guide strolls the Aït Ben Haddou kasbah.

drive. Explore the maze-like **Taourirt Kasbah** and browse local handicrafts on sale at the **Ensemble Artisanal** before having dinner at **Le Petit Riad** and tucking in for the night.

>DAY 2: OUARZAZATE TO MERZOUGA AND ERG CHEBBI

- Start your morning with a tour of **Atlas** and **CLA Film Studios,** keeping an eye out for Hollywood royalty before hopping in the car. Direction: Merzouga.

A group of friends climbs Erg Chebbi to catch the sunset.

- Follow the **N10** north, past Skoura. At Tinejdad, turn off the N10 and follow the **R702** (Route de Jorf) to Erfoud. Continue on, following the signs for Merzouga, about one hour farther along. Total driving time is around 6-8 hours, depending on stops. **Erg Chebbi** is the towering mass of sand at the end of the road in Merzouga. You can't miss it.

- It's best to arrange **desert camping** ahead of time. Guides can meet you at the parking lot or, even better, in one of the local accommodations that often provide covered parking for you while you **camel-ride** into the sunset.

- Dig in for a **camp-cooked meal,** enjoy the **music and bonfire,** and when the **stars** come out, rejoice.

>DAY 3: LONG DRIVE BACK TO MARRAKESH

- Wake up early to watch the **sun rise over the dunes** before heading back to Merzouga for **breakfast** at one of the local accommodations, included in the price of your desert camp.

- Hit the **long road back to Marrakesh,** retracing your steps to **Ouarzazate,** over the **Tizi n'Tichka pass** and on to Marrakesh. You will want to make sure to cross the mountain pass before nightfall. Budget your time accordingly.

- Consider **stopping over for an extra night** in Ouarzazate, nearby **Skoura** or the **Dades Gorge** to break up the drive back. For more information on how to do this, consult the *Moon Morocco* guidebook.

tea service in the desert

BEFORE YOU GO

WHEN TO GO

Morocco is a country with **four distinct seasons,** following other countries in the northern hemisphere, with **summer** lasting June-August, **fall** September-November, **winter** December-February, and **spring** March-May.

FALL

The **beginning of fall** is one of the better travel periods, after the kids have gone back to school and many European vacationers are back to work. Daytime temperatures are about perfect along the coast, averaging 16°C (60°F) to 27°C (80°F), and the **water is generally warm** throughout **September.** It's a real possibility that you'll have an entire beach to yourself. Toward the **end of fall** the Sahara becomes cooler, with **October** generally being an excellent month for **desert excursions. November** is a slower travel month, so deals can sometimes be had with hotels, restaurants, and tours around this period.

WINTER

December is becoming a trendy time to visit Morocco, with many holiday-goers Christmas shopping in the medinas of Marrakesh, though temperatures can be surprisingly **chilly,** averaging 6°C (43°F) at night and 21°C (70°F) during the day. **January** typically

an artisan plies his trade

kicks off the **short ski season** in **Oukaïmeden,** though the rest of the country is quieter, with some hotels and restaurants closing down for the month. More remote roads are sometimes washed out during the **heavy seasonal rains.**

SPRING

Spring is probably the **best all-around time to visit,** with temperatures typically around 15°C (58°F) at night and around 26°C (78°F) throughout the day. The mountain snows have cleared, valleys are in bloom, and the entire country north of the **High Atlas** seems to erupt in shades of green, while the not-too-distant **Sahara** is warming up for the summer.

SUMMER

During the **summer,** temperatures soar inland, especially in cities like **Marrakesh,** averaging 38°C (98°F) with many days well above 40°C (102°F), making travel difficult and unbearably hot. Weather-wise, this is the **best time to be on the coasts. August** is crowded, as many Europeans and Moroccans have the month for vacation. Moroccan families crowd the beaches of **Essaouira,** while Europeans flock to the packaged resort town of **Agadir** and other beaches along the South Atlantic Coast. The **Sahara should be avoided** during the summer, as travel is just too hot, with daytime highs well over 45°C (113°F).

RAMADAN AND OTHER ISLAMIC HOLIDAYS

The busiest travel times for Moroccans, outside of the August vacation, revolve around the Islamic calendar, with the two largest holidays being the holy month of fasting, **Ramadan,** and the biggest holiday of the year, **Eid al-Adha.** Travelers to Morocco will encounter traveling hiccups and delays during these times. However, despite this, for Muslim and non-Muslim travelers curious about Islam, visiting Morocco during Ramadan or any of the other religious holidays can be a rewarding experience. Many mosques have all-night *dikr,* a kind of spiritual chanting done in a group, while many families will open their doors to entertain guests. Some of the liveliest nights in Morocco happen during Ramadan.

the enormous Erg Chebbi sand formation of the Sahara

RAMADAN

During the month of Ramadan, Moroccans are fasting throughout from sunrise to sunset. **Many businesses are closed,** including restaurants, or have shortened opening hours. Traveling by **public transport** can be difficult, with many **delays in service.** The exact dates of Ramadan and other Muslim holidays are not known in Morocco until there is a sighting of the moon by religious officials that matches with Islamic scripture.

- **Currency:** Moroccan dirham (abbreviated as "Dh" in this book and "MAD" on currency exchanges)

- **Conversion rate:** 1Dh = .09 EUR; .095 USD; .084 GBP. Rates fluctuate. A good rule of thumb is that 10Dh is about 1 USD or 1 EUR.

- **Entry requirements:** No visa needed for travelers from the US, Canada, UK, Europe, Australia, or New Zealand. South African travelers need a travel or work visa to enter the country.

- **Emergency numbers:** Morocco has a few standard emergency phone numbers. Each are only a couple of digits long and can be dialed from any Moroccan phone, though English will not generally be spoken. For most emergencies, travelers are best served calling their local consulates.

A man pauses to gather thoughts before prayer.

- **Medical/Fire:** 15

- **City Police:** 19

- **Royal Gendarmerie** (police force outside of major cities): 177

- **Time zone:** GMT (during Ramadan, time is moved back one hour)

- **Electrical system:** European, round 2-prong plugs, 220 volt

- **Opening hours:** Vary dramatically. Most businesses—such as banks, post offices, and pharmacies—keep closely to posted hours, typically 8:30am-3:30pm. Smaller, locally owned businesses will often be open long hours, but will often close for 15 minutes-1 hour for daily prayers (five times a day). Some shops will open as early as sunrise while others will not open until after lunch. In most parts of Morocco, the best times to get things done are usually right before and after sunset.

Roughly speaking, Ramadan should fall between April 23 and May 23 in 2020; between April 12 and May 11 in 2021; and April 2 and May 1 in 2022. The end of Ramadan is marked by **Eid al-Fitr,** often called Eid es-Seghir, or the "little holiday."

EID AL-ADHA

Eid al-Adha, often called plainly the "big holiday" or Eid al-Kabir, is easily the **biggest holiday** in Morocco. It is a **three-day festival** that occurs two moon cycles (or about two months) after the end of Ramadan and is the **biggest feast in the country,** marking when Ibrahim (Abraham) was willing to sacrifice his son for God. **Trains, public buses,** and *grands taxis* are **impossibly full** directly before and after this festival.

BUDGETING

Espresso: 10Dh
Beer: 40-60Dh
Glass of wine: 40Dh+
Sandwich: 15-25Dh
Lunch or dinner: 20-200Dh+
Hotel: 400Dh+
Car rental: 100Dh+
Gasoline/petrol: 12Dh/liter
One-way bus/train fare: 50-120Dh,
variable depending on distance

local cash machine hidden in the souks

GETTING THERE

FROM EUROPE

UK and EU travelers have a selection of **direct flights** with connections from most major European hubs to **Agadir** and **Marrakesh.**

From **Spain** and **France,** it is possible to enter the country by **ferry** to **Tangier** or the Spanish exclaves of **Ceuta** or **Melilla,** where you will then cross the land border into Morocco. Of these options, the quickest, easiest, and most practical is the 35-minute ferry that connects **Tarifa, Spain,** directly with Tangier.

FROM OUTSIDE EUROPE

Most travelers from **Australia, New Zealand, North America,** and **South Africa** will arrive to the **Mohammed V International Airport** in **Casablanca.** Morocco's national airline carrier, Royal Air Maroc, has a monopoly on nonstop flights to and from North America, connecting Casablanca with Boston, New York, Miami, Washington DC, and Montreal. All other carriers in North America, as well as all flights from Australia, New Zealand, and South Africa, stop over in Europe or the Middle East.

GETTING AROUND

Travel within the country is mostly accomplished by **train, bus,** and **car.** Within each city, **walking** is usually the best way to get around, though *petits taxis* are also readily available for longer distances.

BY PLANE

There are a few nonstop in-country flights leaving Casablanca, including **Agadir, Marrakesh,** and **Ouarzazate.**

A musician strums his melody to entertain the crowds.

BY TRAIN AND BUS

There are two primary **train lines.** The first line connects down the Atlantic Coast from Tangier to Casablanca and then turns inland to Marrakesh. The other follows a northeast trajectory from Casablanca through Fez to Oujda in the northeastern corner of the country. The new Al-Boraq high-speed train connects Tangier with Rabat (about 1 hour) and Casablanca (about 2 hours).

Between cities not connected by train there are **local and private buses,** as well as *grands taxis* that connect cities and towns.

BY CAR

Renting a car provides more mobility to travelers. The roads in Morocco are in generally good condition, though lighting is an issue for night driving.

TRAVEL DOCUMENTS

UK, EU, Australian, New Zealand, Canadian, and US nationals need to present a valid **passport** upon entry. Your passport should be valid for at least six months from your planned date of departure from Morocco, though you will not need to present proof of return. Customs officials will stamp a valid **90-day tourist visa** in your passport on arrival.

South African passport holders will need to obtain a **visa** before arriving, and will be required to provide proof of return travel and funds to support their stay in Morocco. Contact the Moroccan Embassy in South Africa for more information.

WHAT TO PACK

CLOTHING

Morocco is called a cold country with a hot sun. The cold is the most surprising element to travelers visiting Morocco for the first time. Outside of the summer months, temperatures can drop, particularly at night. Below-freezing temperatures in parts of the desert and the mountains are common and should be expected. Pack **sweatshirts, hoodies, warm pants, thick socks, waterproof shoes,** and a **waterproof coat** outside of the summer months—especially during the winter. Along the coasts, temperatures are regulated by the ocean and rarely get to freezing, but a light **rain jacket** should be packed along for all seasons for coastal exploration, along with a **bathing suit.**

trekkers setting off from Imlil

SUN PROTECTION

All travelers should pack to protect against the sun. Bring a **wide-brimmed hat, sunglasses,** and **waterproof SPF 100 or higher sunscreen** (though this you can find at most pharmacies), as well as light **long-sleeved shirts** and **pants,** particularly if you plan on going to the desert or going into the higher altitudes of the mountain ranges.

FOR HIKERS AND TREKKERS

Those interested in trekking through the mountains should pack **collapsible trekking poles, waterproof hiking boots,** and **maps** of the region whenever possible. Though not necessary, a good pair of **binoculars** for birding and spying wildlife should be considered.

TOILETRIES AND CREATURE COMFORTS

A pair of **earplugs,** an **eye mask,** and a **light scarf** to use as a shade for bus, train, and *grand taxi* trips will make traveling through the country much more pleasant.

It is a very good idea to travel with **toilet paper,** as many public restrooms in Morocco do not supply it.

ELECTRONICS

Morocco runs on the European **220-volt system,** with electronics having two round plugs. Most electronics, such as laptops and battery chargers, require only a **plug adapter** and do not need a voltage regulator from 110 to 220, though check your device to be sure. Plug adapters can be easily purchased online or at your local electronics store and are a necessity for those looking to bring their cell phones, tablets, laptops, or cameras.

MARRAKESH

Ancient bamboo-covered souks,

an endless array of bazaars, five-star restaurants, lush palm groves, snake charmers, fortune tellers, and characters of all sizes and shapes make up modern-day Marrakesh.

Any visitor to Marrakesh would be forgiven for believing this city sprang directly from the pages of *One Thousand and One Arabian Nights*. The snowcapped peaks of the High Atlas Mountains provide a picturesque backdrop to this living dream that is in a near-constant state of transformation. From the bustling souks, circus-like

HIGHLIGHTS

✪ **JEMAA EL-FNAA:** Spend a night reveling in the carnival charm of Morocco's most famous public square (page 40).

✪ **KOUTOUBIA MOSQUE:** Take in the most well-preserved Almohad-era minaret in all of Morocco (page 40).

✪ **MARRAKESH MUSEUM:** Discover the history, culture, and people of the region in this converted palace (page 43).

✪ **BAHIA PALACE:** The most splendidly decorated of Marrakesh's many palaces was formerly the residence of the sultan's most cherished concubine (page 47).

✪ **MAJORELLE GARDENS:** Take a stroll through this art deco masterpiece curated by famed fashion designer Yves Saint Laurent (page 51).

✪ **MOROCCAN COOKING CLASSES:** Take a piece of Morocco home with you to share with your friends and family by learning how to make your own tajine, *pastilla,* or couscous (page 53).

✪ **STORYTELLING AT CAFÉ CLOCK:** Experience the ancient art of oral storytelling as it has been practiced for generations (page 63).

✪ **THE SOUKS OF MARRAKESH:** It's more than a shopping experience—wandering through the labyrinthine souks is a real cultural pastime (page 66).

✪ **STAYING IN A *RIAD*:** Spend a night, or more, in one of the hundreds of traditional refurbished Moroccan *riad* guesthouses, each offering its own unique touch (page 87).

atmosphere, and frenetic nightlife of the Jemaa el-Fnaa, to the contemplative quiet of the Menara Gardens, to candlelit dinners and spiritual tranquility tucked in the quieter corners of the medina, this is a city that opens like a ripe pomegranate, inviting travelers of all stripes.

Since the Almoravids first crowned it their capital in the 11th century, Marrakesh has played a historically important role in Moroccan and world history. Marrakesh was so identified with Morocco that many travelers referred to it as "Morocco City," while in countries such as Pakistan, the entire country of Morocco is still known as "Marrakesh." As you probably already know, Marrakesh is popularly also called the "Red City," "Pink City," or "Ochre City" because of the red earth used in the construction of the medina and medina walls.

To experience Marrakesh, you no longer have to take the "Marrakesh Express" train from Tangier after a long ferry ride from Spain. Its airport is well-connected with daily flights from over 20 European cities, three per day from Paris alone. The fact is that "Kesh"—as the locals call it—is a "must-see" destination, now firmly established beside London, Paris, Tokyo, or New York. However, Kesh is not a city to simply "see." Rather, it is a place to experience.

Take a stroll through the gardens, learn how to make your own tajine in a cooking class, work on your bartering skills in the souks, inhale the night musk along the medina walls, and then dance your tail off until late into the night. There are countless activities to do, restaurants to try, and accommodations to fit nearly every budget and interest. So maybe it shouldn't come as a surprise that Marrakesh is one of the most popular destinations in the world.

Tourism is nothing new in Marrakesh. Moroccans, foreigners, and traders from around the world have long been coming here for business, pleasure, and a taste of the exotic, making it a great crossroads of language, culture, and civilization. Coupled with a healthy supply of water from the mountains, Marrakesh's strategic location—at the end of the famed Salt Road that crossed the Sahara, near the ports of Agadir and Essaouira, as well as on the major routes north to modern-day Casablanca and Rabat— ensured its importance. Some travelers make their way over the Sahara and to the Atlantic, while others stay in Marrakesh to experience life at the crossroads. The diversity that has marked this city through its long history continues to thrive in its medina and Ville Nouvelle.

As a longtime trade station, the old medina of Marrakesh has evolved over the centuries into a honeycomb of souks, representing a variety of different neighborhoods. Each of the souks was originally the home of an individual group of shops with certain specializations. Metal workers, wood workers, leather workers, spice merchants, and others each had their own distinct district in the medina, recognizable from the sights, sounds, and smells associated with each trade. Today, tourist bazaars are crowding out some of the more specialized businesses, though vestiges of the original souks are still identifiable. Because of the interest from travelers coming to Marrakesh, there has been a small revival of traditional crafts, which is helping to keep these artisan industries alive.

The Ville Nouvelle, which includes the neighborhoods of Gueliz and Hivernage, offers some of the best restaurants in town and a few of the best parks in Morocco, not to mention some of the best nightclubs in Africa. Though there is not a lot of sightseeing to do in the Ville Nouvelle, a trip through the palm groves could easily make it on your itinerary, perhaps coupled with an early morning at the Majorelle Gardens. Shopaholics and foodies should plan on spending some time browsing in the shops and nibbling in the restaurants.

Of course, a stay in Marrakesh would not be complete without a night out on the Jemaa el-Fnaa, the giant plaza that is the carnival heart of the city. Fortune tellers, jugglers, medicine men, musicians, henna artists, storytellers, and snake charmers all gather to entertain the crowds as they have for a millennium. Sip on freshly squeezed orange juice (4Dh) and peer through the veil of smoke from the grilling lamb, chicken, and beef brochettes on offer at the numerous food stands while the Gnawa drumbeat rhythmically draws you further into the festivities. This is a quintessential Marrakeshi scene and something to behold.

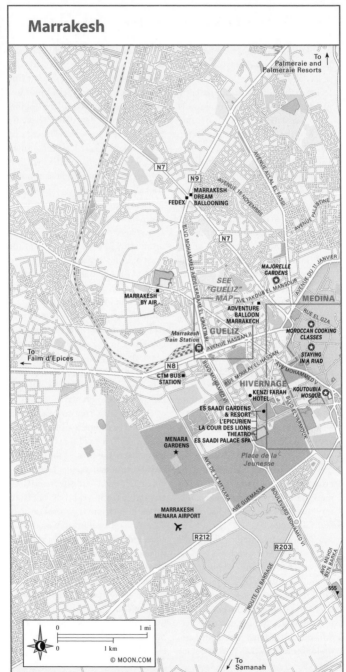

Marrakesh

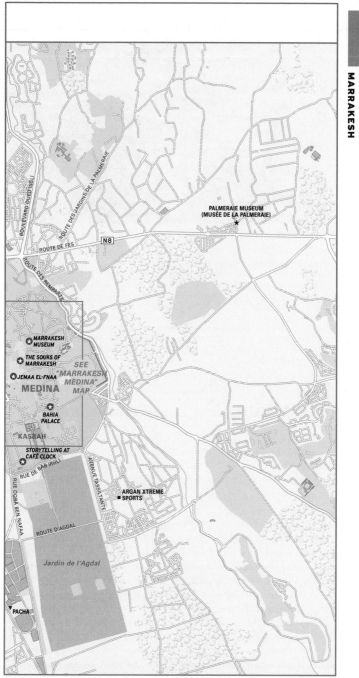

PHOTOGRAPHY ETIQUETTE

taking a photo over the Jemaa el-Fnaa

Among photographers, Morocco is known for being both extremely beautiful and extremely hard to photograph. This is particularly the case when attempting to photograph people. Over the last 20 years, tourism in Morocco has grown exponentially. In some ways, this has been positive, with better public transportation and better citywide infrastructure, as well as the fostering of cross-cultural understanding and exchange. However, over-aggressive tourists with their cameras pointed in the faces of people going about their daily lives have taken a toll. There can sometimes be a real aggression toward photographers. In no place in Morocco is this more apparent than in Marrakesh. Here are a few tips to help you grab the most Instagrammable photos.

ORIENTATION

Like other Moroccan cities, Marrakesh is divided into two parts: the old medina and the Ville Nouvelle.

MEDINA

The old medina of Marrakesh is one of the largest in Morocco. The main square, **Jemaa el-Fnaa,** a UNESCO World Heritage site since 1985, can easily be found—it's hard to miss the towering mass of the Koutoubia Mosque, the central meeting point of the medina. Easily found signs peppered throughout the medina also point the way to the Jemaa el-Fnaa. Streets are usually unnamed; there are many confusing, often frustrating, dead ends; and though the rest of

the medina is divided into neighborhoods, these are generally indistinguishable to most visitors and are not well signed. Many locals, however, do know the neighborhoods, so if you're staying in the medina or looking for a restaurant, it's a good idea to know the name, if only to ask someone to point you in the right direction.

It is incredibly easy to become disoriented in these old medieval cities. Though Google and Apple maps of the Marrakesh medina are quite good, you'll still likely get turned around a time or two. Not putting pressure on yourself to see a bunch of sights makes it easier to stop in at a café or dawdle a bit longer over lunch, or perhaps reserve that much-needed massage, all

- It is respectful to **ask** to photograph a person or a person's shop before taking a photo. Most shop owners will agree, particularly if you've just spent some money in the shop. Strangers on the street will usually decline, but they will be much happier you asked, and you may be surprised: Every once in a while someone will say yes!

- Occasionally you will be asked to **pay,** generally 5-10Dh. In the Jemaa el-Fnaa, it is customary to pay for photos featuring the various monkey handlers and snake charmers. The going rate is 20Dh-100Dh; this is how they make their living. However, if you spend some time here, you probably won't like how they treat the animals.

- Photographers who are polite, ask permission, and tip occasionally when asked generally **make new friends** and have a pleasant experience, though this isn't to say there won't be some aggression, particularly with street photography.

- **Use Darija.** This is a great time to practice. Know your please (*afek*) and thank you (*shokran*) in Moroccan Arabic. It can do wonders, particularly in smaller towns.

- **Shoot landscapes.** If you're obviously shooting a landscape, you likely won't be bothered at all.

- For those interested in street photography, it's a good strategy to **tuck away in a quiet corner,** carefully compose your shot, and wait for the right person to walk by.

- **Be discreet.** If your camera has a silent shutter option, this can be a good way to be more discreet with your photography. Also consider the gear you're using. The bigger and more intimidating, the more likely it is you'll provoke undesirable reactions. A good smartphone camera can work wonders.

- Most people love **selfies.** If you have an experience with someone and would like to mark it with that person by taking a selfie, this has become the standard. Moroccans are no exception to the selfie craze.

- Just remember—even though you're shooting, it's not a war. **Smile and be friendly,** and if someone gives you a hard time, be humble and apologetic.

a scooter jets through the small medina streets

in the name of relaxation, particularly after an adventure in getting lost, which is bound to happen and is part of the experience.

In the medina is where you'll find the majority of sights that are of touristic interest. From the Jemaa el-Fnaa, the popular **souks** of Marrakesh, the traditional **artisans,** and residential neighborhoods lie to the north. To the east are streets lined with cafés, shops, and *riads.* There are residential neighborhoods to be found here as well as the **tanneries.** To the south you'll find the **mellah, kasbah,** and current **royal palace** of the king of Morocco, while to the west sprawls the **Koutoubia complex** and the most elaborate of the **city gardens.**

Gates and Thoroughfares

Several gates enter into the old medina. Bab Jdid leads from the west, past the splendid Koutoubia Gardens down Avenue Houman el Fetouaki. Bab Nkob is perhaps the most used gate, separating the old medina from Gueliz near the Place de la Liberté along Avenue Mohammed V. To the north, near the *gare routière,* are Bab Doukkala and Bab Moussoufa, used often by those arriving by *grand taxi.* There is a handy guarded parking lot near Bab Doukkala for drivers, while the entrance by Bab Moussoufa provides a straight path along Rue el Gaz (which turns into Rue Riad el Arous) to the back of the souks. To the east is Bab Lalla Aouda, near the tanneries, and it's one of the better signed gates in the medina.

Avenue Mohammed V cuts through the medina, right between the Jemaa el-Fnaa and the Koutoubia Mosque.

VILLE NOUVELLE

Avenue Mohammed V is also the main artery leading from the medina into the Ville Nouvelle. The Ville Nouvelle is divided into a few neighborhoods, with Gueliz and Hivernage being the most important.

Gueliz

Gueliz is the most popular section of the Ville Nouvelle, with lots of shopping and popular cafés and restaurants. Gueliz extends north and west from the city beyond the large Place de la Liberté. Here you will find the train station as well as the major bus stations. The train station is along Avenue Hassan II, turning west from Avenue Mohammed V at Place du 18 Novembre. The Supratours station is behind the train station, and just a block south of the Supratours station is the CTM station. Most grands taxis and other bus companies use the gare routière, outside of the medina near Bab Doukkala.

Hivernage

Hivernage is the other neighborhood in the Ville Nouvelle most travelers should know. It's west of the medina, southwest of the Place de la Liberté. The five-star resorts are located here, along with some of the more upscale dining options, bars and nightclubs, and big boulevards. You'll also find the Menara Gardens here.

PLANNING YOUR TIME

Most people spend at least two to three days in Marrakesh. This is just enough time to see the sights, absorb the life in the medina, and make a trip into the Ville Nouvelle to see the Majorelle Gardens, the Palmeraie (Palm Groves), and a few of the other attractions, while also giving yourself enough time to lounge for an afternoon in the luxurious spread of your *riad.* The wide variety of restaurants and the abundant entertainment make longer stays feasible and often (happily) irresistible.

For those looking to spend more time in the area, Marrakesh can serve as a base for a number of other activities, including treks into the High Atlas and longer seaside adventures in Agadir and Essaouira. The more popular day trips are to High Atlas hiking destinations such as the Ourika Valley and Imlil. Though guides are not necessary, they can be helpful, providing insights into the local culture and taking you to some sights and local villages off the trodden tour circuit. Using a guide can also be a time saver for those who want to see more of the country but don't want to spend the time learning the often-confusing network of roads. However, after a few days in Marrakesh, most travelers opt to continue their journey, either heading west to the Atlantic or southeast, up and over the mountains and into the Sahara. Whatever your direction, continuing on from Marrakesh is easy enough, though you may find yourself wishing you had spent a little more time here. Travelers planning on spending a week in Marrakesh only to find themselves passing a lifetime in the Red City are not unheard of.

Itinerary Ideas

MARRAKESH ON DAY 1

1 After an expansive Moroccan breakfast at Riad Boussa, strap on a comfy pair of walking shoes.

2 Meet Saeed, your English-speaking guide from Marrakesh by Locals, at the Koutoubia Mosque and get ready for an exploratory outing to some of the Red City's most iconic landmarks. Your tour will include lunch at a local eatery digging into a Marrakeshi classic: *tangia*.

3 Dive back into the medina and learn some tricks from Saeed to help you navigate the confusing twists and turns of the souks on your own.

4 After a lot of walking, unwind on the terrace of your *riad* enjoying the late afternoon before cozying into La Table Badia and enjoy an exquisite Moroccan dinner, replete with dishes that will defy your taste buds to identify which is the sweet and which is the savory.

5 Stop by the Skybar at Le Salama for a nightcap before testing your medina knowledge to find your way back to your *riad*.

MARRAKESH ON DAY 2

This more relaxed day is full of photo ops. Be sure to pack your camera.

1 Head into Gueliz and hop on the red bus run by Alsa for a quick tour of the medina.

2 Hop off the red bus at the Majorelle Gardens. Get there early for a little quiet. This will be a great spot for a photo op in the gardens with the stunning cobalt blue backdrop.

3 Take the bus out to the Palmeraie. Be sure to grab a seat on the top to

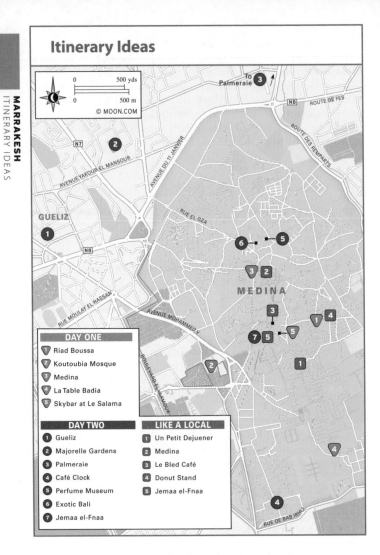

Itinerary Ideas

0 — 500 yds
0 — 500 m
© MOON.COM

To Palmeraie ③

N8 ROUTE DE FES

ROUTE DES REMPARTS

N7

AVENUE YAKOUB EL MANSOUR

AVENUE DU 11 JANVIER

GUELIZ

N8

RUE EL GZA

⑥ — ⑤

MEDINA

③ ②

③

RUE MOULAY EL HASSAN

AVENUE MOHAMMED V

⑦ ⑤ ⑤

① ④

②

BOULEVARD EL MANSOUR

①

④

RUE DE BAB IRHLI

DAY ONE
1 Riad Boussa
2 Koutoubia Mosque
3 Medina
4 La Table Badia
5 Skybar at Le Salama

DAY TWO
1 Gueliz
2 Majorelle Gardens
3 Palmeraie
4 Café Clock
5 Perfume Museum
6 Exotic Bali
7 Jemaa el-Fnaa

LIKE A LOCAL
1 Un Petit Dejuener
2 Medina
3 Le Bled Café
4 Donut Stand
5 Jemaa el-Fnaa

see into some of the more palatial spreads. Dab on a bit of extra sunscreen if needed.

4 For lunch, it would be hard to pass up diving back into the medina for a camel burger at **Café Clock.**

5 After lunch, take in a few museums that capture your fancy, like the offbeat **Perfume Museum.**

6 Relax into dinner at **Exotic Bali** for a taste of the Far East and experience a delicious array of Indonesian food prepared in a beautiful Moroccan *riad*.

7 Head out onto the **Jemaa el-Fnaa** to take in the very best of Marrakesh's nightlife.

MARRAKESH LIKE A LOCAL

1 After waking up at Kammy Hostel, head toward the Jemaa el-Fnaa, but stop for a quick breakfast first at **Un Petit Dejuener.**

2 After a good breakfast, do what any good Moroccan does when they first visit Marrakesh: get lost. Spend your first hours wandering through the souks, dodging scooters, and puzzling your way out of the **medina.** For lunch, ask for the nearest *bissara* **stand** and get elbow-to-elbow with the local workmen eating lunch. Don't be afraid to ask for seconds.

3 Make your way back to the Jemaa el-Fnaa (follow the signs) and sit out on a terrace sipping a coffee or mint tea. **Le Bled Café** is a good spot to delve into the Moroccan art of people-watching.

4 After a coffee, head to the **donut stand** for a fresh, crispy late-afternoon treat.

5 As the sun sets, head out on the **Jemaa el-Fnaa** and enjoy the festive atmosphere, musicians, storytellers, soothsayers, snake charmers, monkey handlers, and the rest of the madness. When hunger calls, head to one of the food stands on the Jemaa el-Fnaa and order up dinner. Just be sure to bargain.

Sights

MEDINA

Though not the largest medina in Morocco—that distinction belongs to Fez—the Marrakesh medina is one of the liveliest. Most of the sights in Marrakesh are within the walls of the medina, as are numerous cafés, restaurants, and renovated *riads*.

Most of the sights in the medina can all be seen in a day, most efficiently with a guide. You can usually book a reliable guide through your lodging. It's more relaxing to spread sightseeing out over a few days, clustering sights with their neighborhoods, while the rest of the time is spent dining, shopping, or just wandering the labyrinthine streets, taking in the Marrakeshi way of life.

The famed Marrakesh souks are gathered north of the Jemaa el-Fnaa. Though many of the original artisans

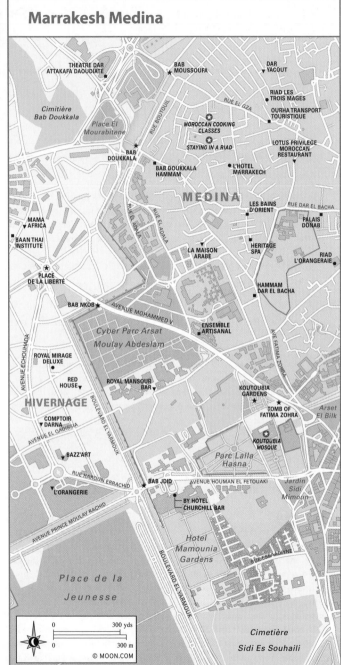

Marrakesh Medina

THEATRE DAR
ATTAKAFA DAOUDIATE

BAB
MOUSSOUFA

DAR
YACOUT

Cimitière
Bab Doukkala

Place El
Mourabitene

RUE EL GZA

RIAD LES
TROIS MAGES

OURHA TRANSPORT
TOURISTIQUE

MOROCCAN COOKING
CLASSES

STAYING IN A RIAD

LOTUS PRIVILEGE
MOROCCAN
RESTAURANT

RUE BOUTOUIL

BAB
DOUKKALA

BAB DOUKKALA
HAMMAM

L'HOTEL
MARRAKECH

MEDINA

RUE DAR EL BACHA

LES BAINS
D'ORIENT

PALAIS
DONAB

MAMA
AFRICA

RUE EL ADALA

RUE EL ADALA

LA MAISON
ARABE

HERITAGE
SPA

RIAD
L'ORANGERAIE

BAAN THAI
INSTITUTE

PLACE
DE LA LIBERTÉ

HAMMAM
DAR EL BACHA

BAB NKOB

AVENUE MOHAMMED V

ENSEMBLE
ARTISANAL

Cyber Parc Arsat
Moulay Abdeslam

AVE FATIMA ZOHRA

AVENUE ECHOUHADA

ROYAL MIRAGE
DELUXE

RED
HOUSE

ROYAL MANSOUR
BAR

KOUTOUBIA
GARDENS

TOMB OF
FATIMA ZOHRA

Arset
El Bilk

HIVERNAGE

BOULEVARD EL YARMOUK

COMPTOIR
DARNA

AVENUE EL QADISSIA

KOUTOUBIA
MOSQUE

BAZZ'ART

RUE HAROUN ERRACHID

Parc Lalla
Hasna

Jardin
Sidi
Mimoun

L'ORANGERIE

BAB JDID

AVENUE HOUMAN EL FETOUAKI

BY HOTEL
CHURCHILL BAR

AVENUE PRINCE MOULAY RACHID

Hotel
Mamounia
Gardens

RUE ESSAADIYNE

BOULEVARD EL YARMOUK

Place de la
Jeunesse

Cimitière
Sidi Es Souhaili

0   300 yds

0   300 m

© MOON.COM

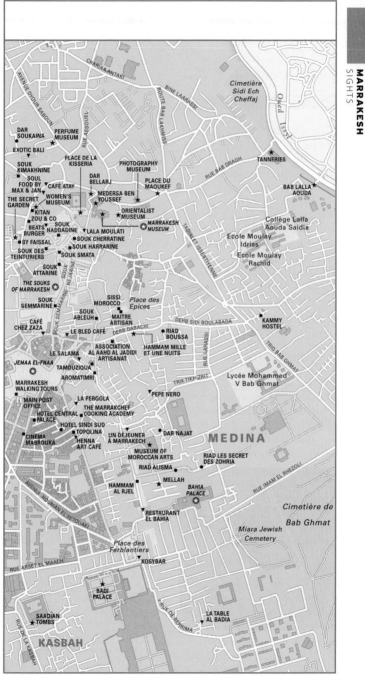

DAR
SOUKAINA

PERFUME
MUSEUM

EXOTIC BALI

SOUK
KIMAKHNINE

SOUL
FOOD BY
MAX & JAN

CAFÉ ATAY

WOMEN'S
MUSEUM

THE SECRET
GARDEN

KITAN
ZOU & CO

BEATS
BURGER
BY FAISSAL

SOUK
HADDADINE

SOUK DES
TEINTURIERS

SOUK
ATTARINE

THE SOUKS
OF MARRAKESH

SOUK
SEMMARINE

CAFÉ
CHEZ ZAZA

SOUK
ABLEUH

LE BLED CAFÉ

LE SALAMA

JEMAA EL-FNAA

TAMOUZIQUA

AROMATIMRI

MARRAKESH
WALKING TOURS

MAIN POST
OFFICE

LA PERGOLA

HOTEL CENTRAL
PALACE

THE MARRAKCHEF
COOKING ACADEMY

HOTEL SINDI SUD

CINÉMA
MABROUKA

TOPOLINA

HENNA
ART CAFÉ

UN DEJEUNER
À MARRAKECH

MUSEUM OF
MOROCCAN ARTS

RIAD ALISMA

HAMMAM
AL RJEL

MELLAH

RESTAURANT
EL BAHIA

PLACE DE LA
KISSERIA

DAR
BELLARJ

MEDERSA BEN
YOUSSEF

LALA MOULATI

SOUK CHERRATINE

SOUK HARRARINE

SOUK SMATA

SISSI
MOROCCO

MAITRE
ARTISAN

ASSOCIATION
AL AAHD AL JADIDI
ARTISANAT

ORIENTALIST
MUSEUM

MARRAKESH
MUSEUM

Place des
Epices

DERB DABACHI

RIAD
BOUSSA

HAMMAM MILLE
ET UNE NUITS

PEPE NERO

DAR NAJAT

PHOTOGRAPHY
MUSEUM

PLACE DU
MAOUKEF

DERB SIDI BOULABADA

KAMMY
HOSTEL

RIAD LES SECRET
DES ZOHRIA

BAHIA
PALACE

CHARIAA ANTAKT

BINE LAARASSI

ROUTE BAB LAKHNISS

RUE ASSOUEL

Cimetière
Sidi Ech
Cheffaj

Oued
Issyl

RUE BAB DBAGH

TANNERIES

BAB LALLA
AOUDA

Collège Lalla
Aouda Saidia

Ecole Moulay
Idriss

Ecole Moulay
Rachid

TABAL ET ISSEBTYENNE

RUE LAFRASSI

TRIQ BAB GHMAT

Lycée Mohammed
V Bab Ghmat

TRIK TIKHIZIRT

MEDINA

RUE IMAM EL RHEZOLI

Cimetière de
Bab Ghmat

Miara Jewish
Cemetery

AVENUE HOUMAN EL RETOUAKI

Place des
Ferblantiers

KOSYBAR

RUE ARSET EL MAACH

BADI
PALACE

RUE DE BERRIMA

SAADIAN
TOMBS

RUE DE LA KASBAH

KASBAH

LA TABLE
AL BADIA

have moved to separate quarters, displaced by the numerous bazaars, vestiges of this artisan history remain. See the Shopping section (page 66) for detailed information about the souks.

See the Shopping section (page 66) for detailed information about the souks.

TOP EXPERIENCE

✪ JEMAA EL-FNAA

The giant plaza comprising the center of the medina is the Jemaa el-Fnaa (also Djemma el-F'nâ and other variations), one of the most storied public squares in history. By day, it looks like little more than a dusty crossways of traffic with *grands taxis* and donkey-pulled carts plodding through the pedestrian traffic. There are usually a few monkey handlers and snake charmers about. The best action doesn't start until late afternoon, after the hottest part of the day, and continues well into the night. This is when most of the performers and musicians really come alive. Food stands grill all sorts of meat, fish, and vegetables, and there are also stands for *harira* soup and freshly squeezed orange juice. The feel of this is something like a large county fair, but mingled with the essentials of Moroccan culture in all of its carnivalesque glory.

the night bustles out on the Jemaa el-Fnaa

Beware of pickpockets in more crowded areas. The LGBT community should be aware that this is also prime cruising ground, particularly for gay men. However, any advances by any Moroccan should be taken with extreme caution, as prostitution is a serious issue in Marrakesh.

✪ KOUTOUBIA MOSQUE

Ave. Mohammed V

The Koutoubia is the mosque and minaret that established the Moroccan style that is seen throughout the country, from the new Hassan II Mosque in Casablanca to the cherished Qaraouiyine Mosque in Fez. This is also one of the best-preserved examples of Almohad architecture. The minaret dates from the mid-12th century. Work was likely begun shortly after the Almohads conquered the Almoravid empire in AD 1150, and continued under the rule of Sultan Moulay Yacoub al-Mansour. One of the more striking features of the mosque is that the stones used in its construction are of visibly varying size. They would have been covered with a coat of plaster and painted—something local authorities were considering when the tower was renovated in 2000—but fortunately they settled for just cleaning the mosque and didn't cover the stones with plaster and paint. Today, the Koutoubia is lit up at night and comes alive.

The tower is an outstanding example of the Almohad style, with other key examples being the unfinished Hassan Tower in Rabat and the Giralda in Sevilla. One of the first things you'll notice are the varying decorative arches centered on the tower. These arches are layered upon each other around the mosque,

the Koutoubia Mosque

because it was not oriented correctly toward Mecca. This mistake in orientation is possibly the same reason why the Tin Mal Mosque found in the High Atlas is no longer in use. Though non-Muslims are free to wander the abandoned Tin Mal Mosque, they are forbidden entrance to the Koutoubia Mosque.

TOMB OF FATIMA ZOHRA
Koutoubia Mosque

Between the busy Avenue Mohammed V and the Koutoubia Mosque lies the Tomb of Fatima Zohra, a traditional white-washed domed mausoleum, popular with the local women who seek her blessing (*baraka*) to conceive children and to help cure illness. Like many of the venerated saints (or marabouts) of Morocco, not much is known about Fatima Zohra. The local myth is that she was the wife of a liberated slave who had become an imam. By day she is said to have been a woman, and by night a wondrous dove. The tomb is closed to non-Muslims, though it is unmissable right next to the pedestrian crosswalk to the Jemaa el-Fnaa and makes for a great meeting point.

KOUTOUBIA GARDENS
Koutoubia Mosque; daily 8am-8pm; free

On the other side of the minaret from the ruins of the mosque are the Koutoubia Gardens. These provide an excellent spot for picnicking and are often used by groups of Moroccan ladies looking for a shaded spot, perhaps after a visit to Fatima Zohra. The gardens are small, though well laid out, and offer plenty of opportunities for photos, but be respectful because local women can be very superstitious about having their photos taken.

framing the windows and varying from floor to floor. Note how the arches change from one side to the other, with each face of the mosque. Those arches on the third floor of the tower on the southeast window have become synonymous with Almohad gates found throughout Morocco and Spain. There are some fascinating stories about the origin of the four gold balls that are stacked atop the minaret, many of which find themselves woven into tall tales spun by the storytellers every night on the Jemaa el-Fnaa. As legend has it, there were originally only three gold balls; however, when al-Mansour's wife accidentally ate during Ramadan, she had her gold jewelry melted down to add a fourth ball to the minaret. When the gold balls were replaced with brass balls nobody seems to know.

The foundations of the mosque next to the minaret were excavated during the renovation and restoration of 2000. The excavation proved one of the architectural theories of the mosque: Evidence was found of the mosque having to have been rebuilt

BEHIND THE SCENES OF THE JEMAA EL-FNAA

Morocco is a country replete with characters, and in no place is this more evident than a night out on the Jemaa el-Fnaa. The large square comes alive at night with **storytellers** and **snake charmers, monkey handlers** and **fortune tellers, musicians** and **henna artists,** as well as more modern carnival entertainments such as **putt-putt golf.** It seems hard to believe that people can make a living these days as a snake charmer, but in Marrakesh, anything is possible. However, there are a few things to consider while making your way around the square.

a water seller on the Jemaa el-Fnaa

Though the snakes and monkeys are a staple of the Jemaa el-Fnaa, those considering animal welfare might want to keep in mind that the hooded cobra snakes used by the snake charmers have their venom pockets removed, essentially killing the snake over the course of a few days. These snakes are bred specifically for the purpose of entertainment, and while they are generally well taken care of because they are the source of income for these performers, the end of the snake's life is thought to be painful. The monkey handlers spend years working with their animals so that they might perform certain tricks, again as entertainment. Some handlers are kinder than others.

Otherwise, entertainment is to be had for people of all ages. Children love the dancers, animals, and musicians, while adults enjoy looking into their future with fortune tellers and discussing their latest henna tattoo with the artist. **Tipping** is the norm. Before **taking photos** or engaging with a performer individually, it's best to agree on a price ahead of time, 20-100Dh depending on what the performer is being asked to do, while tipping 5-10Dh to musicians or storytellers is acceptable.

HOTEL MAMOUNIA GARDENS

Avenue Bab Jdid; 8am-8pm; free

The most elaborate gardens to tour within walking distance from the medina are the Hotel Mamounia Gardens just west of the Koutoubia Mosque, down Avenue Houman el Fetouaki. A nice circuit to do is to pass the Koutoubia Mosque and cut through the Koutoubia Gardens to where the horse-drawn carriage stand is outside the Hotel Mamounia. You can walk through the hotel, taking in the palatial spread, to the gardens out back. In the heat of the day, the hotel's gardens make for a shaded distraction. The well-cultivated garden always provides a fresh, green respite from the dusty medina and heavy roar of traffic. The gardens and hotel can be found directly through Bab Jdid on the west wall of the medina.

PLACE DE LA KISSERIA

North of the souks is the Place de la Kisseria. This central square houses a few of the more interesting sites in Marrakesh, including the Marrakesh Museum and Medersa Ben Youssef. Directly across from the museum is the Ben Youssef Mosque. This mosque was originally built during the Almoravid dynasty in the 12th century and is the oldest mosque in Marrakesh, though not the best preserved—that distinction belongs rightly to the Koutoubia Mosque.

decorative Arabic script in the Medersa Ben Youssef

features an intact dome and latrines dating from AD 1117. It is the oldest building in Marrakesh, and although it's currently closed indefinitely for renovation, visitors can still view the *koubba* (shrine). Located below the current ground level of Marrakesh, this fenced-in ornate domed structure was built at the same time as the original Ben Youssef Mosque for Muslims to do their ablutions before entering the mosque. The interior is richly decorated with floral patterns, including pinecones, palms, and acanthus leaves, though much of this will have to be left to the imagination until it reopens. In the meantime, it's worth looking at if for no other reason than it is the best-preserved piece of Almoravid architecture in all of Morocco.

Though the Almoravids built the mosque, nothing is left of their original design. The Almohad dynasty took over, declared the mosque was oriented poorly, had it destroyed, and built another mosque atop the rubble. This mosque fell into disrepair and was completely rebuilt in the 19th century, leaving nothing behind of the Almoravid or Almohad design. Today, the mosque is largely indistinguishable from many of the mosques in Morocco, though it is still one of the most important in Marrakesh and houses the *kadi* (the judge of the region). It was once the center of Marrakesh. Like other mosques, it is closed to non-Muslims.

On the square next to the mosque is another site of interest, the recently excavated **Almoravid Koubba,** which

✪ Marrakesh Museum (Musée de Marrakech)

Pl. Ben Youssef; tel. 0524/441 893; www.musee.ma; daily 9am-6:30pm; 50Dh

Housed in the restored Dar Menebhi Palace, the Marrakesh Museum was opened in 1997. The Omar Benjelloun Foundation generously financed the elaborate restoration. Today, photos near the museum entrance showcase this restoration work. One wing hosts Moroccan textiles and embroidery as well as Amazigh jewelry. The traditional hammam has been transformed into a rotating exposition gallery featuring many more contemporary Moroccan and international artists. You'll also find a collection of decorative ceramics and ornate daggers. Though there is a lot on display, half of the fun of this museum is walking around the restored palace and taking in the attention to details, such as the *zellij* tile work, enormous carved wood doors, and fine stucco work. Anglophones will likely be

the Almoravid Koubba, the oldest building in Marrakesh

disappointed to find most signs and postings only in French, though for museums in Marrakesh, this is still the standard and should be visited to get a feel for the history and culture of the region.

Medersa Ben Youssef

Kaat Benahid; tel. 0632/251 164; www. medersa-ben-youssef.com; daily 9am-5pm; 70Dh (closed until 2020/21)

The Medersa Ben Youssef was a functioning Quranic school originally built during the Almoravid period in the 12th century. It was in use as a school until the 19th century. During the French protectorate it fell into disrepair and disuse before being restored by the same Omar Benjelloun Foundation that restored the Dar Menebhi Palace. Throughout the *medersa* you'll find photos of the recent restoration as well as beautiful woodwork carved from the cedar trees of the Atlas Mountains throughout the vestibules, cupolas, and main prayer room. Marble, imported from Italy, and the local stucco work provide most of the rest of the decoration, with some complex *zellij* (mosaic) work of various shapes, techniques, and arrangements keeping the eye busy. The *medersa* will be closed until sometime in 2020/21 for a major renovation.

Dar Bellarj

9-7 Zaouiate Lahdar; tel. 0524/444 555; daily 9:30am-12:30pm and 2pm-5:30pm; free

Just outside the Medersa Ben Youssef, the Dar Bellarj, literally meaning "Stork House," is a beautifully restored animal clinic that now serves as a business front for local artisans. Exhibits vary and entrance is usually free, though sometimes a small fee of 15Dh or so might be charged depending on the exhibit. Exhibits are chosen every few months and are generally themed around something like photography or textiles. Check out the gift shop for some wonderful ideas for presents to take back home and to support local artisans. Even with the posted hours, this is one place that is sometimes closed for apparently no reason.

Orientalist Museum

5 Derb El Khamsi; tel. 0524/447 379; daily 9am-7pm; 50Dh

Opened in 2018 in a restored *riad*, this is a small, curious museum that "owns" the orientalist expression generally derided by those sensitive to the "othering" of people. It isn't an overly large collection and mostly features the work of Europeans depicting African and Asian subjects. However, with one work each by the French great Eugène Delacroix and the Spanish master of surrealism Salvador Dalí, as well as a few by the Marrakesh French expat icon Louis Majorelle, I would be hard-pressed not to recommend stopping in to enjoy this collection for any lover of art. Unfortunately, the museum does not currently feature explanatory plaques. Instead, the manager encourages visitors to walk around, guided by their sense of the aesthetic.

Photography Museum (Maison de la Photographie)

46 Rue Bin Lafnadek; tel. 0524/385 721; www.maisondelaphotographie.ma; daily 9:30am-7pm; 50Dh

Following Zaouiate Lahdar from the Dar Bellarj west toward Place du Maoukef will bring you to the Photography Museum. Photographers and those interested in Moroccan history will enjoy the collection of black-and-white photos dating from 1870 to

1950. The curator has so many photos, over 5,000 original prints, that they can't all be shown at once, so they are exhibited by theme, which changes every three months. A short documentary from 1957 about the Amazigh, *Chez les Berbères du Haut-Atlas*, by Daniel Chicault, screens every hour. This was the first time that the Amazigh were filmed in color, and the scenes, even if you don't understand the French narration, are breathtaking. The rooftop terrace has views over Marrakesh with the distant snow-capped mountains of the High Atlas serving as a backdrop. The terrace is open for lunch and serves traditional Moroccan cuisine (80Dh), though a short break for coffee or tea is likely sufficient for most guests.

Perfume Museum
(Musée du Parfum)

2 Derb Chérif, rue Diour Saboun;
tel. 0661/095 352; www.benchaabane.com/
lemuseeduparfum; daily 9am-6pm; 40Dh

Unlike so many museums that are interested in showing you something, the Perfume Museum wants you to experience something else—namely, your sense of smell. Housed in a restored 19th-century *riad,* the museum will immerse you in the world of perfume. By far the most interesting room in this small museum is the darkened room where you inhale the seven scents of Morocco, including saffron, cedar, rose, and other natural fragrances that are all indigenous to the country. Amina is usually around and can tell you a lot about the history and art of perfume-making in Morocco. You'll also have the option of making your own perfume to take home with you (400Dh), which makes for an incredible personalized souvenir. This is an unforgettable olfactory experience, unique in Morocco, that should be on a "must do" list for any visit to Marrakesh.

The Secret Garden
(Le Jardin Secret)

Rue Mouassine 121; tel. 0524/390 040;
www.lejardinsecretmarrakech.com/en; daily
9:30am-6pm or 7:30pm, depending on the
time of the year; 60Dh

With origins dating back nearly 400 years to the Saadian Dynasty, walking into this renovated and rehabilitated garden in the middle of all the bustle of Marrakesh is something of a dream. As you walk around the stately Arab-Andalusian Moroccan palaces, these pinnacles of Moroccan art and architecture, you would be forgiven if you gave yourself a pinch. There are two gardens: an Islamic Garden and an Exotic Garden. The Islamic Garden, divided into four distinct parts designed to help with irrigation, are meant to invoke heaven, as it is narrated in the Quran, and is a sacred place meant for careful contemplation. The Exotic Garden, on the other hand, pays homage to the many experimental gardens that have existed in Marrakesh over the years, each bringing their own special plants, interests, and designs from around the world.

Women's Museum
(Musée de la Femme)

19 rue Sidi Abdel Aziz, Souk Jeltd;
tel. 0524/381 129; www.museedelafemme.ma;
daily 9:30am-6:30pm; 30Dh

A few minutes by foot north of the Jemaa el-Fnaa along one of the busier souk roads you'll find the wonderful Women's Museum. This much-needed museum weaves the culture and artistic importance women have played in "the art of daily life." The three-story museum features a series of carpets on

Two men work leather in the local tanneries.

the ground floor showing the different regions of Morocco while introducing how women incorporated their lives into their art. On the next two floors are ornate shoes from the beginning of the 20th century as well as a selection of pottery, jewelry, *handiras* (highly decorative capes), and other traditional clothing. A series of black-and-white photographs from the French painter Jean Besancenot from the 1930s helps to bring the past of these women to life. The exposition changes every six months, with a terrace café slated to open in early 2020.

Tanneries
Bab Debbaugh; 10am-sunset; free
Farther west along the same road that led from the Place de la Kisseria, past the numerous shops selling everything from bottled water to recycled metal sculptures, and all the way to the exit of the medina near Bab Debbaugh, you'll come to the tanneries of Marrakesh. Marrakesh

tanneries have been working leather hides traditionally for almost a thousand years with little change to the process. Hides are first left to soak in a vat of quicklime, salt, water, and cow urine to make hairs and fat easier to remove. Tanners then leave the hides out to dry. Once dry, they are transferred to a vat of pigeon excrement, which makes the leather softer, before being dipped into a final vat of colored dye. The hides are left to dry in the sun once more and then cut and sold to leatherworkers, who make slippers, bags, purses, belts, wallets, and other products with them. With all the poop, pee, bloody animal hides, and hot sun, it's no wonder that the tanneries smell as rank as they do, and it's obvious why they are so far away from the rest of the medina. You'll likely be given a mint leaf cluster to shove up your nose. This will make the smell more bearable. It's an impressive sight, all the same, and a truly medieval experience.

MELLAH

The mellah, or old Jewish Quarter, is a neighborhood now called Hay Essalam that is spread out to the south of the Jemaa el-Fnaa. To get to the mellah from the Jemaa el-Fnaa, you can either take the southwest passage, Rue Riad Zitoun el Kedim, across from the orange juice stands, and follow the crush of traffic for 15 minutes, or take the infinitely more pleasant Rue de Banques starting near Café de France—keep to the right where it merges at the Café Bakchich and continues on as Rue Riad Zitoun el Jdid. Follow this café- and shop-lined pedestrian thoroughfare until you come to a small park with a few cafés around it. This is the mellah.

Though very few Jews still live in the mellah, there remain several shops dedicated to classically Jewish crafts, including jewelers and a few tailors. After coming to the park, stay to the right to arrive at Place des Ferblantiers, which was once better known as Place de Mellah and the center of the Jewish Quarter. There are several synagogues, some of which have gardens you can visit, though you will likely need a guide to find most of them. The majority are spread to the east of the Place de Ferblantiers around the Jewish Cemetery.

✪ Bahia Palace
(Palais de la Bahia)

5 Rue Riad Zitoun el Jdid; tel. 0524/389 511; www.palais-bahia.com; daily 9am-4:30pm; 70Dh

You'll find the Bahia Palace in the midst of the mellah, just off the Rue Riad Zitoun el Jdid. This ornate palace was given to the concubine Bahia, a favorite of the wealthy vizier Si Moussa Ba Ahmed's harem. The exact dates of the construction are unknown, but it is thought to have been built in two parts. The first section of the palace, known as Dar Si Moussa, was constructed by Ba Ahmed's father between 1859 and 1873, and the palace as it is known today was completed by Ba Ahmed while he was the grand vizier to the sultan by the end of the century.

Be prepared to strain your neck looking up at the beautifully maintained woodcarving, geometric painting, and stucco work throughout the ceilings of the palace. Materials for decorating the Bahia Palace were sourced from across North Africa. Marble was brought from Meknes and was probably originally extracted from Carrara, Italy. This same marble may have previously decorated Moulay Ismail's palace in Meknes and perhaps the ancient city of Volubilis. Marble was also stripped from the nearby Badi Palace. Cedar for the painted ceilings of the palace apartments was commissioned from the Middle Atlas, and glazed terra-cotta tiles arrived from Tetouan. Artisans across North Africa and Andalusia were used in the construction of the palace, though the end

Travelers explore the Bahia Palace.

result is less geometrically harmonic than spatially organic.

The palace is still used by the government, with the current Minister of Culture Affairs residing in a small section of the palace. A few scenes from the Alfred Hitchcock film *The Man Who Knew Too Much* were filmed in the palace. Get here early to avoid the crowds and have a more tranquil stroll through the palace and its gardens.

Museum of Moroccan Arts

Derb Si Saïd; tel. 0524/389 564; Wed.-Mon. 9am-4:45pm; 20Dh

Confusingly also known as the **Dar Si Saïd Museum,** this spacious museum near the Bahia Palace is located in the remodeled house of Si Saïd, brother to the grand vizier Ba Ahmed. You'll find it behind the Préfecture Medina on Rue Riad Zitoun el Jdid. The museum has transformed from an "arts and crafts" museum to one that really specializes in Moroccan carpets. Though you'll be able to find carpets from all around the country, it is the spectacular carpets from Haouz and High Atlas tribes that are truly worth the price of admission. Also be sure to check out the intricate mosaic work upstairs in this remodeled palatial house.

KASBAH

The kasbah comprises the southwest corner of the medina, on the other side of the expanse of the king's palace from the mellah. The **Saadian Tombs** are the most interesting site here. There is also an interesting **Artisan Complex** on the main road cutting through the kasbah (aptly named "Rue de la Kasbah"), as well as several quieter boutique *riads* that are away from the hustle and bustle of the rest of the old medina.

There are a few ways to get to the kasbah from Jemaa el-Fnaa. To take the most direct way, follow the busy Rue Riad Zitoun el Kedim until it ends, and then take a right past the small covered market and follow the road to the horse-drawn carriages. From the horses, you can turn left into the kasbah, though this will cut through a neighborhood where there is a good chance you might get a little turned around. An easier way to navigate, though a bit longer, is to follow Rue Riad Zitoun el Kedima as above, but this time, keep going straight past the horse-drawn carriages until this dumps you out of the medina walls at Rue Sidi Mimoun. You'll see a little post office. Take a left and then another left to immediately enter back through the medina walls, beneath the elaborately arched Bab Ananou and into the kasbah.

the intricate, ornate Saadian Tombs

Saadian Tombs

Rue de la Kasbah; daily 8am-4pm; 70Dh

Originally walled in by Moulay Ismail in the late 17th century and then "rediscovered" by French in 1917, the Saadian Tombs are some of the most ornate tombs in all of Morocco. It is the sheer beauty—or, some might argue, audacity—of their decoration that drives so many tourists here to gape at the gaudy mesh of stucco work, *zellij* tiles, inlaid gold, and Italian marble. The mausoleum consists of three rooms, while the elaborate graves and gravestones spill out into the courtyard and its gardens. About 60 members of the Saadi dynasty (1554-1659) are buried inside the mausoleum. The most famous room is the Room of the 12 Columns, which houses the grave of Ahmad al-Mansour, the best known of the Saadi rulers. He ruled from 1578-1603 and built the nearby Badi Palace. It is rumored that French authorities found the tombs while conducting an aerial survey of Marrakesh. The locals say otherwise, and that they have always known they were here.

Badi Palace (Palais el Badi)

Ksibat Nhass; tel. 0661/350 878; daily 8:30am-12:30pm and 2:30pm-4:30pm; 70Dh

The Badi Palace is the ruined palace of the Saadian sultan Ahmad al-Mansour. Al-Mansour began construction of the palace in 1578 to celebrate his victory over the Portuguese at the famous Battle of the Three Kings in the town of Ksar el-Kbeer near Tangier. The empty palace grounds are a bit more interesting after a tour of the Bahia Palace, where you will see a window into the history that has been preserved and then, when visiting the Badi Palace, see that which has been left to ruin. The ramparts serve as great spots to photograph Marrakesh, and the general lack of crowds ensures a little peace and quiet after the busy medina crowds.

the desolate, though intriguing, Badi Palace

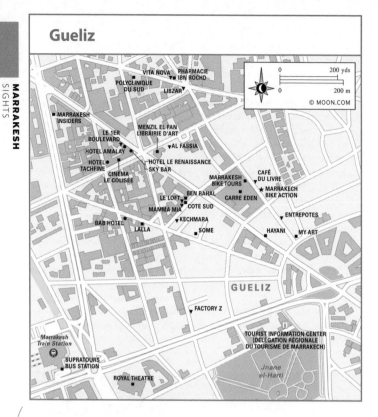

Gueliz

MARRAKESH INSIDERS

VITA NOVA
PHARMACIE IBN ROCHD
POLYCLINIQUE DU SUD
LIBZAR

0   200 yds
0   200 m
© MOON.COM

MENZIL EL FAN
LIBRAIRIE D'ART
LE 1ER BOULEVARD
HOTEL AMALAY
AL FASSIA
HOTEL TACHFINE
CINEMA LE COLISÉE
HOTEL LE RENAISSANCE
SKY BAR
MARRAKESH BIKE TOURS
CAFÉ DU LIVRE
MARRAKECH BIKE ACTION
BEN RAHAL
LE LOFT
COTE SUD
CARRE EDEN
MAMMA MIA
KECHMARA
ENTREPOTES
BAB HOTEL
LALLA
SOME
HAYANI
MY ART

GUELIZ

FACTORY Z

Marrakesh Train Station

TOURIST INFORMATION CENTER (DÉLÉGATION RÉGIONALE DU TOURISME DE MARRAKECH)

SUPRATOURS BUS STATION

Jnane el-Harti

ROYAL THEATRE

The palace has a long history of being looted and sacked. In the 17th century, after the fall of the Saadian dynasty, the palace was stripped of materials and marble was taken, perhaps to Moulay Ismail's palace in Meknes. Today, the coos of pigeons and clacking bills of mating storks enliven this place. There are some projects underway in the palace to renovate some areas and develop gardens.

Admission price does not include access to the small museum (10Dh) and the excellent *minbar* (a type of pulpit sometimes used by imams to deliver their Friday sermons) housed there. The *minbar* is an excellent example of the artistry of the 12th century and has been faithfully restored.

The museum is the best preserved indoor area of the expansive palace grounds. The token admission is worth it for those interested in glimpsing what has been preserved of the palace and for a look at the *minbar*.

GUELIZ AND HIVERNAGE

The Gueliz quarter is a place to live, shop, dine, and party, but not so much for sightseeing—with the exception of a few unique gardens, namely the Majorelle Gardens and the Palmeraie, which should be high on everyone's list of things to see in Marrakesh. If time allows, consider swinging through the Menara Gardens in nearby Hivernage, though perhaps the most animated walk is along Avenue Mohammed V, the main promenade for shopping. Here, everything becomes lively right around sunset as the heat cools and the fragrant trees lining the promenade give off their perfume.

☼ MAJORELLE GARDENS (Jardin Majorelle)

Rue Yves Saint Laurent; tel. 0524/313 047; http://jardinmajorelle.com; daily 8am-6pm May-Sept., 8am-5:30pm Oct.-Apr., 9am-5pm during Ramadan; 70Dh for gardens, additional 30Dh for Berber Museum

The wonderfully art deco Majorelle Gardens is the loving creation of French painter Jacques Majorelle, who began working on the gardens in the 1920s. Majorelle cultivated this garden over 40 years, first opening it to the public in 1947. However, because of health issues, he had to abandon the gardens. The gardens suffered without a caretaker and were nearly destroyed; at one point, there was thought of turning the space into a hotel. Luckily, in 1980, fashion designer Yves Saint Laurent and his partner, Pierre Bergé, purchased the gardens and set about a restoration effort.

Today, the intense cobalt blue walls (incidentally, this particular intense

the distinct cobalt blue of the Majorelle Gardens

shade of blue is called "Majorelle blue" after the French painter), water lilies, lotus flowers, and numerous cacti tucked beneath the shade of the towering palm trees make this a heaven for people and birds alike. However, because of its popularity, the gardens are not quite as relaxing as one might imagine, particularly when buses full of tourists descend onto the property. It is best to go early in the morning, when the crowds are away, the air is fresh, and the blackbirds, house sparrows, warblers, and turtledoves who call these gardens home are at their most active.

There is a small café with a terrace inside the gardens, but it's expensive for what it is. The small **Berber Museum** houses an interesting look at the neighboring culture of the High Atlas Mountains and includes a review of textiles and jewelry. The gift shop has original period photographs for sale, some of them decades old and nearly all of them fascinating, though not cheap. If you've made it all the way to the Majorelle Gardens, it's probably worth your time to pop in for a quick look, though there are better museums in Marrakesh.

During Ramadan, the gardens are open 9am-5pm. The attached Berber Museum is open from 10am-garden closing time. The gardens and museum typically close at 6pm, though from Oct. 1-Apr 30, they close at 5:30pm. It's best to consult the Majorelle Gardens website to be sure of opening and closing hours ahead of your visit and to plan on getting there as early as possible.

MENARA GARDENS

Ave. de la Ménara, Hivernage; daily sunrise-sunset; free

The Menara Gardens are an expansive

Menara Gardens

PALMERAIE

To the northeast of the medina lies the expansive Palmeraie, or palm groves, spread over 12,000 hectares (30,000 acres). This impressive spread of palm trees is the only oasis north of the High Atlas Mountains and is considered throughout North Africa as the most stunning garden in all of Marrakesh, with palm trees seemingly without end. During the Almoravid dynasty in the 11th and 12th centuries, the elaborate underground network of irrigation that allows the vegetation to thrive in this otherwise arid environment was constructed. Several golf courses dot the Palmeraie, along with a few larger resort complexes. For the best view of the Palmeraie, take the double-decker tour buses (tel. 0663/527 797, bustouristique@ also.ma, 145Dh), which you can catch at the Jemaa el-Fnaa just outside the Tourist Information Center on Avenue Mohammed V in the Gueliz neighborhood. The views from the top of the bus really allow you to take in these expansive gardens—just don't forget your sunscreen.

olive grove southwest of the old medina and directly south of the Hivernage neighborhood, abutting the olive groves of Bab Jdid. In 1985, UNESCO declared the 12th-century Almohad gardens, along with the Agdal Gardens of the king's Royal Palace, a World Heritage Site. The 100-hectare (250-acre) grounds are ideal for picnics, where quiet and shade are easily found.

The **Saadian Garden Pavilion** (20Dh) at the edge of a pool, dating from the 16th-century Saadian dynasty, can be entered from roughly 7am-5pm, with proceeds going to the Cultural Foundation for Restoration. There is a terrace view from the garden pavilion overlooking the pool to Marrakesh, while behind the pavilion the High Atlas Mountains soar up over the plain. The pool dates from the Almohad era. It was a favorite with soldiers, who used to train in it, though swimming is not allowed any longer. Camel rides are usually available in the gardens for 40-100Dh, depending on how long the ride is and how good your bargaining skills are.

Palmeraie Museum
(Musée de la Palmeraie)

Dar Tounsi; tel. 0628/031 039 or 0661/095 352; www.benchaabane.com/ musee_palmeraie; daily 9am-6pm; 40Dh

Supported by a generous donation of over 100 pieces of contemporary art by the Benchaabane Foundation, the airy Palmeraie Museum is a surprisingly great museum for families. Housed in a reclaimed French protectorate-era 1940s farm, with lots of green space and a large Andalusian garden, there is lots of room to roam around. There are also art workshops for children as well as educational workshops where children can learn about the environment, the dangers of climate change, and what they can do to help protect it for the future. Workshops are run by Rachida Touijri, a popular local artist. The museum also has a rotating exhibit featuring (usually) contemporary Moroccan artists as well as a permanent collection of contemporary and modern Moroccan artists.

Sports and Recreation

✪ MOROCCAN COOKING CLASSES

One of the best ways to dive in and really experience the culture of Morocco is to learn how to prepare the various salads, tajines, and couscous dishes that you will undoubtedly become familiar with during your travels. Expect to spend at least half a day with any cooking class, as Moroccan cuisine tends to take a while to prepare.

Café Clock
224 Derb Chtouka; tel. 0524/378 367; 300-600Dh

Café Clock runs a varied cooking course in English that includes different salads and tajines, though their course on baking Moroccan breads is perhaps the most interesting. It's a shorter, two-hour course that involves a trip to the 600-year-old neighborhood *farran,* a local oven that is used by the community every day for baking, and the price is considerably less

bread baking in the local public oven

than the asking price for the normal cooking classes at 300Dh.

✪ Faim d'Epices

Douar Old Ali Ben Aich; tel. 0600/048 800; www.faimdepices.com; 550Dh

Discover the secrets of Moroccan spices and a few kitchen shortcuts at Faim d'Epices. The kitchen is about a 20-minute drive from Marrakesh; your tuition for the class includes transportation to and from Marrakesh. The courses include instruction in English on making traditional breads, as well as couscous and various salads, tajines, and sweets. Throughout the day, chef Nezha will tell you about storing all those wonderful spices you'll likely be packing home and give you some culinary history. You'll sip on artisan coffee or mint tea while preparing your meals and finish the afternoon on the terrace among the citrus trees digging into your day's work. It's a full day, with pickup around 10am and drop-off at 4pm, and one of the most enjoyable days you could hope for. A relaxing spa package can be added on to your day; it runs 5pm-8pm and is a nice way to unwind.

La Maison Arabe

1 Derb Assehbé, near Bab Doukkala; tel. 0524/387 010; 600Dh

For classes in the medina, check in with the *dada* (Moroccan Arabic for a woman who manages the cooking and children of a house) at the chic La Maison Arabe. Geared toward both amateurs and professionals, classes work with translators and use modern equipment. Classes start with an explanation of the seasonal menu, typically with one of the Moroccan salads and a tajine of your choice (or forgo the salad and make a dessert instead). You'll take a tour of the local

market to pick fresh ingredients, make a quick stop at the spice market, and then get to work. After slaving away, you'll eat the fruits of your labor poolside in the elaborate setting of this upmarket *riad*.

Spices are out for a cooking class.

Rouge Cafe Cooking

Various locations in the medina; www.rougetravel.com; 200Dh

If you're looking for a more homey experience that feels as though it was taught by a good friend (or maybe your mom's friend), then check out this humble course offering. Classes begin at 10am, as is usual, to give you enough time to go to the local market to pick out the fresh ingredients with your chef. This is a friendly budget option popular with students and travelers staying at hostels. The environment is much more laugh-aloud than your typical serious-faced courses held throughout the Red City. Relax. Have a laugh. And make a delicious Moroccan tajine for lunch. The classes are run by a family that owns a number of *riads* and hostels throughout the medina, so locations of the classes change depending on demand and space available. It's best to contact through their website. For the cooking classes, look at "Marrakesh Activities" under "Excursions," or just go straight to the "Contact Us" page and write them from there.

The Marrakchef Cooking Academy

Riad Monceau, 7/8 derb Chaabane, Riad Zitoun Lakdim; tel. 0524/429 646; www.riad-monceau.com; 500Dh

For beginning chefs or the next Julia Child, this friendly series of classes held in the opulent setting of the Riad Monceau provides the perfect setting for just about anyone to learn all about Moroccan spices and cuisine. Led by Rachida Sahnoune, chef at Restaurant Riad Monceau, the workshops are limited to only a few participants to make sure that everyone gets their hands dirty, so to speak. Workshops run about 3.5 hours, with one in the morning starting at 10am and another in the evening beginning at 5:30pm. In these workshops, you'll learn about the entire process of making one starter and one main, and do it yourself from start to finish. There are also shorter Moroccan pastry workshops available in the afternoons at 2:30pm. Consult the website to combine a morning cooking class with an afternoon hammam.

HAMMAMS

There are still traditional hammams throughout the medina of Marrakesh. These are simple affairs, with a steam room and scrubbing available for 10-20Dh. Though they're intended for locals, many travelers find an experience in a real Moroccan hammam something memorable. You can ask at your accommodations for the closest neighborhood hammam. Local hammams usually do not have websites or phone numbers. You will also be expected to bring your own spa gear, including soap and towel.

MEDINA
Bab Doukkala Hammam

southeast corner of the Bab Doukkala Mosque; daily, men 8pm-midnight, women noon-7pm; 10Dh

The Bab Doukkala Hammam is a great option to experience a local hammam for the centrality to many of the *riads* in the north part of the souks. This is one of the largest local public hammams, though as all of the public hammams tend to be, it seems like it could use a big scrub-down itself. Scrubbing (20Dh) and massages (50Dh) are usually available, and the attendants understand enough English so that communication, though limited, is better than at most other local hammam options.

Hammam al Rjel

Place Sidi Boudchich along Rue Assouel; open daily sunrise-midnight; 10Dh

This large neighborhood hammam is for men only, as the name indicates. For men looking to experience this bathing ritual, it is a good, clean option. Do remember that when in the public bath, men should always keep their privates covered. This might seem odd at first, but you'll get used to it quickly. Definitely splurge on a massage while you're here (50Dh). English is extremely limited, though if the massage is too hard, they will understand "ouch."

Hammam Dar el Bacha

20 Rue Fatima Zohra; daily, men 7am-1pm and 9pm-midnight, women 2pm-9pm; 10Dh

This local favorite keeps on charming, particularly for female tourists looking to have a bathing experience where they'll be able to interact with local women. The people of Marrakesh are known throughout Morocco for their sense of humor, which comes across with stories and laughter while they are enjoying the public bath and sharing local gossip. One of the friendliest local baths in town. Make sure to bring your hammam kit!

Heritage Spa

40 Arset Aouzal (near Bab Doukkala); tel. 0524/384 333; www.heritagespamarrakech. com; daily 10am-8pm, by reservation only; 300Dh

Located inside a luxurious, almost palatial setting, this Moroccan spa offers an upscale version of the local hammam, complete with 45-minute beauty treatments. The "Hammam Beldi Detox" is one of the most popular of these, offering a black-soap scrub with argan oil and bitter orange, which is said to make the skin more taut and youthful. Afterward, a deep-cleansing mask made of traditional *ghassoul* clay is applied. The experience is not 100 percent Moroccan, particularly the massages that offer up treats such as a "Hot Herbal Tea Bag" massage and traditional Chinese foot massages. That said, you might want to consider splurging for the "4 Hands Sultan's Harem" massage that will leave you feeling divine. English is well-spoken here.

Les Bains d'Orient

241 Arset Aouzal; tel. 0524/387 679; www.les-bainsdorient.com; daily 10am-8pm, by reservation only; 200Dh

Here, the traditional Moroccan hammam is seen as an heir to the baths of ancient Rome and Greece. The hammam, literally a source of heat, is a real place of life in Eastern culture. Here, they like to meet not only to relax, but to chat and share. Whereas some of the other upscale spas have done away with this social aspect of the traditional hammam, here they attempt to keep it alive. You'll enter the first heat room, where the humidity reaches 100 percent and the temperature can climb to over 40°C (105°F). Relax on Turkish slab benches and take deep breaths while the pores of your skin gradually expand to let out all the toxins in the body. Chat with your friends and take in this experience—capped, of course, by a full-body scrub and quick 15-minute massage.

Hammam Mille et Une Nuits

58 Derb Derbachi; tel. 0524/443 079 or 0524/443 080; www.spa-hammam1001nuits.com; daily 9am-8pm, by reservation only; 150Dh

Located just a few steps from the Jemaa el-Fnaa, this is a charming spa set in an ornate, traditional Moroccan building that dates back to 1842. The service, though, is anything but traditional. It offers up the full gamut of what you might expect in a spa in North America or Europe, complete with manicures, pedicures, hair styling and coloring, and epilation for both men and women, as well as a more Moroccan-style hammam. To get ready for your big night out, this is the one-stop shop to get all your spa services met.

HIVERNAGE
Es Saadi Palace Spa

Rue Ibrahim el Mazini; tel. 0524/337 400; www.essaadi.com; daily 8am-9pm, by appointment only; 400Dh

A considerably less traditional, though completely enjoyable, spa experience can be had at some of the palatial hotels in Hivernage. The cream of the crop is the Es Saadi Palace Spa. The grounds of this spa are enormous, featuring a thermal spa, high-tech swimming pool with multiple water pathways, thermal heat baths, dedicated rooms for massage, open terraces for yoga, a total workout gym, and a mirrored room for indoor yoga or dance. This is holistic body care at its finest.

Royal Mirage Deluxe

Rue de Paris; tel. 0524/425 400; daily 8am-9pm, by appointment only; 400Dh

One of the better excuses to make your way into the Royal Mirage Deluxe is to make a reservation at their spa. Indulge in a California or Thai massage, and while you're at it, add in a facial, a body scrub, and a relaxing 30 minutes in the traditional Moroccan steam room. With all the heat and humidity, your body will feel refreshed and your skin wide open, and when you make your way out of the spa and back into the opulence of the hotel, you'll be sure to leave feeling like spoiled royalty.

GULIZ
Baan Thai Institute

Apt. 13, Résidence Les Jasmins, 4th fl., on the corner of Ave. Mohammed V and Rue Oum Errabia Gueliz; tel. 0524/433 304; open daily by appointment only; 350Dh

If you want to relax after a rough day shopping on the bustling streets of Gueliz, the Baan Thai Institute is perfectly located, just on the main drag of Avenue Mohammed V near the Carre Eden shopping center, though in a drab, workaday building. As expected, a Thai massage is the norm in this surprisingly wonderful spa, and it helps that most of the staff speak some English; 500Dh will get you a full Thai massage and a couple of hours of serious pampering.

GOLF
Samanah

Menara; tel. 0524/483 200; www.samanah.com; 650Dh

Marrakesh has quickly become the European golfer's destination of choice, with a growing number of world-class courses to choose from. The near-constant sunshine, distant snow peaks of the High Atlas, unbeatable culture, and relative inexpensiveness all add up to unforgettable days on the links. Most courses are at resorts, with multiday golf packages available for about 4,000Dh. However, the stress that these courses put on Morocco's unstable water resources is something to be concerned about, despite what good they do for the economy and preservation of green spaces. The 18-hole Samanah Golf is a Jack Nicklaus-designed course and is surprisingly one of the less busy golf courses in Marrakesh, despite winning the International Golf Development of the Year award in 2011.

Palmeraie Resort Golf

Circuit de la Palmeraie; tel. 0524/368 766; www.palmeraiemarrakech.com; 700Dh

Featuring 27 holes over 77 hectares with panoramic views over the distant High Atlas Mountains, not to mention the 11 lakes on the course, there is a lot to like about this elaborate construction. You will find several restaurants catering to different sorts of budgets and tastes at the resort, as well as a high-end spa. If you're looking to hit the links, this would be a great day out for any golf lover.

HOT-AIR BALLOONS

If the budget allows, a hot-air balloon ride over Marrakesh and the Houaz Plain to watch the sun rise can be an enchanting experience. It's not

HOW TO HAMMAM LIKE A LOCAL

To bathe like the locals, head to one of the many inexpensive hammams (Moroccan baths, generally 10Dh) spread throughout the old medina. For just a few dirhams, you can take part in the bathing ritual and be part of a real cultural experience. You will want to come prepared with the following:

- flip-flops or sandals

- a plastic bucket

- a cup (traditionally this would be brass, but any cup will do)

- a towel

- a *kis* (the scrubbing glove)

- *savon bildi* (black soap)

- *rhassoul* (clay soap)

- shampoo

- conditioner

- shower gel or soap bar

- something to cover your lower half (bathing suit or underwear, though keep in mind they might get stained if you're going to have henna applied or might get stretched out because of the steam)

- a clean change of clothes

- an orange to eat while you are relaxing in the cooling room before you change into fresh clothes

The typical hammam consists of four rooms: changing room, cool room, warm room, and hot room. When you first enter the steamy confines of the hammam, you will strip down to your bathing suit or underwear and put your belongings in a cubicle in the changing room. Next, you can apply the *savon bildi* in the cool room and then head into the warm room, or go straight to the warm room, where you can rinse and scrub. Some people just head straight for the hot room and do everything there while they breathe in the steam. The basic idea is to gradually increase the temperature of the air and water as you go from room to room, while washing using your bucket and cup. Usually, there will be someone on hand in the changing room to lead you through the hammam ritual: soaping, rinsing, and exfoliating. They will also vigorously (if not violently) rub you down for a small charge of 40-50Dh. Most locals opt to do everything themselves, usually going with a friend or family member to have a chat while they are scrubbing down.

quite a magic carpet, but it's as close as you can get. Rides are generally 40 minutes-1 hour long. Balloons can be canceled at the last minute due to high winds or an unexpected visit from the royal family. In case of cancelation, you will be refunded promptly by each of the companies listed.

Adventure Balloon Marrakech

tel. 0691/707 744; email: info@ adventureballoonmarrakech.com or

adventureballoonmarrakech@gmail.com;
http://adventureballoonmarrakech.com;
2,000Dh

The friendly services of this outfit begin with an early morning pickup (around 6am) by 4x4 from your accommodation to make sure you can see the sunrise. You'll be served a light breakfast while watching the balloon inflate and hearing the usual safety talk by the balloon's pilot. The real treat, of course, is being able to watch the sun crest from behind the peaks of the High Atlas Mountains. Children under 12 get 50 percent off. A traditional Moroccan breakfast is served afterward.

Ciel d'Afrique

Imm. Ali, Appt. 4, 2e Étage., Route de Targa -
Victor Hugo; tel. 0524/432 843;
email: contact@cieldafrique.info;
www.cieldafrique.info; 2,000Dh

For a full-on VIP treatment, look no further than Ciel d'Afrique. They've been running balloon rides since 1990 and have evolved to be the premier luxury hot-air balloon tour operator in the country. Though their "Classic" flights are enjoyable, they are in a shared balloon that can fit up to 20 people. The real splurge is to go for a private balloon ride (minimum of two people, 4,920Dh per person) with your loved ones or good friends. Amazingly enough, the balloons all have Wi-Fi on board, so you can even share the moment with your friends back home.

Marrakesh by Air

Residence Bel Air, #11 Apt. 5, Sergent Levet
Street (Victor Hugo); tel. 0652/129 721;
https://marrakechbyair.com; 2,050Dh

The standard flights on offer by Marrakesh by Air are well done, offering charming service and spectacular views. While they do offer services for large groups, like many other hot-air balloon operators, the value isn't quite there. Children under 10 receive a 50 percent discount.

Marrakech Dream Ballooning

Rue Ibn Aïcha, résidence Alhadika Alkobra,
imm G, n°12, Guéliz; tel. 0524/422 946;
email: info@marrakech-ballooning.com;
http://marrakech-ballooning.com; 2,050Dh

Like all of the other hot-air balloon companies, Marrakech Dream Ballooning includes pickup and dropoff at your accommodations with their packages, as well as coffee and tea service and a safety briefing before takeoff. However, what sets them apart are the post-balloon festivities, which include not only a giant breakfast spread in a traditional Moroccan tent, but also a camel ride through the palm groves. All in all, it makes for an incredibly memorable morning in Marrakesh.

PUBLIC POOLS

When the heat turns up, and your accommodation doesn't have a plunge pool or swimming pool, there's only one thing to do: search for water. In the summer, temperatures can soar to 50°C (120°F), making a refreshing dip in a swimming pool something of a midday ritual... or necessity. The most convenient pools will be in your accommodation. Many, but not all, accommodations in Marrakesh have pools; be sure to ask ahead to see if yours does. If not, check into some of these public options.

Palais Donab

53 Dar el Bacha; tel. 0524/441 897;
www.palaisdonab.com; daily 11:30am-3pm;
150Dh pp

If your accommodations don't have

a pool or you're just looking for a place to chillax, pop into the Palais Donab. There is an attached hotel, restaurant, and lounge, but the real draw here is being able to be pool-side in the middle of the medina for 150Dh (per person). The price of admission includes towels and sun beds, but you'll have to pack your own sunscreen.

Palmeraie Resorts
Circuit de la Palmeraie; tel. 0524/334 343; www.palmeraieresorts.com; 150Dh pp

If you're looking to enjoy some sun, party a bit, shake your moneymaker, and sit down to a luxe meal, check out the pool at Nikki Beach in this resort tucked into the palm groves. It boasts three swimming pools, tennis courts, lounge spaces, and a DJ that spins the latest cuts all day long. This is not a great place for kids, but ladies might be interested in the resort's midweek escape on Tuesdays with a complementary pool bed and open bar from 11am to 1pm. Gentlemen, don't worry, you have your own deal on Thursdays from noon-1pm.

TOURS AND GUIDES
GUIDED CITY TOURS
Marrakesh by Locals
tel. 0659/165 696; www.marrakechbylocals.com; 200Dh

For guided tours of Marrakesh, this new walking tour outfit is incredible. They run two different types of tours, both of which are for those interested in the culture and history from a local perspective. One is a walking tour for families and friends who want to be in privacy and do not want to "share" their guide with someone else; the other tour is for travelers who prefer to share the experience with like-minded souls.

Marrakesh Walking Tours
tel. 0606/548 155; www.marrakechwalkingtours.com; 1,000Dh

Though a touch more expensive than many of its counterparts, Marrakesh Walking Tours stands out thanks to the head guide, Khalid, who is professional in every respect, speaking fluent English (which is not always the case with tour guides) and possessing a deep knowledge of his city's art, culture, and history that is wonderful to behold. For a real treat, instead of booking the regular (and expensive) full-day Historic and Cultural tour, consider the vibrant night tour of the Jemaa el-Fnaa instead. Not only is this half the price (500Dh), but this tour will give you insight into the circus vibe of Marrakesh's most popular hangout spot that you will not find anywhere else.

✪ Marrakesh Food Tour
tel. 0666/261 545; https://marrakechfoodtours.com; 600Dh

If you're anything like me, you probably like to travel through your stomach. Lucky for us, resident Marrakesh expat and influential blogger Amanda Mouttaki has put together a tour just for us. Tours are limited to around eight people and usually meet in the Jemaa el-Fnaa. From this busy plaza, you'll quickly dive into the local souks to sample Marrakesh's slow-cooked specialty *tangia* and the ever-popular Moroccan donuts, *sfeng,* to a number of other dishes scattered throughout the medina that will leave your belly happy and your taste buds glowing.

BIKING
Bike tours have become increasingly popular over the last few years. They can be a wonderful, eco-friendly way to get out and explore the surrounding

a guide giving instructions to a group

Hiring a guide anywhere in Morocco, particularly in Marrakesh, can be a little tricky. The market is crowded with self-proclaimed experts and locals trying to make a quick buck and who are not afraid to overcharge for their services. When in doubt, you can ask to see the **certification** given by the Moroccan Ministry of Tourism or play it safe and stick with one of the guides listed here.

One of the common local cons is to pose as a guide, particularly in and around the Jemaa el-Fnaa. Though policing has gotten better in recent years, many travelers to Marrakesh often fall prey to one of these local conmen. Though occasionally the prices will be higher than those of licensed guides, the real issue is that many of these faux guides have not been certified or schooled and thus often spew lots of misinformation. To get the real scoop on Marrakesh, or any other Moroccan city, make sure to contact a certified local guide or company.

One of the best travel strategies is to **reserve a guided tour** for your first full day in Marrakesh. This way, as you're learning more of the culture and history, you'll also be able to have a friendly face to help orient you in the confusing medina.

Because of the rising popularity of Marrakesh, there can be a scarcity of guides during busy seasons (spring, fall, and winter holidays) and during festivals. It is best to **arrange for a guided tour ahead of your arrival.** The guides listed throughout this guidebook have all been vetted, speak English unless otherwise noted, and are certified whenever certification is available.

palm groves and the further reaches of Marrakesh. E-bikes have become increasingly popular. For those looking to bike into the mountains, this is the e-ticket.

✪ Marrakesh Bike Tours

44 Rue Tarik Ben Ziad; tel. 0667/797 035 or 0661/240 145; www.marrakech-city-bike-tour.com; 250Dh for group city tour, 400Dh for private guided city tour

Located next to the Carre Eden shopping center, this outfit has become the go-to company for those looking to explore the Red City on two wheels. By far the best deal is the friendly group city tour, though private tours are also available. You'll want to make sure to book the morning tour (10am) on hotter days, as tours are around three hours long. The afternoon tour (3pm) is in the hottest part of the day and should only be attempted in hot months

TOURING MARRAKESH BY BUS

The red double-decker buses run by **Alsa** (tel. 0524/335 270, www.alsa.ma, daily, 9am-sunset), seen throughout the city, provide a relaxing way to see many of the sights from the comfort of a cushy bus seat, though they also double as a handy way to get to distant parts of the Ville Nouvelle. **Tickets** are available to purchase (145Dh for a day pass, 165Dh for a two-day pass) when you board the bus, which leaves every 20-30 minutes every day from the station in Gueliz across from the Tourist Information Center on Avenue Mohammed V.

There are two bus circuits. The **Historic Tour** makes stops at the Jemaa el-Fnaa, the tourist office, Menara Gardens, and the train station, and the **Oasis Tour** makes a circuit through the Palmeraie. Each bus takes approximately one hour to make a full circuit. Your ticket is valid for 24 hours, and for those who want to see more of the city but don't want to deal with unreliable taxis or figuring out the local bus schedule, this can be a huge timesaver. For people wishing to tour the Palmeraie, the views from the top of the bus can't be beat. They allow you to peer over some of the walls that otherwise obscure many of the elaborate villas spread throughout this giant palm grove.

by those with a predisposition for self-harm. Otherwise, the guided tours will keep you safe on the busy Marrakeshi roads while showing off some of the best that the Red City has to offer.

Argan Xtreme Sports

Rue Fatima al Fihria; tel. 0524/400 207; www.argansports.com; bike rental 200Dh/ day, tours from 300Dh

To rent a bike, check in with Argan Xtreme Sports, who can set you up with a bike to get around the city for around 200Dh a day. They also arrange more extreme bike tours throughout the High Atlas Mountains and around Morocco. The Palmeraie Tour (300Dh) is a great way to circuit through the vast palm groves of Marrakesh. For those looking to really challenge themselves, perhaps imagining a future outing with the Tour de France, this is your outfit.

MOTORCYCLE SIDECAR TOURS
Marrakech Insiders

tel. 0669/699 374; http://marrakechinsiders. com/en; 1,500Dh per sidecar

For a bespoke, exclusive experience, hop on one of the sidecars of this fun tour outfit and speed around the streets of Marrakesh and the local palm groves. There is literally no other tour like this in all of Morocco. Every ride is custom-made based on your time constraints and interests. You could explore all the way into the High Atlas Mountains if you wanted. For an especially interesting day, look into the "High Flyer Combo" on the company's website: it combines a morning hot-air balloon ride led by Ciel d'Afrique with an afternoon tour on the sidecars, giving you the opportunity to explore Marrakesh by land and by air in the same day. Rides usually meet at Grand Café de la Poste in Gueliz, though pickup at your accommodation can be arranged for 200Dh.

Entertainment and Events

On arriving, pick up a copy of *Marrakech Pocket* from your hotel or the Tourist Information Center. This monthly publication lists all of the upcoming events in the city, though only in French. There seems to be a festival at least once a month, some larger than others. It's also worth knowing that some of the nightclubs, particularly 555 (tel. 0678/181 085, www.beachclub555.com), occasionally host concerts.

PERFORMING ARTS

✪ Storytelling at Café Clock
224 Derb Chtouka; tel. 0655/210 172; www.cafeclock.com; free

Every Thursday night at 7pm, Café Clock hosts one of the most culturally interesting events around town. Professional storytellers from the Jemaa el-Fnaa come and weave their tales for audiences in English and Moroccan Arabic. Other weekly events include traditional music on Sundays (6pm); jam sessions on Wednesdays, where you can bring an instrument and play with a cast of characters from around the world (7pm); and Saturday night live local music (6pm).

Royal Theatre
Ave. Hassan II; tel. 0524/431 516

Designed by renowned Tunisian architect Charles Boccara, this truly royal theater is inspired by Roman art and decadence, as belied by the imposing cupola and Romanesque columns. The outdoor amphitheater of the Theatre Royal seats 1,200 and is a focal point for cultural events in the Red City,

hosting shows, receptions, concerts, ballet, and other exhibitions throughout the year. An indoor 800-seat opera house is supposedly in the works, but there has been no update about this since the Royal Theatre's opening in 2001, after nearly 25 years of construction and a myriad of delays.

Theatre Dar Attakafa Daoudite
Dar Attakafa Daoudite, Ave du 11 Janvier; tel. 0669/267 709 or 0662/782 662

Considerably popular with the local French expat community, this theater has a number of shows throughout the year that focus on unison and cultural plurality—fitting, as the name of the theater means "house of culture." Beyond the francophone plays and music that grace the calendar, there is also an exceptional library that hosts events and readings, though largely in French as well.

CINEMAS

Cinéma Mabrouka
77 rue Bab Agnaou; 25Dh

This throwback movie house is part of a small revival taking place around Morocco. It is the only theater that shows primarily Moroccan and French films, though popular French-dubbed Hollywood productions do appear from time to time. It's best to look up their Facebook page for the latest showings.

Cinéma le Colisée
corner of Blvd. Zerktouni and rue Mohammed el-Beqal; tel. 0524/448 893; 35Dh

If you'd like to escape the hot

The last great storyteller performs at Café Clock.

Morocco has long been a land of stories and storytellers. Oral storytelling is an art that is passed from generation to generation, with storytellers becoming masters of the form, of keeping an audience hypnotized and on-edge, before delivering the final revelation, moral, or lesson. Stories are often told by women in the privacy of their homes, but in public, it is a craft of men and it is a high art. However, it is also a dying art. Aging storytellers are anxious to find young people to take over their craft.

Oral storytelling, or *hiyakat,* can trace its roots far back, before the written word, in the cradle of civilization on the Persian Peninsula. In Morocco, the roots trace back to the storied **Jemaa el-Fnaa.** Storytellers have sat in this popular square, plying their trade late into the night, for generations. They spin their tales among the snake charmers, musicians, and fortune tellers as their fathers and forefathers have, telling stories of intrigue, of sultans and harems, adventures of Sindibad, and genies that arise from bottles with little more than a dusting off, often with disastrous results.

Storytellers generally apprentice for five or more years, learning how to charm an audience, how to work on their breath and speech cadence, to understand when to lower their voice to a whisper and then when to unleash the wrath of the heavens with a thunderous roar. Professional storytellers have a thousand or more stories, not unlike their muse, **Scheherazade,** perhaps the most famous story of them all. You'll hear versions of the famed stories of *1,001 Nights,* as well as tales of the birth of the Sahara and of Aicha Rmada, a local version of Cinderella. There is a rekindled interest in Moroccan storytelling, particularly in Marrakesh, with **Café Clock** leading the revival.

afternoon in an air-conditioned movie theater, check out this cinema. While they do show movies in English, they are not great about publicizing the times, so it's best to stop by and ask about the schedule. The people working here are extremely helpful. A variety of films are shown here, from local Moroccan to French and the standard Hollywood fare.

FESTIVALS AND EVENTS

International Marathon (Marathon Internationale)

Dar Talib Daoudiat, Unité 4; www.marathon-marrakech.com; Jan.; 700Dh

In January, Marrakesh hosts this annual marathon that will take you on a very flat course that makes a circuit around the old city of Marrakesh and through the nearby palm groves.

During the race, every 5 kilometers (3mi) there are refreshment points with water and orange slices. Medals are awarded to all ranked runners. There are other events, including a children's race and half-marathon, that are also a lot of fun for sporty families. Check the website for more information and to sign up.

Formula E Grand Prix

various locations around the city; Jan.;
free-600Dh

Electric car racing has taken the world by quiet, silent storm, and Marrakesh is no different. Every January, the ABB FIA Formula E Championship returns to the Red City for "sand, souks, and a spectacular showdown." In just a few short years, the Formula E Grand Prix has become the must-see car racing action. And with the backdrop of majestic Marrakesh, there isn't a more beautiful environment for a 2.99-kilometer (1.18-mi) circuit with 12 turns and some of racing's longest straightaways. Though there are a number of free venues available to watch the race, viewing cannot be guaranteed. For guaranteed viewing, you'll want to buy a grandstand ticket.

International Festival of Contemporary Dance

various locations around the city; Mar.; free

Contemporary dance has really taken hold throughout North Africa and the Middle East. The love for dance is expressed in the annual International Festival of Contemporary Dance, held every March throughout the city. For a few days, the city is transformed by bobbing heads, swaying hips, and twisting torsos spinning like dervishes in the Jemaa el-Fnaa. Most events are public and free, though some private shows in theaters have a cover charge.

Marrakesh Laughs (Marrakech du Rire)

various locations around the city;
May or June; 150Dh and up

Created by comedian Jamel Debbouze in 2011, this is a very popular event for francophones from around the world who are looking for a night of laughter and spectacle. The event is televised, watched by an estimated 3 million people and syndicated throughout the year. Though comedy and music sketches take place around the city, the headliners perform at the amphitheater of the **Royal Theatre**. Performers are mostly Moroccan and French who all share the love for a great *jeu du mots*.

Popular Arts Festival

various locations around the city;
June or July; free

The Popular Arts Festival showcases talents typically seen in the Jemaa el-Fnaa and exports them into the palatial digs of the **Badi Palace** (Ksibat Nhass, tel. 0661/350 878) and **Royal Theatre** (Ave. Hassan II, tel. 0524/431 516) every June or July. The energy around this festival is palpable, and it seems to be all anyone talks about for the weeks leading up to it. Performers of all stripes—storytellers and snake charmers, fire eaters and Gnawa musicians—descend on the city to swallow flames in the famed city square and belly dance in the transformed ruin of the Badi Palace in the plush confines of the Royal Theater. Those lucky enough to be in Marrakesh over the course of this festival are in for a carnival treat.

International Film Festival

www.festivalmarrakech.info/en; Nov. or Dec.; free-200Dh

The International Film Festival, held late November or early December every year, brings together a diverse collection of filmmakers from around the world to screen films in English, French, Arabic, and other languages. The festival honors strong performers, with a list of recipients including Sharon Stone, Juliette Binoche, Hirokazu Kore-Eda, Mohamed Khouyi, Fernando Solanas, and Jeremy Irons. The festival works with local Moroccan film studios, such as Atlas Film Studios in Ouarzazate. Inquire at your accommodations for ticket availability.

Shopping

One of the charms (and hassles) of Morocco is having to barter. Prices are nearly always negotiable. The entire act is a great dance, with partners taking turns with the lead, spinning one another around until a final price is agreed upon. Moroccan dancing partners, at least when it comes to the realm of shopping, are notoriously aggressive and demanding. Like in a good dance, you are expected to be equally aggressive and demanding. Don't be rude, but be firm with a price you think is fair. Whatever prices you and the shopkeeper start out at generally signal that a "fair price" will be arrived at somewhere in the middle.

MEDINA
✪ THE SOUKS OF MARRAKESH

If crowds aren't your thing, consider going to the souks on a Friday afternoon, when the medina is much more subdued and many, though not all, of the stores are closed. Otherwise, be sure to slip on your best pair of walking shoes and shop till you drop.

Souk Ableuh

From the Jemaa el-Fnaa, head north past the Café de France and keep to the left past the Terraces de l'Alhambra restaurant, where you'll enter the Souk Ableuh, the first of the many souks of Marrakesh. This souk is relatively tame, with a selection of bazaars, and it's mostly a busy thoroughfare to the main souks beginning with the longer Rue Smarine. You'll see a row of olive sellers with mounds of deliciously spicy olives, reflecting the Souk Ableuh's predominant historical trade.

bamboo-covered souks

Ornate pottery is a popular gift item.

Souk Semmarine

Past the Souk Ableuh you'll duck through archways and come to the clearly marked Souk Semmarine. This is basically a road that turns into two other souks: Souk Nejjarine and Souk el Kebir. Most of the smaller souks run off of this main artery formed by these three souks. Above, slats in the bamboo covering over the souks let in slivers of sun, the bamboo providing just enough shade to keep shoppers cool throughout the long, hot afternoons. These main three souks are filled with pottery and pastry sellers, as well as larger bazaars catering to tourists with all manner of traditional Moroccan goods. At the junction where the souk road forks, you will find the Souk Attarine complex just through Souk Stalia to the left. If you continue straight ahead, you will find the Souk Laghzel (the wool and former slave market), as well as the Souk Zrabia (the carpet souk) on the right, before arriving at Souk Cherratine, which connects with the Souk Attarine, forming a connected circuit.

Souk Cherratine

The Souk Cherratine connects with the main Souk Semmarine road, at this point now called Souk el Kebir. This area is the primary reserve of leatherworkers and their goods. Camel-skin bags and goat-hide coats are all on offer here, though prices can be outrageous. Some smaller items, such as wallets and belts, are 20-100Dh, while purses and clutches typically run 100-300Dh, depending on the type of leather used and the decoration. Camel leather is the most expensive, with goat and sheep being a close second and cow the cheapest and most common. A well-made leather bag big enough for your laptop should cost 200-300Dh, though you will almost always have to bargain to get that kind of price. Like carpet dealers, leather sellers can be notoriously aggressive with their pricing. Don't be surprised if you hear 2,000Dh for a leather jacket that should be half that price.

Souk Smata

Running nearly parallel to the Souk el Kebir, south about midway through Souk Cherratine, is the Souk Smata or the Souk des Babouches, a series of shops dedicated to the lovely Moroccan slippers you've likely seen everywhere. The traditional slippers of Marrakesh are cream, while saffron yellow ones are favored by the people from Fez. Today, you can find slippers in a wide range of styles and colors. Some slippers are meant to be worn indoors, while others have rubber soles, making it possible to wear them outside of the house. The shop owners in this souk are typically friendly and mostly honest with pricing. If you're buying multiple pairs of slippers, discounts will be available.

Souk Attarine

Located in the northwest of the souk complex, the Souk Attarine now houses shops selling silver teapots,

the colorful souks of Marrakesh

Here is a quick list of souk goods and a considerably fair price for each, though some souk items are of notoriously poor quality, and that's something to watch out for. As they say in Morocco, "Not everything that sparkles is gold."

- **Carpets:** Prices vary with size; 3-meter by 4-meter (roughly 10-ft by 13-ft) carpets are typically around 1,000-3,000Dh, though certain more ornate carpets, such as carpets from Tazenakht and Rabat, can fetch 2-4 times as much. Of all the sellers in the souks, carpet-sellers are notoriously the most aggressive and often start with outrageous prices, like 20,000Dh.

brass lanterns, and other metal works. However, the few **spice stands** that are still around, with their fragrant pyramidal towers of spice, give a hint to the real historical importance of this souk. Spices were, and still are, one of the more valued commodities in the Moroccan household kitchen.

Souk des Teinturiers

Down the busy street leading to the decorative Moussine Fountain from Souk Attarine is Souk des Teinturiers, or the **Dyers Souk.** Traditionally, this is where wool and silk were naturally dyed into bright reds, indigo blues, saffron yellows, and a kaleidoscope of other colors. Historically, this was a well-known souk for its rich, deep purple dye, sourced from nearby Essaouira. Today, the dyes are largely

chemical, though a few keep to tradition. The wool is likely imported from Australia, and the "silk" is more rayon than anything else, though shopkeepers will insist on calling it cactus silk. This is the best souk to find a light scarf to wrap around your head. If you're

the colorful Dyer's Souk

68

- **Ceramics:** Decorative plates and bowls, typically from Fez and Safi, will cost anywhere from 40Dh (small plate or bowl) to 200Dh (large plate or bowl). Some bowls from Fez, distinguished by the heavier white clay and blue-and-green flower motifs, can cost up to 400Dh.

- **Moroccan slippers (*belghas* or *babouches*):** These cost 50Dh for indoor slippers, and 90Dh for outdoor versions with rubber soles. Beware of paper-soled indoor *belghas*, which will quickly wear out. The embroidered slippers from Tafraoute will generally cost 150Dh.

- **Scarves:** Light scarves range from 40-100Dh.

- **Shisha pipes:** It costs 150Dh for a small one, though large ones can cost as much as 500Dh, depending on ornateness.

- **Silver jewelry:** The price is always negotiable, but silver jewelry is sold by the gram, and 15-20Dh a gram is reasonable. Sterling silver will be stamped with the number 925. All other silver is of mixed quality and should be substantially less.

- **Spices:** Cost varies with type and quality. Good **saffron** can be had for less than 10Dh a gram. Most other spices are less than 50Dh for a kilogram. It's best to say how much you want in dirhams—order 5Dh of one spice or 10Dh of another. Often, you will be surprised by the quantity.

- **Tajines:** You'll pay 25-40Dh for a plain clay tajine. Beware of the decorative glazed tajines, as they may contain lead; these should not be used to prepare or serve food. The two- or three-piece tiny tajines for spices are typically 20-30Dh.

- **Teapots:** Cost runs from 100Dh (small) to 200Dh (large).

lucky, one of the owners or boys in the neighborhood will show you to a rooftop for a spectacularly colorful view of the souk. A tip of 5-10Dh is customary for this unbeatable photo op.

Souk des Chaudronniers

You can still hear the pounding of hammers on metal at the Souk des Chaudronniers, or **metal workers' souk,** just north of the Soutk Attarine. Here, copper and bronze are still pounded into bowls, plates, spoons, and all manner of shapes to be used around the home. Workers can be particularly sensitive to having their photos taken, so be careful. After a few minutes in the heat of the action when the workers are at their most furious, pounding and tapping incessantly into the metal, the overwhelming orchestra can induce headaches. Perhaps this is where metal music got its start? Though headache-inducing, a stop by the Souk des Chaudronniers provides a fascinating glimpse into the art of metal sculpting.

Souk Kimakhnine

Farther north from the Souk Attarine, along Souk Kchachabia in the quietest area of the souk complex, you'll find the Souk Kimakhnine, a souk still dedicated to making traditional Middle Eastern **musical instruments** such as ouds (lutes), *watars* (a type of acoustic guitar), *tarboukas* (goblet drums), and all manner of Moroccan-specific instruments. This is an absolute must-stop for musicians and one of the favorite souks for kids, where the owners will happily let them bang on drums or try their hands at plucking notes on the *watar*.

Souk Haddadine

Next to Souk Kimakhnine is Souk Haddadine, another one of the lesser-visited souks in Marrakesh. This souk and the smaller Souk Chouari form the Woodworker and Blacksmith Souks. The alleyways here smell of freshly cut pine wood and are some of the quietest places in the medina, making a stroll through here surprisingly relaxing. Peek into the shops, where some workers are cutting wood to fit while others are painting decorative motifs. Meanwhile, the blacksmiths forge wrought iron into window grates and coat hangers.

Souk Harrarine

Formerly the silk market (from whence it gets its name), today's Souk Harrarine has become a market for popular, geometrically intricate light fixtures. There are light fixtures of all types, from those that wouldn't look out of place in a grand palace to smaller lights that would be at home on a nightstand, cozily illuminating your bedroom.

TRADITIONAL GOODS AND HANDICRAFTS
Ensemble Artisanal

Ave. Mohammed V; tel. 0524/443 503;
Mon.-Sat. 9am-7pm, Sun. 9am-1pm

If you're looking for traditional Moroccan goods but find shopping in the souks intimidating—and rightfully so—make your way to the Ensemble Artisanal. You'll find well-made Moroccan products, such as leather bags and decorated pottery, for government-established prices. If you want to be a little more familiar

colorful leather stools

An artisan carves intricate stucco.

with standard prices, it's a good idea to duck into the Ensemble Artisanal to see the prices of goods before attempting haggling in the souks. You can window shop all you like, wonderfully hassle free. The Ensemble Artisanal is a short five-minute walk from the Jemaa el-Fnaa, north from the Koutoubia Mosque on Avenue Mohammed V across from the Cyber Park.

Association Al Aahd al Jadidi Artisanat
Derb Derbachi; tel. 0524/392 741;
Mon.-Sun. 10am-9pm
This is the artisans' district, and is located at the entrance of Derb Dabachi, left after the covered part as you're walking away from the Jemaa el-Fnaa. Here, you can find all sorts of products made from straw and bamboo, as well as some hand-whittled spoons and hand-carved cutting boards in walnut, lemon tree, and other woods. You'll find all sorts of wooden kitchen utensils here, perfect for that chef du

cuisine you left back home. The craftsmen here all work on-site, so you can meet the people behind the work.

Maitre Artisan
60 de la place des Epices;
Sat.-Thurs. 9am-8pm
If you have become intrigued by the local use of *tadelahkt* (a type of plaster), master Marrakeshi artisan Abdelghafour offers *tadelahkt* objects of very high quality and in very pretty colors. He does a lot of work for exporting, particularly to France, so he is used to demanding standards. You will also be able to take home supple leather poofs, silver nickel wall sconces, ceramic boxes, and trays and intricate boxes made of glass and metal.

ARGAN OIL
Aromatimri
27 rue des banques Kennaria; 0524/387 282;
Mon.-Sat. 10:30am-10pm, Sun. 11am-10pm
Easily found near the Jemaa el-Fnaa square, this shop is for those looking

for good quality **argan oil**, above all else. There are other quality cosmetics on offer from Youssef, the kind store owner, with some of the popular traditional Moroccan beautification products, such as kohl and rose water, found in large supply.

BOUTIQUES AND FASHION
Sissi Morocco
Place des Epices; tel. 0615/226 520;
Mon.-Fri. 9am-6pm
This shop is extremely popular with the expat crowd. Sana, the incredible saleswoman you'll usually find here, will be happy to direct you to whatever you need. The cushions in particular are well done, with a subtle Moroccan minimalist touch. You can also find bags, wallets, and even some new clothes here. This is the kind of shop that you can walk into not wanting a thing, and then come out with your arms full. Buyer be warned!

Kitan
11 Derb Smara Kandil Sidi Abdelaziz;
tel. 0664/623 969; www.kitansouk.co.uk;
daily 10am-8pm
Founded by Mai, a Japanese woman, in 2015, this has quickly become a trendy shop in Marrakesh. Here you will find a nice selection of cotton and linen tunics, as well as other traditional clothes, with exceptional craftsmanship. The designs done here by Mai are a bit finer and more minimalist than what you'll find in other similar places around Morocco.

Zou & Co
11 Souk Jeld Sdid Abdel Aziz;
tel. 0524/428 662; daily 10am-8pm
This upscale concept store in the medina offers a contemporary take on many Morocco classics, from plates fashioned from olive and walnut wood to stylish ceramics, fashionable linens, and one-of-a-kind mirrors. This is a great stop for shoppers who are looking for something that wouldn't be out of place in a Parisian apartment.

Topolina
134 Dar el Bacha; www.topolina.shop;
daily 10am-8pm
For funky Japanese-Moroccan-fusion fashion, check out this boutique shop not far off the Jemaa el-Fnaa. You'll find hip takes on Moroccan shoes with prints that will leave your feet dizzy to big sacks with matching kimono-style robes that would look great on the street or on the beach.

LINEN AND FABRICS
By Faissal
119 Rue Mouassine; tel. 0696-972001;
daily 10am-7pm
If you're looking for all-natural, 100 percent cotton, linen, or wool fabrics to take home, pop in for a peek here. Faissal offers bolts of fabric done in a bright array of colors. He makes them all in a workshop near the shop. The cotton-linen blends are nice, but the 100 percent cotton threads are where his work truly stands out.

MUSICAL INSTRUMENTS
Tamouziqua
84 Kennaria Touala; tel. 0671/518 724;
daily 10am-9pm
Tamouziqua is easy to miss. It's one of the many stores dealing in musical instruments, though where many of the other shops along Kennaria Touala also sell flamenco guitars from Spain and Fender knock-offs from China, Mustapha Mimani is still making *watars, gimbris,* and Moroccan drums the old-fashioned way, with carved, notched wood and stretched animal hides. Look for the cubbyhole shop

carpets for sale in the souks

raised a couple of feet off the street and listen for the banging of drums. Mustapha also gives music lessons for those looking to find their Gharnati or maybe Gnawi soul.

GUELIZ

Gueliz has quickly become the go-to shopping district in Marrakesh's *ville nouvelle*, with the popular Avenue Mohammed V lined with shopping centers. There is a sort of **outdoor shopping mall** along the Place du 16 Novembre, which features many brand names familiar to Europeans and North Americans. Farther up Avenue Mohammed V is the new **Carre Eden** shopping center, another popular stop for name-brand goods, as well as the Marrakesh branch of Starbucks. For traditional Moroccan goods, duck through the alleyway across from the Carre Eden for a selection of bazaar goods, including handsome pottery, embroidered kaftans, and decorative Moroccan pottery, often for prices far less than you'll find in the medina.

CARPETS
Ben Rahal

24 Rue de la Liberté; tel. 0524/433 273; www.benrahalart.com; Mon.-Sat. 9:30am-1pm and 3pm-8pm

If carpets are your thing, head to the reputable Ben Rahal. This is one of the best shops in Marrakesh and maybe in all of Morocco. The service is informative and friendly, without being pushy. Bruce Willis, Bill Murray, and Kate Hudson have all shopped here. Carpet selection includes some Moroccan standards as well as some of the most diverse, truly unique pieces you'll find anywhere. The prices are higher than in some of the smaller villages, but quality will be assured. You can get a spectacular piece for around 5,000Dh.

BOUTIQUES AND FASHION
Carre Eden

Ave. Mohammed V; tel. 0524/487 246; www. carreedenshoppingcenter.com; Sun.-Thu. 10am-9pm and Sat.-Sun. 10am-10pm

Some might argue that the best way

to get a glimpse of the contemporary culture and fashion of any place you visit is to head to the local mall. Housing a number of stores popular in Turkey and France, it's easy to see where Morocco's love for fast fashion is imported from. With Marrakesh's sprawling resident Starbucks serving up familiar icy-cold caffeinated Frappucinos, this can be a good stop to perk up and shop for some wardrobe basics.

Some

76 Boulevard El Mansour Eddahbi;
Mon.-Fri. 9am-7pm

Tucked down a quiet side street sits this slow concept store. With a blend of artisanal heritage goods sourced from around Marrakesh, as well as some new old-fashioned quality ceramics, cozy furniture, and warm light fixtures, this two-story cocooning store might well be the place where you find everything you need for that home makeover you've been waiting on.

Cote Sud

Rue de la Liberté; tel. 0524/438 448;
daily 10am-7pm

Resident Marrakesh design aficionada Sabine offers up some fabulously crafted home decor, bags for men and women, jewelry, and a number of accessories, all made by Moroccan craftspeople. For a thoughtful gift for that special someone back home, pick up a souvenir that speaks to your love for the local artisans.

Lalla

35 Boulevard El Mansour Eddahbi;
Mon.-Sat. 9am-7pm

Sometimes a girl just needs a new bag. Lalla offers up a variety of sacks to please all comers, from funky hand-stiched cotton totes and suppulent leather satchels to elegant, understated evening bags. If you're in the market for something to sling over your shoulder, the chances are that you'll find just the thing here.

Hayani

213 Boulevard Mohamed;
Mon.-Sat. 10am-7pm

If you're more of a shoe diva than Carrie and Kim (Bradshaw and Kardashian, respectively), you'll want to check out Hayani. They specialize in Moroccan-made, high-quality sandals, ballerinas, city shoes, and boots. Sizes are all in European, so it would be helpful to know your European size before stepping in.

FURNITURE
My Art

Pl. du 16 November at Rue Tarek Ibn Zyad;
tel. 0524/449 181; Mon.-Sat. 10am-1pm
and 3pm-7pm

For upscale, handcrafted artisan furnishings, such as tables, lamps, and leather sofas, as well as some other handicraft items, check out My Art. It features exceptional home decor crafted by Moroccans to contemporary European tastes.

BOOKSTORES
Menzil el Fan Librairie d'Art

55 Blvd. Zerktouni, next to the restaurant
Al-Fassia; tel. 0524/446 792; Mon.-Sat.
9am-12:30pm and 3pm-7pm

One of the best bookstores in Marrakesh is the eclectic Menzil el Fan Librairie d'Art. Shelves of coffee-table books—mostly dedicated to Moroccan handicrafts—line the walls. Some great art deco posters from the French protectorate era go for 70Dh.

Food

Inspired by the taste buds of the millions of people from hundreds of nationalities that visit the city each year, Marrakesh is the place to dine out on great fusion-fueled menus. French bistros and Italian pizza joints cozy up with sushi restaurants, Chinese noodle dives, and Balinese cuisine, making the entire culinary vibe of Marrakesh (somewhat surprisingly, for first-time visitors) truly international. It wouldn't be a mistake to say that the food scene in Marrakesh is perhaps the most eclectic in the entire country. If you're spending a long time in Morocco, you would be wise to check out a few of the international options as, outside of some of the bigger cities, your choices throughout the rest of the country are generally limited to Moroccan fare.

For traditional Moroccan food in Marrakesh, there are some really nice Moroccan restaurants. The functioning restaurants in high-end *riads* are well worth checking out as the atmosphere of dining in beautifully restored *riads* is part of the Marrakesh experience. For couples and close friends, these cozy restaurants often make for the most memorable nights out.

MEDINA

There are several places to eat around the medina, though an evening snack on the Jemaa el-Fnaa itself is an experience not to be missed. Most cafés in the busier parts of the medina and around the city serve some sort of breakfast, lunch, or dinner from around 8am until 10pm or so, while reservations will be needed for most of the fine-dining establishments tucked into the numerous *riads* and hotels. If you don't have a phone, you can either have someone at your lodging make a reservation for you or stop by the restaurant the day before and make a reservation in person.

In the kasbah and the mellah, choices are pretty limited outside of the individual *riads,* which will usually make lunches or dinners on demand, even for non-guests. This can be a great way to see a few different *riads.* You can expect a well-done tajine for around 100Dh, and possibly, depending on the restaurant and *riad,* a good wine might be had.

CAFÉS AND LIGHT BITES
Café Atay
62 Rue Amsefah; tel. 0661/344 246; daily 10am-10pm; 60Dh

A good option around the souks is Café Atay, which serves tea. (*Atay* is "tea" in Moroccan Arabic.) The menu includes a variety of simple sandwiches and pastries, but don't miss the surprisingly competent coffee, which can be just the sort of caffeine jolt you might need after a day in the souks. The double-decker terraces serve to elevate above the hum of activity below, giving some great views over the medina, and the free Wi-Fi is handy.

Le Bled Café
6 Kennaria Dabachi; tel. 0524/368 346; daily 10am-10pm; 40Dh

Just a short walk off the Jemaa el-Fnaa, Le Bled Café is one of the quieter options, where hearty tuna sand-wiches and veggie pizzas are made with a smile, along with coffee and freshly squeezed juice. The terrace of this café, and the popular **Bakchich Café** next door, make for great people-watching just off the plaza with a light lunch or just a tea or coffee.

❂ Henna Art Café

35 Derb Sqaya, off Rue Riad Zitoun el Kedim;
tel. 0666/779 304;
www.marrakechhennaartcafe.com;
daily 11am-8pm; 60Dh

South of the Jemaa el-Fnaa you'll find the wonderful Henna Art Café, a veri-table haven for vegetarians and vegans. Offerings include copious simple yet delicious salads and falafel (how is this not more popular around Morocco?). The service is friendly, and the entire café really does its best to show off local artists; American artist Lori Gordon curates the gallery's rotating exhibi-tions. It's best to come in early or mid-afternoon for the best terrace seating.

Un Déjeuner à Marrakech

corner of Rue Kennaria and Douar Graoua;
tel. 0524/378 387; daily 11am-10pm; 50Dh

Un Déjeuner à Marrakech has favor-ites for a late breakfast, lunch, or light dinner. The menu includes omelets, salads, and fresh juice mixes, includ-ing beet root, cucumber, and mint. Vegetarian and gluten-free options are available. Seating inside can be a smoke-free reprieve from the hot sun, but the shaded terrace views on the roof over the medina and to the High Atlas are worth the climb.

MOROCCAN
Café Chez ZaZa

21 Bab Fteuh; tel. 0673/081 716;
daily noon-midnight; 80Dh

Just a bit north of the Jemaa el-Fnaa

you'll find Café Chez ZaZa. The lively terrace looks over the rooftop of the medina, and the waiters, most of whom know more than just a bit of English, will make sure you are well looked after. The menu is traditional Moroccan. Vegetarians will delight in the veggie *pastillas,* a rare find in Morocco, as well as the fresh, clean salads. This is perhaps the best place around the souks for lunch, so the terrace tends to fill up by 2pm.

Lala Moulati

1 Talaa Ibn Youssef, Souk Chaaria;
tel. 0524/385 012; daily 9am-10pm; 70Dh

For people-watching, it doesn't get any more comfy than this bakery café. For a coffee and cookie, stick to the down-stairs window-front bar and take in the busy medina street outside. Head upstairs or to the terrace for a quick breakfast or lunch. The menu is full of familiar favorites to keep the kids happy, from spaghetti Bolognese and cheese pizzas to burgers and pancakes. Though tajines and *pastillas* are on the menu, you can find better elsewhere for half the price.

Lotus Privilege Moroccan Restaurant

9 Derb Sidi Ben Hamdouche; tel. 0661/997
919; www.restaurantlotusprivilege.com;
daily 7pm-1am; 250Dh

Book at least one or two days ahead of time for a seat at Lotus Privilege Moroccan Restaurant. You might even need to hire a guide to lead you to the restaurant, buried in the kas-bah neighborhood. Dinner is served in the cool confines of the starlit patio pool. At 8pm, live Tarab Al-Andalusi (Moroccan music with Andalusian roots) stirs the soul while whirling dervishes spin to the beat. The menu features traditional

Moroccan food revisited, such as a succulent John Dory fish tajine with spicy Moroccan *charmoula*. The food is good, but make no mistake—this is a place you come to for the show.

Restaurant El Bahia

Ansa el Bahia; tel. 0524/378 679; daily noon-4pm and 7:30pm-11:30pm; 150Dh

The Restaurant El Bahia near the Bahia Palace serves competent, though overpriced, tajines. This place is popular with tour groups; when they arrive, it can make service crawl to a halt. The palatial digs are nice and worth skipping the terrace for. Grab a courtyard seat and snack on some spicy olives while your tajine simmers. The menu features Moroccan wines, and let's be honest, after a hot day of touring the souk, sometimes a glass of crisp white wine is all you really need.

✪ La Table Al Badia

135 Derb Ahl Souss; tel. 0524/390 110; www. riadalbadia.com; daily 7:30pm-11pm; 300Dh

For authentic home-cooked Moroccan cuisine, check out La Table Al Badia in the Riad Al Badia. Samira, the chef, heads to the souk every day to hand-pick fresh meat and produce. Succulent lamb that falls off the bone and crispy meat-stuffed pastries are just a couple of the tricks up Samira's sleeve. During the few cold months, you'll dine fireside, as the Marrakesh nights can get chilly. Otherwise, you'll dine outside on the palatial terrace under the dim lights and the stars. Reservations are required the morning of your intended dinner at the very latest. Most dietary needs, such as vegetarian or gluten-free, can be accommodated.

INTERNATIONAL
✪ Pepe Nero

17 Derb Cherkaoui Douar Graoua; tel. 0524/389 067; www.pepenero-marrakech. com; daily dinner seating at 8pm; 200Dh

For an upscale *riad* dining experience, Pepe Nero is just the trick. An Italian-Moroccan fusion menu is served in this beautifully restored *riad*. Dine outdoors beneath a cover of stars; the long central pool and fountain are lit up at night, surrounded by candlelit dining tables. Choose from two menus created by the friendly Cordon Bleu-trained chef, Khalid: The Il Bel Paese menu features Italian dishes, such as mouthwatering saffron carnaroli risotto. The Ville Rouge menu focuses on Moroccan classics revisited, such as pigeon *pastilla* and slow-roasted shoulder of lamb. If you were going to splurge on one restaurant in the medina, it would be this one. Call ahead for reservations.

✪ Exotic Bali

56 Derb Chentouf; tel. 0666/044 882; http://exotic-bali.com; daily noon-10pm; 200Dh

If your hunger pangs steer you toward something farther east, look no further than Exotic Bali. Located on the far end of the souks, the tranquil, moonlit terrace is the perfect spot to unwind while Balinese chef Andy Gustiandi whips up some fresh mint-infused spring rolls to get you started. You'll likely be surrounded by in-the-know French travelers who always seem to have a nose for the hottest restaurants in town. Though the *ikan kukus sumedang* (steamed white fish with *sumedang* sauce or coconut cream) is the chef's specialty, you'd be forgiven for digging into the succulent *daging rendang padang* (slow-cooked beef with coconut and veggies in a creamy *padang* sauce) that just falls apart, not unlike a perfect pot roast. As you might expect from an Indonesian restaurant, there are also tons of options here for vegetarians and vegans alike. This is a can't-miss restaurant for those interested in Marrakesh's burgeoning international dining scene and for those seeking something a world away from the neighborhood *tajine*. No alcohol is served.

Beats Burger

35 Souk Jeld Kimakhine; tel. 0524/391 213; www.beatsburger.com; daily noon-10pm; 100Dh

After a long morning in the souks, sometimes you just want a burger, and Beats Burger fills that craving. From classic cheeseburgers and homemade chicken nuggets to vegetarian-friendly bagels slathered with cream cheese and stuffed with cooked tomatoes, eggplant, zucchini, and peppers, this is a stop that has a little something for everyone. Stop in for an easy lunch in the medina with bright, Beat-era inspired decor. Free Wi-Fi is available. For a little more quiet, brave the spiral staircase to the intimate terrace, and if you like spicy foods, make sure to order your sandwich with the harissa mayonnaise. No alcohol is served.

the welcoming chill found at Beats Burger

Soul Food by Max & Jan

16 rue Amsefa, Sidi Abdelziz; www. maxandjan.com; daily 10am-11pm; 150Dh

Americans shouldn't be fooled by the name. This is Moroccan-style "soul food," with a slow cooked beef *tangia* taking center stage. There is only rooftop terrace dining here, so for rainy days or particularly hot days, it's perhaps better to look elsewhere. Otherwise, a charming, expansive terrace greets you decorated with *bouchourette* carpets from around Morocco, adding to the hip, funky vibe Soul Food carries over from the Max & Jan Concept Store on the ground floor. If you're in the neighborhood, consider stopping in between 4pm-6pm for a tea or coffee with a pastry (80Dh).

GUELIZ

The dining options in Gueliz, like its hotels, are largely budget and mid-range, with very few upscale dining choices available. Some cafés have a real European feel. If you're looking to pass some time people-watching or digging into a vacation read, there are far fewer hassles with sellers and beggars, making this a good place to relax or meet up with friends.

CAFÉS AND LIGHT BITES

Café les Négociants, Café Atlas, and Café la Renaissance are all at Place Abdelmoumen. Their competing positions across from each other evoke Parisian cafés, such as the well-known Café Flore and Deux Magots. Café Atlas, recently remodeled, is the clear winner of this art deco showdown. The wide patio and renovated interior make for a pleasant late-morning coffee or light early-evening snack. Café les Négociants is the local favorite, and the Renaissance is a tad more upscale

eating out on the Jemaa el-Fnaa

It might seem overly touristy, but the food stalls in the Jemaa el-Fnaa actually existed long before tourism ever took root. The smoke from the grills wafting over the carnivalesque square is as familiar a sight to the locals as the nearby Koutoubia Mosque.

Prices will fluctuate wildly depending on your negotiation skills. In principle, you should **agree to a price** for everything before eating. A typical meal costs 30-50Dh, and a plate of **grilled meats** large enough for 3-4 people to share can run 100-150Dh. Other options include a small bowl of **snail soup** (5Dh), *harira* (5Dh), and one of the most refreshing glasses of freshly squeezed **orange juice** you've ever had (4Dh).

Feel free to walk around the stalls and inquire about the food on offer; high-pressured sales are the name of the game, with everyone promising to feed you "the best" in Marrakesh, but it's all largely friendly. Several stands have been featured in travel guides and on websites, though in practice, the food is pretty much the same across the board. The only real issue you might run into is the occasional owner trying to charge more for olives and bread, which are typically free, or having you pay for a full plate instead of half plate, though if you agree on a price ahead of time, this can be avoided.

The stands are controlled by the Moroccan government, so cleanliness is generally okay, though as a rule stick to the soups, fried foods, and meats; **stay away from the seafood or anything uncooked,** as there are no refrigerators to keep food cold, and in the heat bacteria can be a problem if anything is undercooked. It might also be a good idea to **forgo the silverware,** as it is often washed with the same water all day long; instead, **eat with your hands.** For sauces, **use a piece of bread** to scoop up your food, just like the locals.

with a diverse clientele, many from the attached hotel.

Le 1er Boulevard

19 Immeuble Jakar, Ave. Mohammed V;
daily 7am-10pm; 25Dh

If you're staying around Gueliz and need a place to go out for breakfast or a light lunch, Le 1er Boulevard is a good, clean café. Nothing on the menu will knock your socks off, but sometimes simple is good enough. Service starts

at 8am. Continental breakfast, including a freshly squeezed orange juice, is the staple here.

Café du Livre

44 Rue Tariq Ibn Ziad; tel. 0524/446 921;
Mon.-Sat. 11am-midnight; 20Dh

A tour of the Marrakeshi café scene wouldn't be complete without mentioning the haven of English-speakers, Café du Livre, near the Carre Eden shopping center. Whether you're looking for other Anglophones to hang out with, want to curl up among shelves of familiar books, or plan to drop in on the popular quiz night, the newly remodeled café is a gem of modern Marrakesh, with light sandwiches served throughout the day.

MOROCCAN
✪ Libzar

28 Rue Moulay Ali; tel. 0524/420 402; daily noon-3pm and 7pm-11:30pm; 250Dh

There are a few restaurants where you can find really excellent Moroccan food outside of a Moroccan house. Libzar is one of them. If this is your first Moroccan dining experience, most others will likely pale in comparison afterward. The elaborate menu features seven traditional starter salads, as well as classic tajines such as beef and prune, done to perfection. There's great attention to detail throughout the expansive dining room and in the *zellij* and stucco work. The menu includes a list of local Moroccan wines to pair with dinner.

Al Fassia

Blvd. Mohamed Zerktouni; tel. 0544/434 060; daily 8pm-midnight; 300Dh

Another excellent option for Moroccan dining is Al Fassia. It's nearly always busy, and deservedly so. The menu features tajines and couscous dishes, but the setting inside this restored palace, the all-female service, and the ability to order à la carte (instead of an entire five-course meal) set it apart from the crowd. The restaurant can be a bit hard to find. It's a short walk down a shopping alley just off the boulevard, across from the Franco-Belge hotel by Café SBJ. If it's on the menu, go for the lamb with roasted plum.

Kechmara

3 Rue de la Liberté; tel. 0524/422 532; www. kechmara.com; Mon.-Sat. 10am-1am; 130Dh

Down the street from Le Loft and Mamma Mia is Kechmara, an industrial joint that wouldn't look out of place in Brooklyn or Camden Town. The menu is upscale pub food, including fish-and-chips and sizzling duck-sausage hot dogs. The indoor smoking can be a problem for some. Luckily, there are a few seats on the street and an upstairs terrace.

Dar Yacout

79 Sidi Ahmed Soussi; tel. 0524/392 929; www.daryacout.com; Tues.-Sun. 7pm-11pm, reservations highly recommended; 700Dh

Set against the backdrop of a 17th-century palace restored by American architect Bill Willis, this is a venerable establishment of Marrakeshi fine dining. Enchanting Moroccan decor adorns a setting complete with nooks, crannies, and private lounges coupled with breathtaking panoramic views from the terrace overlooking the medina, Jemaa el-Fnaa, and the High Atlas Mountains. It features a gastronomic menu with a fantastic succession of flavors and the type of service you would expect at this level of dining. The set menu, with wine pairings included, changes nightly, keeping seasonal and traditionally Moroccan. There are typically options for vegetarians and seafood lovers, though make sure you contact them ahead of time. If the lamb is on the menu, you are in for a mouthwatering, slow-cooked treat.

INTERNATIONAL
Vita Nova

36 Rue Ibn Aïcha; tel. 0524/423 939; daily noon-3pm and 7pm-midnight; 80Dh

Sleek Vita Nova features favorite

French-Moroccan fusion food is fine-dining in Marrakesh.

contemporary French bistro menu serves easy-to-like favorites, such as a chicken cordon bleu and a cheeseburger that would be right at home in the Marais in Paris. There is a non-smoking section upstairs. With the rotating indie-favorite and international music jams, the vibe is definitely European. All in all, a great escape from the fare of the medina and the standard Moroccan plates.

HIVERNAGE

The Hivernage district in Ville Nouvelle, with all of its spacious, all-inclusive high-end hotels, is not unlike what you'd find in Vegas, minus the gambling (though there is a bit of that). Most of the restaurants in this area veer toward fine dining, and many offer nightly shows with live music and belly dancers—just the thing to get your night in Marrakesh off to a banging success! Each of these hotels has at least one restaurant, if not two or three, on their property. For those interested in seeing what some of these palatial spreads look like on the inside, a meal out can be a great way to get a peek at a property. Dress appropriately and make reservations.

MOROCCAN
La Cour des Lions
Es-Saadi Palace, Rue Ibrahim El Mazini; tel. 0663/055 704; www.essaadi.com; daily 8pm-4am; 500Dh
Make your way to the top of the impressive Es-Saadi Palace to tuck in for a five-star meal at the immaculate La Cour des Lions. Don't be surprised by a decor all in stone lace and carved plaster and the charm of the panoramic view of the pool, garden, and lights of the city. Before dining, enjoy an aperitif in the sumptuous living room or out on one of the two terraces.

Italian classics, such as spaghetti alla carbonara, as well as some of the best pizzas in Marrakesh. The Diavoli is a spicy, devilishly good pizza. The wine list isn't as extensive as that of some of the other restaurants in the neighborhood, but the homemade ice cream makes up for it. Make no mistake, though, you are coming here for the food and not the service, which can be a hit-or-miss affair.

Mamma Mia
18 Rue de la Liberté; tel. 0524/434 454; daily noon-3:30pm and 7pm-11:30pm; 150Dh
The Marrakeshi Italian restaurant staple Mama Mia serves up pastas, as well as Italian lamb shank. Of course, it's the homemade, wood-fired pizzas that tend to steal the show. They're a big hit with the kids. Thankfully, the first floor is nonsmoking in this rustic local favorite. The red-and-white checkered cloths seal the Italian authenticity. If you're looking for an Italian *séjour* from couscous, look no further.

Le Loft
20 Rue de la Liberté; tel. 0524/434 216; www.restaurant-loft.com; daily noon-midnight; 140Dh
Le Loft keeps the distressed-elegance vibe of the neighborhood with lots of exposed wood and brick. The

A little later, discover a menu created by the chef, Fatéma Hal, who charms nightly with forgotten dishes from traditional Moroccan cuisine. For a real gastronomic journey, order one of the set menus that have been carefully crafted for a balanced meal that will hit all the taste buds. The Saint-Pierre *bastilla,* with its crispy filo dough, is a particular standout.

Red House

Corner of el Yarmouk and rue Abdelaziz Elmalzouzi; tel. 0524/437 040/41; http://theredhousemarrakech.com; daily 7pm-midnight; 200Dh

Though there is an international menu, *menu d'ailleurs,* you'll want to stick to the Moroccan staples at Red House. Not that the international menu is bad—the shrimp bisque and seafood risotto are excellent—it's just that the Moroccan menu is that good! Dive in for the chef's take on the local specialty, *tanjia,* a slow-cooked wonder of lamb that melts in your mouth. For families, this is a good spot for kids, with staples like penne pasta if your little ones have less-than-adventurous taste buds. Families should try to sit outside near the pool, while couples will want to cozy up inside the warmly lit, geometrically ornate interior of this former Moroccan family home-turned-guest palace. There is belly dancing and live music most nights.

INTERNATIONAL
Bazz'Art

Corner of el Yarmouk and rue Abdelaziz Elmalzouzi; tel. 0622/426 200; daily 8am-midnight; 200Dh

Featuring a large breakfast buffet, this is a spot for coffee lovers to lounge, whether outside by the pool or inside with the Moroccan-European-fusion decor. The breakfast spread features some Moroccan classics, such as Moroccan donuts (*sfinge*) and Moroccan pancakes (*beghrir*), though for the most part, it has more of a continental breakfast feel, with lots of croissants and fresh fruit. Lunch and dinner (with a DJ) are possible here, but breakfast is really where it's at.

l'Orangerie

Hotel Sofitel, Rue Harroun Errachid; tel. 0663/055 704; daily 7pm-11:30pm; 400Dh

This gourmet fusion restaurant blends the cosmopolitan French cuisine of chef Dominique Oudin with the rich gastronomy of Moroccan chef Ahmed Ed-Defaa. Though the hotel itself lacks some of the innate Moroccan charm of the other big hotels in Hivernage, the hushed dining space is a welcome retreat for those seeking a quieter dining experience in this neighborhood.

Comptoir Darna

Ave Echouada; tel. 0524/437 702 or 0524/437 710; www.comptoirmarrakech. com; daily 7:30pm-1am; 400Dh

With a bold, sweeping staircase linking the upstairs and downstairs dining rooms and perhaps the most entertaining, family-friendly nightly belly dancing performances, this checks all the boxes for lively ambiance. The menu doesn't disappoint, either. Though you could have a multi-course traditional Moroccan dinner, the international courses, including a rich, creamy lobster ravioli, are top notch. The servers are all multilingual, making ordering in English a snap. At midnight, the attached patio opens up into a club, if you're looking to continue the party. It can keep you dancing until the early morning hours.

Moroccan donuts, *sfinge*, are a great street food pick-me-up.

Bars and Nightlife

Nightlife in Marrakesh is the best in Morocco and famed around the world. Its reputation is fully earned. The nightclubs are as good, if not better, than clubs you might find in London, Paris, Tokyo, New York, or other world capitals. The DJs spinning are generally some of the best in the world, many of them international, though there are fantastic home-grown DJs as well. There are not as many clubs as you might find in these other nightlife hotspots, but what Marrakesh lacks in quantity, it makes up for in over-the-top splendor, likely one of the reasons it maintains the reputation is does.

However, fun does come at a price, often in the form of exorbitant drink prices and high cover charges. You can plan on paying 250Dh or more for cover charges, with drinks typically 100Dh and up. Thankfully, most cover charges do include a drink. If you reserve an entire table with bottle service, cover will be free. This can make a lot of sense for groups of friends looking for a great night out. Keep in mind that though the doors typically open in most nightclubs around midnight, the party never gets going until about 2am.

If going out, use a reasonable amount of caution, particularly with strangers. Spiked drinks are not a real concern, though occasionally there are stories about this. Prostitution (both male and female) is rampant. Beware of engaging in any suspicious conversation. The local police force does take prostitution seriously, and there are efforts to curb prostitution and other illegal activities. Have fun. Dance the night away. Just don't do anything really stupid.

BARS

MEDINA

KosyBar

47 Place des Ferblantiers; tel. 0524/380 324; www.kosybar.com; daily 11am-1am

One of the better rooftop terraces you can find in the medina to sip on some cold suds. The menu is largely limited to beers and wines, but on a hot day, sometimes nothing can beat a cold beer or crisp glass of chardonnay. The service is occasionally forgetful. Don't be afraid to remind them that you ordered that second glass. You could consider Kosybar for a light lunch or dinner, as well, but the afternoon thirst quencher is really where it's at.

La Pergola

7/8 Derb Chaabane, Riad Monceau; tel. 0524/429 646; lapergolamarrakech.com; daily 11am-midnight; 120Dh

Located in the stunning Riad Monceau, this rooftop jazz bar has set the standard for what a great medina bar should be. Local chef Rachida Sahnoune has her fingerprints all over the bistro menu, with beautiful planks of cold cuts and cheeses, Moroccan-inspired tapas, and a frayed beef burger done in the style of the local specialty *tangia*. For cocktails, your new addiction might just be the "Love in the Orange Grove," a specialty cocktail using fresh ginger purée, local sugar cane, fresh-squeezed orange juice, Moroccan orange flower essence, Cointreau, and champagne. Come here on Wednesdays for live jazz music and any other day of the week for jazzy accents. Get here for happy hour, 5:30-7:30pm, to enjoy buy-one-get-one glasses of your favorite drink.

GUELIZ

Entrepotes

62 rue Tarik Ibn Zaid; tel. 0663/731 542; daily 6pm-2am; 100Dh

This is the kind of restaurant that you might visit once at the beginning of your trip and then want to revisit before you depart. This probably has to do with the incredible service, though the international theme might have something to do with it as well. Come for the hip, trendy vibe and smiling service, but stick around for the mojitos and *tapas del mar,* a collection of appetizer dishes all featuring seafood. The terrace seating is highly preferred. You'll want to make reservations or show up earlier in the evening for the best seats. Smoking is allowed inside, as in all bars in Morocco.

Mama Africa

Rue Oum Errabia; tel. 0524/457 382 or 0604/092 509; daily noon-midnight; 70Dh

This is a funky, eclectic, colorful, hip sort of joint that is a bit rough around the edges... and only serves nonalcoholic mocktails. However, most nights they have some great background music, usually local reggae or traditional Moroccan music, and, as long as you don't mind the wait, snacks that are a good change from the typical fare, served straight from the motherland. If you haven't hung out at popular cafés in other parts of Morocco or Africa, you might not be prepared for the truly local flavor. This is a more traditional-style Moroccan/African "bar," complete with a little grunge around the edges. I like it, but it's not for everybody. If you happen by here in the mornings, sometimes they're open and you can get a great coffee.

HIVERNAGE
Churchill Bar

Mamounia Palace, Ave. Bab Jdid; tel.
0524/388 600; www.mamounia.com;
daily 6pm-1am; 200Dh

The incredible Mamounia Palace hotel has a long history of political intrigue that would make for a fine setting for a World War II thriller. Winston Churchill, from whom the bar takes its name, negotiated with American President Franklin D. Roosevelt for three days here, which led to D-Day. The small bar, with its classy jazz music, leopard skin carpet, padded red leather walls, and black velvet armchairs, is like something straight from the '40s. However, it can get crowded quickly. If you want to duck out from the crowds, head to the wonderful outside pool bar for a break. There is a strict dress code that is enforced: men are not permitted to sport shorts or sandals, no matter how hot (or fashionable).

L'Epicurien

Rue Ibrahim El Mazini; tel. 0663/055 704;
www.essaadi.com; daily 8pm-4am; 150Dh

Wrapped in cozy felt and adorned with crystal chandeliers, hand-carved mahogany pieces, and enormous mirrors, another great high-end bar in the Hivernage neighborhood is l'Epicurien, in the famous setting of the Es-Saadi Palace. Live concerts are put on nearly nightly by the locally iconic band the Kech Experience, who play an international, energetic set. This is more of a laid-back experience than the neighboring over-the-top nightclub, Theatro. Limit yourself to the drinks here, as the food is overpriced and quality is not guaranteed. For an even more relaxed bar experience, come around opening time before the band kicks off its set.

Royal Mansour Bar

Royal Mansour, Rue Abou Abbas El Sebti;
tel. 0524/808 282; www.royalmansour.com/
en; daily 11am-1am; 250Dh

This might be the most elegant bar in the world, where British style is livened up with a bespoke Moroccan touch. Whether you're wanting to chat with friends, take part in exquisite tastings, or just enjoy some soothing piano music, this is something of a dream bar, though your pocketbook won't think so. It's the sort of place you can imagine James Bond swaggering down the balustrade to order a martini—shaken, of course. Drinks here are expensive, often 150Dh or more. The bar closes at midnight, making this a romantic stop for a nightcap or a calm start to the storm of the local nightclub scene.

Sky Bar

Hotel Renaissance, corner of Ave.
Mohammed V and Blvd. Zerktouni;
tel. 0524/337 777; www.renaissance-hotel-
marrakech.com; daily 11am-1am; 200Dh

If a great view over Marrakesh and the High Atlas Mountains with a cold beverage sweating from your warm hands is the sort of thing that appeals to you, then head straight up the (admittedly really impressive) elevator to the Sky Bar at Hotel Renaissance. Skip the food at the attached restaurant, Aqua Pazza. It is overpriced and not great, but the views here make it a worthwhile stop for that late afternoon bottle, or perhaps even to catch a sunset.

CLUBS AND LIVE MUSIC
GUELIZ
Factory Z

92 rue Yougoslavie; tel. 0669/254 236;
daily 7:30pm-2:30am; 100Dh

This self-described "coyote bar" has

Americana in spades, from exposed brick walls to lots of bright chrome. You can find dancers bumping, grinding, and grooving on every one of this bar's three levels. Live music happens nearly every week (check their Instagram feed for the best updates, @factoryzmarrakech) with guest DJs spinning some of the most popular jams from the US and Europe.

HIVERNAGE
555

Hôtel Ushuaia, Blvd. Mohammed VI;
tel. 0678/181 085; www.beachclub555.com;
10pm-late; 200Dh

Continuing the party is never a problem at 555. Guest DJs are drawn from around the world, with a heavier emphasis on the American hip-hop and rap scene. Snoop Dogg and Jay-Z have even thrown down here. There is also a dinner spectacle worth checking out, with flashy dancers and outrageous costumes. Doors open at 11:30pm. Every night, groups of four or more ladies get in free, with free drinks all night long, making it a good stop for girls' night out.

Le Salama

40 Rue des Banques; tel. 0524/391 300 or
0657/733 879; www.le-salama.com;
daily noon-midnight; 200Dh

This is one of very few places around the Jemaa El-Fnaa square that offers beer, wine, and spirits. You could have dinner here (300Dh), but the real gem is the rooftop terrace, dubbed the Skybar. While overlooking the medina of Marrakesh, you can enjoy hookah

and cocktails. In fact, these are some of the best cocktails in town, including strawberry mojitos. Local DJs spin some contemporary favorites, while most nights belly dancers will also perform.

Pacha

Blvd. Mohammed VI; tel. 0566/110 288;
www.pachamarrakech.com; 11pm-4am;
200Dh

Pacha holds claim to being the biggest nightclub in Africa. If your favorite big-name European DJ is spinning in Morocco, this is likely the place. Doors open at 11pm, but the party doesn't start until well after midnight. Drinks are more overpriced than usual. Thursday night is ladies' night with free entry for women.

TheatrO

Rue Ibrahim El Mazini; tel. 0524/448 811;
www.theatromarrakech.com;
daily 11:30pm-5am; 250Dh

If Pacha seems overwhelming, try the slightly more intimate TheatrO. With some of the bolder art directions—circus-style acrobats and fire-spitting dancers—this is the spot for many European party-goers. The owners have an inspired philosophy of "reinventing the party each night," which is based on the original Theatre Es Saadi, Marrakesh's first dance hall, established over 60 years ago. The weekly calendar features a rotating ladies' night. Table reservations with champagne service are available starting at 10,000Dh.

✪ CHOOSING A *RIAD*

To get all the way to Marrakesh and not experience at least one or two nights in one of the estimated 1,600 renovated **riads** and **dars** that have been retrofitted into unique guesthouses would be a mistake. Each one of these guesthouses, once a home to generations of Moroccan families, reflects its wonder in a distinct way. These unique accommodations provide a fantastic value, and with their setting in the Marrakesh medina are the best-located properties in the city.

Many owners, both foreign and Moroccan, have decided to maintain a rustic charm to their guesthouses. Others have transformed their *riads* into luxurious five-star retreats, while still others have stripped the houses down to their barest essentials, lending a minimalist appeal that highlights the architecture of these old homes. Generally speaking, each of these *riads* and *dars* offers a sort of Orientalist fantasy, fused with European decadence that meets warm Moroccan hospitality. The **staff** of these *riads* are nearly always friendly, and for most travelers, the real highlight of their trip to Marrakesh is staying in one of these renovated *riads*.

You'll find these guesthouses spread throughout the **medina,** tucked down the pedestrian side streets, often in the quieter corners of the sprawling old city. As you walk down run-down medina streets and approach the aged door for the first time, you'll have no hint as to the wonders waiting for you just on the other side. Here you'll find some of my personal favorites for staying in the Red City, though truthfully with so many choices for guesthouses in Marrakesh, it's hard to go wrong. Nearly every single one I've stayed at, even ones I'm not listing in this guide, have provided excellent **value.**

Accommodations

MEDINA
UNDER 400DH
✪ Kammy Hostel
26 Derb Sekkaya; tel. 0654/215 440 or 0623/143 375; 55Dh for a dorm-style bed

For those looking for a down-home budget experience, the Kammy Hostel is an absolute gem. The rooms are a little cozy, with 4-8 sleeping in bunks. There are four rooms, with one room reserved for only women (85Dh). The management group of Shakira (from the U.S.) and Nacer (from Marrakesh) are a superb team, happy to look out for you and to make sure that you'll find the best deals in town. There is an upstairs terrace to chill out on. This is a quieter hostel than most in Morocco, making it a welcome reprieve from

the cacophony of the souks outside. Breakfast and Wi-Fi are included, though like most hostels you'll want to remember to pack your own towel (you can rent one for 10Dh if needed, however) and soaps. Lunch and dinner are also available, with Karima whipping up one of the most delicious *tangias* in all of Morocco.

Hotel Sindi Sud
109 Derb Sidi Bouloukate, just off Riad Zitoun Lakdim; tel. 0524/443 337; 100Dh d

There are few really outstanding budget accommodations in Marrakesh, but the Hotel Sindi Sud is one of them. Just a short walk south from the Jemaa el-Fnaa, the lodgings are simple, and for shoestring travelers, it's possible to sleep on the terrace for just 30Dh a night. The *riad* is impeccably clean, making it a real steal at this price range. Bathrooms are shared, and there is Wi-Fi. The staff here are incredibly friendly, and, if they have a moment, will help you find your way around the confusing environs of the Marrakesh medina.

Hotel Central Palace

59 Sidi Bouloukate;
tel. 0524/440 235; 150Dh d pp

A long-time backpacker favorite is the Hotel Central Palace. Just a five-minute walk south of Jemaa el-Fnaa, this remodeled *riad* features simple rooms with comfortable beds and shared bathrooms, though cleanliness can sometimes be an issue. There is no air-conditioning or heating in the simple rooms, so nights tend to be hot in the summer and cold in the winter—pack accordingly. The bathrooms are cleaned every day but can become filthy quickly; some might want to pay the 50Dh extra for the rooms with en suite bathrooms.

400-800DH
Dar Soukaina

19 & 24 Derb Lhammam;
tel. 0524/376 055; 400Dh d

There are two houses here, directly across the street from each other, with the same name ownership. Each has its charm, with verdant open-air patios and helpful staff. This is a great-value proposition with all the charm of a Moroccan *riad,* and usually available for much less than other *riads* closer to the Jemaa el-Fnaa. Avoid the ground floor rooms as they can be a bit humid. Families might consider renting two rooms close together, such as the Cumin and Cannelle rooms.

Breakfast, air-conditioning, and Wi-Fi are included.

the interior garden of Dar Soukaina

Riad Alisma

50 Rue de la Bahia; tel. 0524/378 935;
www.riadalisma.com; 500Dh d

The 18th-century Riad Alisma has been renovated to great effect with *mashrabiya*—latticed woodwork that covers the windows and hints at the splendor inside. There is a lot to like about this boutique *riad*. It's a favorite with French travelers passing through Marrakesh, and it's easy to see why. Lining the central patio, rooms are calm, with plenty of beige and brown. The *riad* is large enough so that there

a great place to relax at Riad Alisma

are plenty of private nooks to curl up and enjoy a quiet stay. Wi-Fi, air-conditioning, and breakfast are included with your stay.

Dar Najat
18 Douar Graoua, Derb Lalla Chacha; tel. 0524/375 085; 650Dh d

The owner of the Dar Najat has channeled the desert heritage of Morocco's Sahrawi tribes throughout this quaint *riad.* There's plenty of beige mud-brick, plus masks imported from Mali, though bathrooms are more traditional *zellij* work. Though a bit off the beaten path, it is in a quiet part of the medina, which ensures a restful night of sleep. The staff is friendly, the service prompt, and your every need seen to in this wonderfully relaxing little slice of the Sahara. Wi-Fi, air-conditioning, and breakfast are all included with your stay.

Riad Les Trois Mages
11 Derb Jamal Riad Laarousse; tel. 0524/389 297; www.lestroismages.com; 800Dh d

For the price point, this is probably one of the best deals in Marrakesh. The English-speaking staff, including the ever-hospitable Aziz, will help you find a restaurant or particular shop in the. For budget-minded travelers and those that abhor waste, you'll be happy to know that if you have dinner in the *riad,* they'll keep your leftovers and reheat them for you the next day for lunch. The *riad* itself has a few different lounge areas, an open-air interior patio, a heated pool, and even a baby grand piano. Lush fabrics, fluffy towels, and carpets form part of the ambiance. But what really sets this *riad* apart is Saïda, the French-trained cook who whips up some of the finest Moroccan food in the city with an international flair and the freshest ingredients selected that day from the market. Wi-Fi, air-conditioning, and breakfast included with your stay.

✪ Riad Boussa
192 Derb Jdid; tel. 0524/380 823; www.riadboussa.com; 800Dh d

Just off the main thoroughfare of Derb Derbachi, Riad Boussa is a classic *riad,* full of understated elegance. The welcoming staff and delicious homemade breakfast add to this intimate property, with five bedrooms, an outdoor patio, and rooftop terrace for sun worshippers. All of this is thanks to Brigitte, the tireless owner, and Marrakesh resident for nearly 15 years. Brigitte has made this a popular choice for solo female travelers and has a way of making you feel right at home. You will sleep and eat like royalty here, but what really makes this a can't-miss *riad* in Marrakesh is Brigitte's incredible wealth of information about her adopted hometown, which she happily shares with anyone. There are few foreigners who know the medina and love it as much as she does. Probably the best value is the Tehmara room with its splendid bathtub, while the Limoun suite with its double bed on the mezzanine is perfect for a small family. Wi-Fi, air-conditioning, and breakfast are all included with your stay.

OVER 800DH
✪ Riad les Secret des Zoraida
32 Jnane ben Chegra; tel. 0673/656 552; http://riadlesecretdezoraida.com; 900Dh d

The ladies running the Riad les Secret des Zohria deserve some sort of award for one of the most charming *riads* in Marrakesh. Besides the wonderful and kind service, the taste in Moroccan-style decor is unmatched in Marrakesh. Touches such as fresh flowers in the rooms and the heated swimming pool, one of the very few in the medina, add up to a special stay. Accommodations include air-conditioning, Wi-Fi, and breakfast, as well as mint tea on arrival. If you're looking to complete your relaxing stay with a nice long bath, consider upgrading to one of the suites for 400Dh or so more.

Riad l'Orangeraie

61 Rue Sidi Yamani; tel. 0661/238 789; www.riadorangeraie.com; 1,400Dh d

The two brothers running Riad l'Orangeraie have thought of seemingly everything, including giving guests prepaid cell phones to use during their stay. Rooms all have top-of-the-line beds nestled in the clean lines and elegant decor of Moroccan-European fusion. The staff will happily walk you to any place in the medina, making getting to and from restaurants less stressful. If you were going to splurge on one *riad* in Marrakesh, this would be the one. Rooftop terraces give views over the High Atlas Mountains, and below there are two courtyards, one with a shaded swimming pool.

✪ L'Hotel Marrakech

41 Derb Sidi Lahcen ou Ali Bab Doukkala; tel. 0524/387 880; www.l-hotelmarrakech.com; 2,000Dh

Originally the central part of a Caidal Palace, this historic 19th-century *riad* is an elegant treat in the midst of Morocco's busiest medina. Escape from the hustle of the medina in this charming retreat that combines the perfect blend of great food, cozy comfort, and top-level service. The elegance of this property is not only found in the detailed renovation work

Luckily, most rooftop terraces have straw sunhats.

carried out by local Moroccan craftsman, with high, ornate ceilings, but the antique furniture, touch-soft linens, and attention to warm lighting give a homey feeling that is reminiscent of those grand hotels of the 1920s and '30s. Typically, the hotel has a three-night minimum stay, so for shorter stays, do inquire ahead of time. Air-conditioning, Wi-Fi, heating, and breakfast are all present, though you should make it a priority to also indulge in at least one dinner as part of your stay.

GUELIZ

UNDER 400DH
Hotel Tachfine

corner of Blvd. Zerktouni and Rue Mohamed El Beqqal; tel. 0524/447 188; 270Dh d

For a no-nonsense stay, the reasonable Hotel Tachfine, though outdated, is a good spot for active travelers who are going to spend most of their time out of their rooms. Beds are comfortable, rooms clean, and showers hot. Most of the rooms feature small terraces. Street-side rooms can be noisy, as the Tachfine looks right over some of the more popular neighborhood restaurants and bars. For nonsmokers, the smoking can be an issue here.

✪ Hotel Amalay

87 Ave. Mohammed V; tel. 0524/448 685; www.amalay-hotel.com; 350Dh d

With comfy beds and cozy rooms, the Hotel Amalay is one of the better options outside of the medina for its price range. The rooms, though seemingly trapped in the 1970s-era decor, are cleaned every day and include fresh towels and soaps. The staff is friendly; they occasionally have problems with other booking agencies, so it's best to book direct if possible. The restaurant downstairs is forgettable, though a light breakfast is served with your stay. Streets along the avenue are a bit noisier than the ones out back. Air-conditioning can be hit-or-miss, something to think about in the hot summer months. Wi-Fi and breakfast are all included with your stay. This is one of the better deals in Marrakesh.

400-800DH
By Hotel

Rue Ben Aïcha; tel. 0524/339 151; http://by-marrakech.hotels-marrakesh.com; 710Dh d

The By Hotel is a touch of modern amid the 1970s architecture of the Gueliz district. The large glass doors give way to a chic salon with clean lines and a baby grand piano at your disposal. Youssef, the manager, is friendly and can help you with anything from taxis to restaurant recommendations. Rooms feel a bit cramped with no real views, but the beds and linens are all brand-new. The small, shaded pool on the back patio is perfect for cooling off on those hot Marrakesh afternoons. If you are looking for more modern accommodations, this is the best value for the money. Air-conditioning, Wi-Fi, and breakfast are included with your stay.

OVER 800DH
Bab Hotel

corner of Blvd. El Mansour Eddahbi and Rue Mohamed El Beqqal; tel. 0524/435 250; http://babhotelmarrakech.ma; 1,100Dh d

For a boutique B&B experience, the Bab Hotel might be just the ticket. The swank sky bar, chill poolside, and Los Angeles feel to this hotel make it something a bit different in Gueliz. The sky terrace provides lots of shade, while the rooms are as sleek as the contemporary-design coffee-table books lying about. The all-white rooms with solid black-framed beds and colored throw pillows will provide a comfortable, hip place to crash for a few nights. Air-conditioning, Wi-Fi, TV, and breakfast are included with your stay.

Hotel Le Renaissance

89 Blvd. Zerktouni, corner of Ave. Mohammed V; tel. 0524/337 777; www.renaissance-hotel-Marrakech.com; 1,500Dh d

The recently remodeled Hotel Le Renaissance, in the middle of the Gueliz shopping district, offers standard, modern rooms. There was little done to keep the protectorate-era architecture and design, though the art deco 1970s suite (room 503) is worth considering splurging for; it has a spacious living room, a separate dressing room, and curvy furnishings that will make you feel groovy. Some balconies have views over Marrakesh to the High Atlas. The on-site spa has a full-service Moroccan hammam, with *gommage* exfoliation, massage, and body scrubbing. Air-conditioning, Wi-Fi, TV, and breakfast are included with your stay.

the delicate, sumptuous interior of l'Hotel Marrakech

HIVERNAGE

400-800DH
Kenzi Farah Hotel

Ave. de Président Kennedy; tel. 0524/447 400; 800Dh d

The standard rooms here have spectacular views over the city, pool, and gardens. The rooms are what you'd expect from a three-star hotel anywhere in the world, if sometimes a little on the musty side. Consider splurging for the suites with king-size beds and jacuzzi tub bathrooms (1,200Dh and up). This is the first five-star hotel in Marrakesh and it retains all the services, though a remodel is likely in order to update the restaurants, bars, and palace grounds, which are good, but fall short of five-star quality. Outside of the high season, considerable discounts are available and worth checking into. Air-conditioning, Wi-Fi, TV, and breakfast are included with your stay.

OVER 800DH
Es Saadi Gardens & Resort

Rue Ibrahim el Mazini; tel. 0524/337 400; www.essaadi.com; 1,500Dh d

For a palatial experience, head to one of the best luxury resorts in Marrakesh. You'll find *zellij*-tiled rooms, sauna tubs, spacious gardens with winding paths, a five-star hammam, and the soothing strums of the resident oud player in the enormous reception area. This is a place to bump shoulders with the rich and famous or play at being king or queen for a day, if your budget allows. While the standard rooms are pleasant, the junior suites and private villas are a modern fantasy come to life, though you'll have to part with 4,000Dh or so a night for the privilege of living this fantasy. The private villas come with a golf cart to shuttle you around the vast property. Air-conditioning, Wi-Fi, TV, and breakfast are included with your stay. The on-site spa is one of the absolute best in Morocco.

Information and Services

The city code for Marrakesh and the area is 24.

Tourist Information Center (Délégation Régionale du Tourisme de Marrakech)

Pl. Abdelmoumen Ben Ali; tel. 0524/436 131; www.visitmorocco.com; Mon.-Fri. 8:30am-4:30pm

The Tourist Information Center can be found at the plaza where Avenue Mohammed V and Boulevard Mohamed Zerktouni meet. The office has some maps and updated information about city events, particularly about the numerous festivals, concerts, and gallery showings. If you're looking for the latest pulse for events while you're in town, be sure to stop by. Service is friendly and incredibly helpful.

POST OFFICES AND COURIER SERVICES

The main post office is at Place du 16 Novembre in Gueliz. In the medina, you can find a convenient post office on the south side of the Jemaa el-Fnaa near the horse-drawn carriages. There are also post offices at the train station and airport. Post offices keep the same hours (Mon.-Fri. 9am-4:30pm, Sat. 9:30am-12pm, abbreviated during Ramadan). FedEx (Blvd. 113 Ave. Abdelkrim El Khattabi, tel. 0524/448 257, Mon.-Fri. 8am-noon and 2pm-6:30pm, Sat. 8am-12:15pm) has a branch in Gueliz, east of Place Abdelmoumen Ben Ali.

MONEY

Cash machines are ubiquitous around Marrakesh, though they distribute only 100- and 200-dirham notes. Most large hotels will change currency at the bank rates. Most Moroccan banks now charge a 20-25Dh withdrawal fee.

In the medina, you'll find several banks with ATMs conveniently located on the south side of the Jemaa el-Fnaa, including Banque Populaire (Mon.-Fri. 8:15am-4:30pm), Bank Al Maghrib (Mon.-Fri. 8:15am-3:30pm), and BMCE (Mon.-Fri. 8:15am-6:30pm, Sat.-Sun. 9am-6pm, Ramadan 9am-5pm). For travelers checks, foreign currency exchanges, and other services, it's best to use BMCE. Banks are also found in Gueliz along Avenue Mohammed V. You'll find Attijarwafa Bank (Mon.-Fri. 8:15am-3:45pm, Ramadan 9:15am-2:30pm) and Wafacash Currency Exchange with Western Union (Mon.-Fri. 8am-7pm and Sat. 9am-4pm), as well as the Banque Populaire and BMCE.

Credit cards are accepted more widely around Marrakesh than in some other cities, though there will often be a surcharge of 5 percent added on to any sale. In principle, it's best to use cash whenever possible.

SAFETY

Marrakesh is a very safe city and is patrolled by police, both uniformed and undercover, in part to protect tourists and also to combat prostitution, drug use, and petty crimes, which do unfortunately remain an issue. Most nightclubs have a number of prostitutes working, both male and female. Single partygoers, as usual, should keep a close eye on their drink. Pickpocketing and petty theft can be a concern. Keep valuables locked up in your lodgings or tucked away some-place safe.

HOSPITALS, CLINICS, AND PHARMACIES

In dire circumstances, head directly for the private clinic Polyclinique du Sud (2 Rue Yougoslavie, tel. 0524/447 619) in Gueliz for emergency services.

Pharmacies are spread throughout the city on seemingly every street corner. They can prove to be indispensable in Marrakesh, particularly after a little too much sun, when the need for SPF 140 sunscreen and lip balm arises. Most pharmacies are open daily 8am-6pm, though they sometimes close for lunch.

In the medina, the easiest pharmacy to find is the Pharmacie la Place on the south side of the Jemaa el-Fnaa next to the Banque Populaire. Pharmacy Jnane Benchagra is on Derb el Hammam, and Pharmacy Ksar Al Hamra is near Bab Agnaou.

In Gueliz, you'll find the Pharmacie Centrale on the corner of Avenue Mohammed V and Rue de la Liberté near the Carre Eden. The Pharmacie Ibn Rochd (36 Rue Ibn Aïcha) is another good neighborhood pharmacy.

In Hivernage, you can find Pharmacie Natura on the corner of Avenue El Kadissia and Avenue Echouhada, across from Café Extra Blatt.

Transportation

GETTING THERE

BY PLANE
Marrakesh Menara International Airport

about 5 kilometers (3mi) west of the city center; tel. 0544/447 910

The Marrakesh Menara International Airport offers direct flights to London, Dublin, Oslo, Copenhagen, Stockholm, Paris, Madrid, and other European hubs with various carriers, including low-budget carriers such as Air Arabia (www.airarabia.com), Easy Jet (www.easyjet.com), Transavia (www.transavia.com), and Ryan Air (www.ryanair.com). Travelers arriving direct from North America and other non-European regions will have to transfer planes at the Mohammed V International Airport in Casablanca. Royal Air Maroc (www.royalairmaroc.com) offers direct in-country daily flights

to Casablanca and Fez as well as in-country flights to Agadir, Dakhla, Ouarzazate, and Tangier.

You can usually get a SIM card for your phone for free with Orange, INWI, or Maroc Telecom next to baggage claim. You'll be able to charge this while you're on the go around the entire country. There are money exchange offices and ATMs just beyond the customs area. It's a good idea to exchange some local currency before heading out of the airport.

The local 19 Airport Bus runs daily every 30 minutes 7am-9:30pm (30Dh single, 50Dh round-trip), with service to the Jemaa el-Fnaa. Leave from the main exit of the airport and cross the parking lot. There is usually a bus parked, but if there isn't, just wait next to the entrance to the paid portion of the parking

the Marrakesh International Airport

From North America

All direct flights into Morocco from North America arrive first in Casablanca via Royal Air Maroc (tel. 0522/489 751, www.royalairmaroc.com) and have a short layover before connecting with a short flight (45min) to Marrakesh. From the Casablanca airport, it's also possible to take the train to Marrakesh. Often, it's quicker to take the train as the layover in Casablanca can be lengthy. It's possible to avoid Casablanca altogether and travel through a European hub, such as Madrid or London, or a Middle East hub. Typically, flights through Europe are less expensive than direct flights from North America to Casablanca, and are highly recommended. Flights from Europe (see above) can land directly in Marrakesh, making this a preferable alternative to landing in Casablanca.

From Australia, New Zealand, and South Africa

It's possible to avoid Casablanca altogether and travel through a European hub, such as Madrid or London, or a Middle East hub, such as Dubai, by choosing a ticket directly to Marrakesh. This is a preferable alternative to landing in Casablanca.

A great travel strategy is to break up your trip to Morocco with weekend layovers in and out of Europe. Consider booking a round-trip ticket from a European hub, such as Paris, and then purchase a second round trip from the European hub of your choice with one of the low-cost carriers. Just make sure to leave yourself a day or two on either end of your Morocco trip to explore the European city of your choice and to give yourself plenty of time in case one of your flights is delayed or canceled.

lot. There are no other stops on the route, but if your hotel is along the route, just ask the driver to drop you off. Most drivers know the hotels along the route and can tell you if your hotel is one of them. If you're staying in the medina, this is the best option to and from the airport. Taxis will often try to charge exorbitant fares; 50Dh is a good price to/from the airport (though the metered fare is usually around 25Dh), and you can expect to pay a surcharge of 50 percent after sunset.

From the UK and Europe

Marrakesh is extremely well connected with nearly all major airports in Europe. Most European cities are 3-4 hours away, often connecting via low-cost airlines such as Easy Jet (www.easyjet.com), Ryan Air (www.ryanair.com), Transavia (www.transavia.com), and Vueling (www.vueling.com). If you're looking to get out of Marrakesh and travel around the country, consider booking a one-way ticket into Marrakesh and then your return ticket from another city, such as Fez or Tangier. This way, you can maximize your travel time in-country and make a circuit with Marrakesh as your southernmost destination.

CONNECTING THROUGH EUROPE

For travelers coming to Marrakesh on long flights, a great travel strategy is to break it up with **weekend layovers** in and out of Europe. Many airlines do not have direct flights into Marrakesh, but instead connect through one of the many **European travel hubs,** such as Dublin, Frankfurt, London, Madrid, Paris, or Rome. This means that you're likely to have a long layover in Europe already. Why not extend that layover a bit and spend a weekend in one of your favorite cities while **adjusting to the local time zone**? Morocco is, after all, on the same time zone as the UK and just an hour different from France, Germany, and Italy.

If you want to potentially **save money** on your plane ticket, consider booking a round-trip ticket to and from a European hub, such as Paris. There are often really good deals to be found coming from North America or Australia to Europe. Take advantage of these sales and then purchase a second round trip from the European hub of your choice with one of the many reliable **low-cost carriers** serving Marrakesh from Europe. Just make sure to leave yourself a day or two on either end of your Morocco trip to explore the European city of your choice and to give yourself a little time on the off chance one of your flights is delayed or canceled. Another thing to keep in mind is that a few of the low-cost carriers use alternative airports that are often smaller, which generally means shorter customs and security lines, but sometimes inconvenient locations. It's best to double-check the location of the airports that your chosen low-cost carrier uses.

BY CAR

Coming by car, Marrakesh is an easy drive along the autoroutes from **Casablanca** (243km/151mi, 2.5hr) and **Rabat** (328km/204mi, 3.5hr), while **Agadir** (242km/150mi, 2.5hr) and **Essaouira** (177km/110mi, 2.5hr) are shorter drives and popular day-trips outside of Marrakesh. **Ouarzazate** (198km/123mi, 3.5hr), **Meknes** (469km/291mi, 5hr), **Fez** (529km/329mi, 6hr), and **Tangier** (572km/355mi, 7.5hr) are longer drives requiring half a day to a full day. The mountain pass to Ouarzazate should be driven with extreme caution, particularly during winter months and during storms. Night driving is always dangerous, though the roads to Ouarzazate and Agadir are particularly accident prone.

BY BUS

The new **CTM bus station** (tel. 0800/0900 30, www.ctm.ma) is just south of the train station on Rue Abou Baker Seddik and Rue Ibn el Cadi in Gueliz. Check the scheduled information online or at the station for specific departure information and for "premium" coach buses that are a bit more comfortable and come with onboard Wi-Fi. Some of the more popular bus runs include: Agadir (3hr, 18 daily, 105Dh, premium available), Essaouira (2.5hr, 2 daily, 75Dh), Fez (5.5hr, 6 daily, 170Dh, premium available), Casablanca (4hr, 16 daily, 80Dh, premium available), Ouarzazate (4.5hr, 47 daily, 85Dh), Rabat (4.5hr, 10 daily, 140Dh, premium available), and Tangier (9.5hr, 3 daily, 230Dh).

Supratours (tel. 0890/203 040, www.oncf.ma) is popular, particularly with those traveling by train. Supratours operates in conjunction with ONCF, the train company, and the **bus station** is directly behind the Marrakesh train station (due west just off Avenue Hassan II) in Gueliz, making connections easy. Popular runs include Agadir (3hr, 12 daily, 110Dh), Essaouira (3hr, 6 daily, 80Dh), and Ouarzazate (4.5hr, 3 daily, 90Dh).

BY TRAIN

Marrakesh serves as the southern terminus for the national train run by

ONCF (tel. 0890/203 040, www.oncf.
ma). The train station is along Avenue
Hassan II in Gueliz, turning west from
Avenue Mohammed V at Place du 18
Novembre. From Marrakesh, some of
the more popular train lines run to
and from Casablanca (3.5hr, 9 daily,
2nd/1st-class 90Dh/140Dh), Rabat
(4.5hr, 9 daily, 120Dh/185Dh), Meknes
(7hr, 8 daily, 174Dh/265Dh), and Fez
(8hr, 8 daily, 195Dh/295Dh).

Trains also leave to Tangier (9.5hr,
7 daily, 205Dh/310Dh), though most
trains change at Casa Voyageurs or
Sidi Kacem. Conveniently, the only direct train to Tangier is the overnight
train that leaves Marrakesh at 8:45pm
and arrives in Tangier at 7am without
a change. It's best to book the *"voiture-
lit single/double"* or *"couchette"* sleeping cars at the train station a day or
two before departure. These cannot be purchased online but must be
purchased at the train station. Prices
per bed start at 350Dh, and beds can
sell out quickly during peak summer
travel season.

GETTING AROUND
BY WALKING
Pack a good pair of walking shoes. The
majority of the sprawling Marrakesh
medina is only navigable by foot, and
that's how you'll experience the myriad souks, twisting alleyways, and up-
beat medina life. Avenue Mohammed
V, with its wide sidewalk and continuous traffic, is the main thoroughfare
between the medina and the animated
strip in Gueliz. For quieter walks, consider an outing through the guarded
palaces breaking the sidewalks of
Hivernage.

BY *PETIT TAXI* AND CARRIAGE
The sand-colored *petits taxis* of
Marrakesh are the quickest way

A woman pushes a stroller in the medina.

around town. Fares typically run
10Dh-40Dh, depending on the length
of the drive. Always ask the driver to
use the counter, and keep in mind that
prices go up by 50 percent at night.
Most drivers are friendly and will
use the meter, though they have been
known to take advantage of tourists
late at night, particularly if they think
the tourist has had a few drinks. Taxis
are easy to spot outside of most medina gates. During the day they will
even cut across the Jemaa el-Fnaa
looking for fares. In general, it is best
to try to flag down a moving taxi, as
the taxis waiting for fares are more
likely to try to extort you by charging
for any baggage you might have, by not
using the counter, or by claiming that
they don't have change. In general,
in Marrakesh, the older and more
beat-up the taxi (and driver!) look, the
more honest they typically are.

A horse-drawn carriage, or
calèche, is a fun way to get around,
with a tour typically taking you on
an hour-long trip around the medina
walls. Prices are typically 150Dh per
hour but are always negotiable. Make
sure you agree on a price before taking off. There are stands for *calèches*
around the medina at the Koutoubia
Mosque, just off the Jemaa el-Fnaa,
near Bab Doukkala, and inside Bab

Agnaou along Rue Arset el Maach. You'll also find stands in Hivernage across from the Hotel Al-Andalous on Avenue du Président Kennedy and along Place de la Liberté.

BY LOCAL BUS

The public bus run by Alsa (tel. 0524/335 270, www.alsa.ma, 4Dh) is an option for getting around, particularly between Gueliz and the medina. Nearly all of the local bus lines converge around the Koutoubia Mosque. From here, you can take bus 1 or 15 to Gueliz or the 19 to the airport (30Dh). If you want to cut quickly across the medina, take bus 2 to Bab Lahkmiss. The other two convenient buses are the 11 and 7, which will take you pretty close to the Majorelle Gardens. Interestingly, Marrakesh is the first city in Africa to have 100 percent electric buses. The transition is slow but encouraging.

BY *GRAND TAXI*

For destinations outside of Marrakesh, such as day trips into the nearby High Atlas Mountains, consider taking a *grand taxi*. It is always possible to negotiate the price for the entire taxi, which is a good idea for small groups traveling together. Night prices often increase by 50-100 percent. Fares to less popular destinations vary, and you'll likely have to negotiate with the driver and agree to pay for a partial rate for his return.

Most *grands taxis* for the High Atlas leave from the Route Secondaire N501 outside of the kasbah. Follow Bab Agnaou and Bab er Rob past the Sidi Es Souheïli Cemetery, or take a *petit taxi,* asking the driver for the "Imlil *grand taxi.*" From this station, you can catch *grands taxis* to Asni (1hr, 51km/31mi, 30Dh), Imlil (1.5hr, 66km/41mi, 40Dh), Ourika Valley (Setti Fatma, 1hr, 65km/40mi, 40Dh), and Oukaïmeden (1.5hr, 79km/49mi, 60Dh). Taxis for other destinations leave from the *gare routière* outside of Bab Doukkala.

BY CAR

Driving in Marrakesh is hectic all times of the day. Many forms of traffic will be generally unfamiliar to drivers from North America, Europe, and Australia. Notoriously aggressive scooter drivers bob in and out of streets packed with four-door sedans, horse-drawn carriages, donkeys, and kamikaze pedestrians. Streets are not well marked. Even with GPS guidance, the going can be difficult and it's all too easy to get lost in the chaos. That said, somehow everything works out and most travelers chalk up this frantic driving to something that adds to their unforgettable experience.

Most hotels in the Ville Nouvelle offer free parking for guests, and around the medina there are guarded parking lots. Across from the Koutoubia Mosque along Trek el Koutoubia is one of the more convenient guarded parking lots near the Jemaa el-Fnaa. There is also parking through Bab Doukkala along Rue el Adala near the horse-drawn carriages and through Bab el Khemis off Rue Assouel. Parking is typically 50Dh a day, including overnight. You can pay in advance, but always request a ticket.

Car Rentals

Car hires are best reserved before you depart. Unless you're really in a pinch, stick with international companies like Hertz or Avis. The local outfits are often hit-or-miss with the level of service, and their cars are often a bit worse for the wear. Avis

ROAD RULES AND DRIVING TIPS

If you've never driven in a developing country, **buckle up.** I mean that seriously. You'll want to make sure your seat belt is securely fastened at all times for you and your passengers, especially because police have been giving frequent **citations** for not wearing seat belts in recent years. Let's be honest: driving in Morocco can be a little bit of a harrowing experience. Seat belt safety should go without question.

You won't need an international driver's license to drive in Morocco, but you will need to **carry your license or driving permit from home.** Moroccans drive on the right side of the road, with the driver being situated on the left side of the car, like in North America. Moroccans give way to faster traffic on the left, though in practice, particularly in the cities, you will most often want to stay in the left-most lane to avoid potential hazards coming from the right.

Here are a few more tips to help you drive safely and avoid some of the more common traffic infractions:

- Practice good **defensive driving** techniques at all times. Many Moroccan drivers can be aggressive and will follow too close to the cars in front of them, as well as sometimes pass in dangerous locations, such as on blind turns.

- **City driving** is particularly hectic. Give yourself plenty of time to get to your destination. It helps to have a copilot to assist with navigation. If you miss a turn, don't panic. Calmly continue on until you find a place to turn around.

- **Roundabouts** are common throughout cities. Though when there is a lot of traffic, it can feel like the only rule is the rule of the jungle. Don't be intimidated by these large roundabouts, but do practice caution.

- Be prepared to **share the road.** You'll see livestock, cyclists, pedestrians, donkeys pulling carts, and horse-drawn carriages.

- **Countryside driving** is much more relaxing. You will have to be vigilant about herds of sheep, cattle, goats, and camels crossing the roads. Camels in particular can be very dangerous in the desert region after sunset.

- **Pay careful attention to the posted speed,** usually 30-40kph (20-30mph) in the cities and 60-100kph (45-60mph) in the countryside. Police will give **citations** for anything typically 5-10kph (3-6mph) over the posted speed limit and have traps near speed changes.

- **Plan to be pulled over at least one time by a police officer** flagging you down. This is usually a stop just to check your papers. Stops like this are most often found on main arteries just as you are exiting from or arriving to a city.

- **Keep 1,000Dh cash on you, minimum.** Most infractions are payable only in cash. You will receive a receipt in turn. Most fines are between 200-400Dh.

- Some **gas stations** will not accept international credit or debit cards. For this reason, you will want to make sure you have enough cash for at least one fill-up. A normal four-door sedan or 4x4 will cost around 600Dh to fill the tank.

- **Avoid night driving** if at all possible. Hazards such as speed bumps, large potholes, or slow-moving camels are often not visible, and the lack of road lighting, particularly outside of the major cities, can be a problem.

Morocco is a wonderful country in which to road-trip, with incredible scenery and kind people you'll meet along the way. As long as you remain confident, relaxed, and vigilant, you'll have an extraordinary experience.

(www.avis.com), **Budget** (www.budget.com), **EuropCar** (www.europcar.com), **Right Cars** (www.right-cars.com), and **Sixt** (www.sixt.com) all operate directly from the airport. You can find the **Hertz** branch office (154 Ave. Mohammed V, tel. 0663/614 209) in Gueliz, near the Carre Eden.

Basic car **insurance** will be provided by the supplier, limited to covering theft, third-party damage, and liability, but with a 10,000Dh (around £800/$1000 USD) deposit that will be blocked on your credit card until you return the car. Check with your credit card company to see if they provide rental car insurance. Many companies do this as part of a normal rental transaction when traveling. If your credit card provider does not, consider taking out a separate insurance policy. You will want to make sure you keep all of your paperwork easily accessible, as you'll likely be stopped by the local police at least once to check that all of your paperwork is in order. It goes without saying that you should remember your **driver's license.** You won't need an international driver's license. A valid driver's license from your country of residence will do.

Small groups might consider a van with driver. This can be an easy way to get around and, if splitting the cost, can be quite affordable. Typical transports cost 500-800Dh a day, and a driver an additional 200-300Dh.

Transport Rentals

Ourha Transport Touristique (129 Ave. Imm el Bakouri, Khalid ibnou el walid Gueliz, tel. 0524/446 345 or 0666/164 173, transportouhra@menara.ma, 800Dh per day) offers new, comfortable vans for rent with drivers that understand enough English to make getting around a lot easier and for a fair price.

OUIRGANE VALLEY

The Ouirgane Valley is known for

being green year-round with acres of olive groves and almond trees. This is the first valley you cross on the road leading through the N'Fis Valley, where you can find the ancient Tin Mal Mosque, one of the very few religious sites in Morocco accessible to non-Muslims and one of the most interesting architectural sites to be found outside Marrakesh.

In the middle of the valley you'll find a small town by the same name, Ouirgane, with a few cafés and some humble lodgings. Dotted

HIGHLIGHTS

✪ **TIN MAL MOSQUE:** Tucked into the folds of the N'Fis Valley, this abandoned mosque is the original inspiration for the architecture of mosques throughout Morocco, Spain, and even France (page 106).

✪ **SPRINGTIME HIKING:** When the flowers are in bloom, it's time to hit the trails of the High Atlas (page 108).

✪ **MOUNTAIN GETAWAYS:** A night spent in one of the many excellent accommodations in the valley is sure to please the soul (page 110).

throughout the valley are some of the choicest lodgings outside of Marrakesh. Moroccans and foreigners, mostly French, have established guesthouses on sprawling acreage, with many emphasizing gardens and eco-friendly lodging. Most feature gardens and swimming pools. One of the distinct features of Ouirgane is a small lake, Lalla Takerkoust, that has formed to the northwest edge of the town. This is a manmade lake created by the dam built by the state to regulate the much-needed water for Marrakesh.

ORIENTATION

Located a short two-hour drive south of Marrakesh, the Ouirgane Valley is in the foothills of the High Atlas Mountains. To the east of the valley lies Morocco's tallest peak, Toubkal Mountain, visible on clear days, while to the west you can find the Kik Plateau. From Ouirgane, another hour drive south brings you to Ijoukak and Tin Mal. Conifers and evergreens dot the rangy landscape with the snowcapped peaks of the High Atlas. Rocky outcrops often give way to terraced fields and large groves of fruit trees and other seasonal crops. Because of its altitude, under 2,000 meters (6,500ft), this is a region that is cooler than Marrakesh, making it

a real breath of fresh air in the suffocating heat of mid-summer. In winter, snow is possible, though rare.

PLANNING YOUR TIME

Because of its excellent location just an hour away from Marrakesh, the Ouirgane Valley makes for a wonderful day trip outside of Marrakesh. Because there is limited bus service, this is a much less touristed area of the High Atlas than the Ourika Valley to the east. A car is needed to best navigate this remote region, but once there, most travelers will appreciate the great hiking and mountain biking trails in the region, many of them in continuous use from members of the local communities riding donkeys, horses, and mules between villages. Hiking and biking throughout the region can be done by nearly all levels. The terrain is mountainous, though not treacherously so, with most hikes perfectly doable for families of all ages and those in decent shape with no mobility restrictions. Most hikes can be done in half-day increments.

Though Tin Mal can be done by itself as a day trip from Marrakesh, it's preferable if you can overnight in the valley to couple a day out at Tin Mal with a day of hiking through the region.

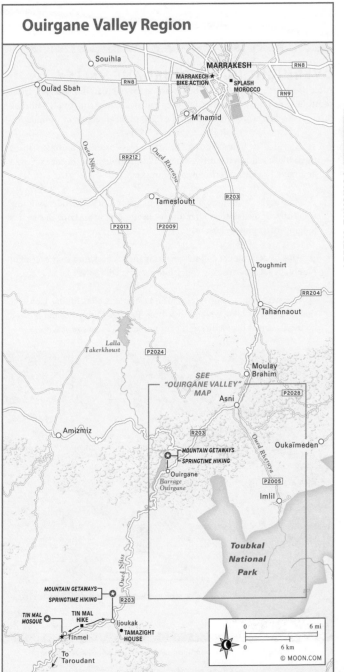

Itinerary Idea

OVERNIGHT IN THE OUIRGANE VALLEY

After breakfast in Marrakesh, you'll want to hit the road immediately. Head south in your rental car, following the road signs for Asni. You'll continue through the village of Asni, south on the R203 in the direction of Taroudant.

1 Spend a few hours touring Tin Mal, a classic, ornate mosque. This is the farthest south you'll drive. After walking through the mosque's curved archways, head back north toward Marrakesh.

2 Stop at the Tamazight House in Ijoukak for lunch. Consider spinning some of your own pottery after lunch—in addition to amazing meals, this lodging offers pottery lessons.

3 Hop back in the car and stop in Ouirgane to check into your overnight mountain getaway, treating yourself to a stay at Domaine Malika.

4 The next day, wake up refreshed and ready for a bit of hiking. Consider the Kik Plateau hike, which leaves from Barrage Ouirgane, and is a 6-8 hour hike across the picturesque plateau that will leave you at Asni.

The Tin Mal Mosque is an ancient ruin, and one of the few mosques non-Muslims may visit.

Itinerary Idea

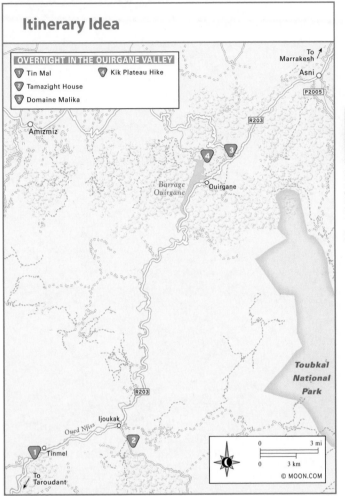

OVERNIGHT IN THE OUIRGANE VALLEY

1 Tin Mal
2 Tamazight House
3 Domaine Malika
4 Kik Plateau Hike

To Marrakesh

Asni

P2005

Amizmiz

R203

4 3

Barrage Ouirgane   Ouirgane

Toubkal National Park

R203

Ijoukak

Oued Nfiss

2

1 Tinmel

To Taroudant

0   3 mi
0   3 km

© MOON.COM

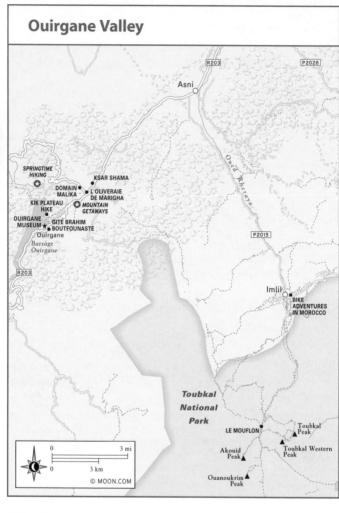

Ouirgane Valley

Sights

✪ TIN MAL MOSQUE

daily 9am-5pm; 20Dh suggested donation

The historically important and wonderfully ornate Tin Mal Mosque is one of the very few mosques in Morocco that non-Muslims can visit. Dubbed Timguida Toumlilt (White Mosque) by the Soussi tribes in the area, it was built by the powerful Abdelmoumen Ibn Ali in 1156, during the Almohad dynasty. The prototypical Moroccan mosque is based on the Tin Mal

the mihrab of the Tin Mal Mosque

you can see the typical designs of the Almohad era, such as the scallop and rosette, which are repeated on the Koutoubia Mosque and the Giralda in Spain. However, the mihrab (and the rest of the mosque) is oriented to the southeast, many degrees away from Mecca. This is a possible reason why the mosque is no longer in use.

The mosque lies just off the main road, a short drive uphill at the edge of town. It is customary to honk your horn as you approach the site to let the guardian know that there are visitors in case he isn't at the site. From the main road linking Marrakesh to Taroudant, the Tin Mal Mosque is unmissable. It lies in the small town of Tin Mal, about 15-20 minutes south of Ijoukak along the west side of the R203.

Mosque, making it an important architectural and historical monument and the reason why it is listed tentatively with UNESCO as a World Heritage Site. Some restoration work was done in 1991, though throughout the mosque there is still no roof.

The layout of the mosque is a classic of Almohad design. Curved archways form a series of decorative naves that connect with a central aisle, which leads to the decorative *mihrab* (a niche in the wall that indicates the direction to Mecca, toward which the faithful pray) and to the fountain where ablutions would have been performed. The mosque was originally split into two halves, one for women and the other for men, likely with a muslin veil dividing the fountain so that both men and women could perform their ablutions prior to prayer. The mihrab is the most well-preserved part of the mosque, with decorated archways radiating from it as well as ornate stucco work original to the period of construction. At this mihrab

OUIRGANE MUSEUM
Ouirgane center; daily 9am-sunset; 10Dh

The ramshackle Ouirgane Museum is alongside the road in Ouirgane. If you've never seen an old olive press, now is your chance. There is one giant press on display here, dating from the 19th century. It was traditionally powered by a donkey, which would circle around the press to operate the wheel that extracted the oil from the locally grown olives. Pots, tools, and other accessories used for the job hang in this little museum, though there is no posted information and the caretaker's English, French, and Spanish are limited. The olive press once served many of the olive trees that were flooded when the local dam was built. This is a somewhat interesting diversion for a few minutes, but no more.

Sports and Recreation

✪ HIKING

Kik Plateau Hike

Distance: 23km/14mi, one way
Hiking Time: 6-8 hours
Trailhead: Barrage Ouirgane. Park at a local hotel and follow the mule route north on the northern edge of the lake

This trail follows a series of mule tracks that offer a glimpse into the local population, with some unique scenery. The trail begins easily enough along the N'Fis River before turning left up into a series of salt mines. You'll follow the tracks up to Tizi Ouzla, a small village, before passing another village, Tizi Ouadoua. Here, you'll fork to the right along the rise of the plateau for some stunning views before descending to Asni. Check out the Cordee Map (cordee.co.uk) for the High Atlas and Marrakesh or download a topographic map on your favorite app beforehand. Experienced hikers should feel comfortable enough without a map: for the entirety of the hike, the main road, R203, that connects Marrakesh to Taroudant, will be to the east, providing an easy landmark if you should lose your way. There is quite a bit of uphill toward the beginning of the hike, though no scree or anything requiring scrambling. On the plateau, there is exposure to the sun without much in the way of shade. Plan accordingly. From Asni, a taxi back to the Barrage Ouirgane to pick up your car is easy enough to find (20Dh).

springtime in the High Atlas Mountains

Tin Mal Hike

Distance: 8km/5mi, one way

Hiking Time: 2 hours

Trailhead: West of the Tin Mal Mosque,
follow the path behind the Ba Adam Café

This largely downhill hike takes you from Tin Mal to Ijoukak, following mule tracks running along the west side of the main road, R203, making it nearly impossible to lose your way. You'll pass through some terraced farmland, through a rocky gorge, and along the N'Fis River. This is one of the easiest hikes in the region and is best done in the morning, so you can plan on a visit to the mosque before making the hike to Ijoukak, where you can dig into a well-earned lunch. Most hikers will want to retrace their footsteps on the trail back to the car (2.5 hours, light uphill), though from Ijoukak you will be able to ask for a taxi back to Tin Mal (15Dh) to the car.

MOUNTAIN BIKING
Bike Adventures in Morocco

tel. 0524/485 786 or 0666/238 200;
www.bikeadventuresinmorocco.com;
700-1,400Dh

Lahcen Jellah, one of the most knowledgeable certified mountain guides in the region, is now based out of Marrakesh. He started this company that offers a wide range of High Atlas tours. They specialize in mountain biking, though cross-country, free-ride mountain, and road biking are possibilities as well. Treks run from one-day outings to two-week excursions, with rates ranging from 700-1,400Dh per person a day, depending on equipment requirements and group size. Bike Adventures carries the latest Cannondale bikes, and new

Mountain biking is a popular activity in the region.

equipment is purchased every year. For multi-day bike trips, all meals are included—and Lahcen happens to be one of the better chefs in the mountains, too!

✪ Marrakech Bike Action

tel. 0667/797 035 or 0661/240 145; https://
marrakechbikeaction.com; 1,490Dh
pp 2-3 people; 1,090Dh pp 4-8 people

Based out of Marrakesh, this outfit has become a go-to company for those looking to explore the High Atlas Mountains on two wheels. They were the first company to have electronically assisted biking (e-biking), which is great if you're not a hardcore biker but still like the idea of venturing through the mountains more romantically than by car. The e-bikes have a motor that kicks in to help you on those long, tough hills. The bikes are totally customizable, and the motor isn't heavy and can be turned on and off, making it a great solution for couples or families with mixed levels of abilities.

The Ouirgane Valley has some of the best accommodations in the High Atlas. All of them include a **demi-pension** (breakfast and dinner) unless otherwise noted, with the kind of service and locations that make disconnecting and enjoying a mountain getaway a wonderful addition to your Marrakesh vacation. Whether in the depths of a **snowy winter** or the soaring temperatures of a **Moroccan summer,** the accommodations in this chapter are great places to get away from it all.

RAFTING
Splash Morocco Rafting
tel. 0618/964 252; http://moroccoadventuretours.com; 900Dh

Splash Morocco Rafting has great gear and may be the most family-friendly outfitter for rafting. They have a wonderful route down the **N'Fis River.** Rafting this river is suitable for beginners. This can be done as a day trip from Marrakesh, and can be an exciting way to interact with the locals who live along the river. The tour stops for lunch, to chit-chat, sip on a tea, or barter for goods.

Food and Accommodations

Restaurants in this region are all of the rustic café variety, with hearty meals for a fraction of the price of what you'll find in other parts of Morocco; a standard tajine generally runs 25-40Dh. For the best lunches and dinners, it's best to reserve at one of the accommodations listed below the day before.

OUIRGANE
✪ Gite Brahim Boutfounaste
tel. 0676/622 790 or 0524/485 937; 150Dh pp

In the middle of the town of Ouirgane lies Gite Brahim Boutfounaste. The most notable feature of this *gîte* is the traditional public hammam (20Dh), which offers you a chance to scrub down after a few days of hiking through the park and valley. You'll find terrace views over the valley and unsophisticated, though friendly, service. The showers have hot water, and Wi-Fi is available throughout the grounds. The owner, Hamid, will make sure you're well taken care of. Lodging includes breakfast and dinner. The small fireplace in the salon does a surprisingly good job of warming the place up on cold winter nights.

Le Mouflon
Souk l'Hamis; tel. 0524/484 371; 400Dh d

A short turn off the main road will bring you to the door of this rustic café, restaurant, and hotel. Perhaps the best budget option in the region, the restaurant is a local staple, a family tradition that has been serving up hearty tajines since the 1950s. Chef Rachida has followed in her father's footsteps in the restaurant, with meals served outside in the stunning backyard garden when the weather allows (45Dh). The couscous is recommended, though you'll need to call ahead and reserve. They only make it in Moroccan family-style, meant to serve four people (50Dh per person, 200Dh for the plate). Rooms here are simple but warm enough for the cold nights, so you can snuggle down before hitting the trails. Couples not taking advantage of the included breakfast and dinner can deduct 150Dh per night for the cost of meals. All in all, a great bargain for couples and good friends.

chairs in a mountain kasbah

Ksar Shama

58km from Asni on the Taroudant road, Marigha; tel. 0524/485 032; www. ksarshama.com; 800Dh d

The Ksar Shama is another option for those seeking refuge in the mountains in a cultivated garden. The property is quieter than some of the other options, with fewer tour groups and day-trippers from Marrakesh. The rooms are notably larger, as are the beds, making it a good option for those in need of more space. Some of the rooms feature separate salons that have two banquettes, perfect for kids, while other rooms are darker, with fewer windows and a combined salon/living room. Breakfast, Wi-Fi, and air-conditioning are included with your stay. The service can be a little slow, though perfectly friendly. The on-site restaurant and spa are serviceable and can be visited by non-guests, though reservations are needed.

L'Oliveraie de Marigha

59km from Asni on the Taroudant road, Douar Imarigha; tel. 0524/484 281; www. oliveraie-de-marigha.com; 900Dh d

The expansive L'Oliveraie de Marigha features plenty of room to spread out, even with the tour groups that occasionally stay in the numerous bungalows. The cabana bar and poolside seats sprinkled throughout the olive grove all add up to the feeling of really being away from it all. The restaurant has a varied seasonal menu with a mix of French classics and Moroccan favorites (220Dh, reservations required). A lunch next to the pool is particularly welcome. Breakfast is included with your stay, and discounts are sometimes available, particularly outside of the busier seasons.

✪ Domaine Malika

59km from Asni on the Taroudant road, Marigha; tel. 0524/485 921 or 0661/493 541; www.domainemalika.com; 1,550Dh d

Tucked just half a kilometer off the main road, Domaine Malika is a charming luxury guesthouse nestled into the Ouirgane Valley. The property features large, modern salons with a rustic touch for groups to gather. There is plenty of natural light, with windows everywhere you turn. In the rooms, beds have lush linens and you'll find plush towels hanging in the bathroom. The bathtubs are big enough for two, making this a perfect location for a romantic mountain getaway. Lodging includes breakfast, air-conditioning, TV, and Wi-Fi, as well as access to the swimming pool. The private hammam on site offers facials, scrubs, massages, and other services on reservation. If the budget allows, the splurge is well worth it.

IJOUKAK
Tamazight House
near Tigmmi n'Tmazirte; tel. 0668/253 421 or 0633/552 129; 260Dh s, 500Dh d

For overnight stays, the Tamazight House is a simple, homey option. The staff is friendly and the beds, though a bit old, are clean and comfortable with secondhand bedding. The rooms are all nonsmoking. The location makes it a good stopover for hikers, independent budget travelers, and small groups, and breakfast and dinner are included. The property uses solar power for the hot water, making it somewhat eco-friendly. Interestingly, there are pottery lessons available, with classes of up

the rustic pottery made in Ijoukak

to five people (50Dh an hour per person). Lessons usually run three hours. Lunches and dinners can be reserved and are highly recommended.

Transportation

GETTING THERE

There is no reliable public transport outside of the *grands taxis* into Asni (1hr, 63km/39mi, 15Dh), the primary village of the Ouirgane Valley. The easiest way to get to the valley is by car, along the winding road (R203) that leads from Marrakesh (63km/39mi, 1hr) to distant Taroudant farther south. Nearly all of the major sights are along this road, and the more tucked-away accommodations are well-signed. The road is well-maintained, though hairpin turns and the occasional rockslide mean it's better to limit driving to the daytime, when visibility is clearer.

GETTING AROUND

Whether you have arrived in the region by car or *grand taxi,* if you are looking for any sort of public transportation, whether around the Ouirgane Valley or into Toubkal National Park, the best place to find a *grand taxi* is Asni.

OURIKA VALLEY

One of the most popular day trips from Marrakesh is an outing to the Ourika Valley. The valley follows a series of villages—Ourika, Oualmes, and Setti Fatma—up the Ourika River into the High Atlas Mountains. Because of the altitude and the location in the protected cover of the mountains, locals often come here to catch a break from the hot Marrakesh summers. There are several hotels, cafés, and shops along the route, as well as some light hiking up to a stunning series of waterfalls, making for plenty of activities for just about everyone, and

HIGHLIGHTS

✪ **SETTI FATMA WATERFALLS:** Take a springtime hike through this series of seven connecting cascades (page 117).

✪ **SETTI FATMA MOUSSEM:** If you're visiting in August, try to attend this lively festival (page 118).

✪ **LUNCH IN A MOUNTAIN VILLA:** Disconnect and unwind with a homey lunch at Ourika Garden Mountain Villa (page 118).

perhaps the perfect day trip from the bustle of the Red City.

ORIENTATION

The road leading from Marrakesh (P2017) will take you almost directly south, passing through the main towns of **Ourika, Oualmes,** and **Setti Fatma** along the way. Ourika, nestled right into the foothills of the High Atlas, is the first town you will hit, about an hour's drive after leaving Marrakesh. From here the road winds up to Oualmes and ends at Setti Fatma, home of the waterfalls.

PLANNING YOUR TIME

The valley lies just a short **two-hour drive** from Marrakesh. This is an **easy day trip** that can be done with a group, with a guide (see a list of guides in the Toubkal National Park, who all cover this hike as well, on page 130), or all by your lonesome. If you're hiking the waterfalls, you'll want to make sure to **leave early** enough to make a full day at the falls. Though you could chance public transportation, like much of the region around

climbing into the High Atlas Mountains

Marrakesh, it's best to **rent your own car.**

Because of its close location to Marrakesh, the Ourika Valley is popular with internationals and locals alike. It's best to come **midweek** to **avoid the larger weekend crowds. Springtime,** as with so much of the High Atlas, is when this region really shines, while in August the popular **Setti Fatma Moussem** makes this a must-see destination.

Ourika Valley

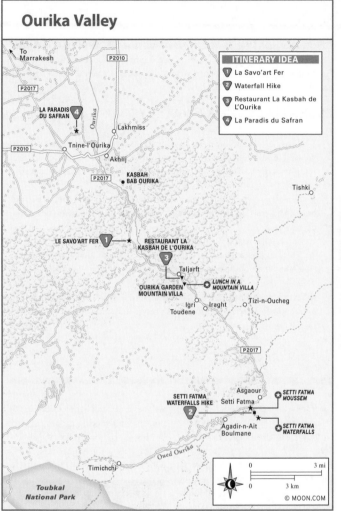

ITINERARY IDEA

1 La Savo'art Fer
2 Waterfall Hike
3 Restaurant La Kasbah de L'Ourika
4 La Paradis du Safran

To Marrakesh

P2010

P2017

LA PARADIS DU SAFRAN 4

Ourika

Lakhmiss

Tnine-l'Ourika

P2010

Akhlij

P2017

KASBAH BAB OURIKA

Tishki

LE SAVO'ART FER 1

RESTAURANT LA KASBAH DE L'OURIKA 3

Taljarft

OURIKA GARDEN MOUNTAIN VILLA

LUNCH IN A MOUNTAIN VILLA

Igri Toudene

Iraght

Tizi-n-Oucheg

P2017

Asgaour

SETTI FATMA WATERFALLS HIKE 2

Setti Fatma

SETTI FATMA MOUSSEM

Agadir-n-Ait Boulmane

SETTI FATMA WATERFALLS

Oued Ourika

Timichchi

Toubkal National Park

0   3 mi
0   3 km

© MOON.COM

Itinerary Idea

Before your trip to the Ourika Valley, make sure you call ahead to Le Savo'art Fer, a gallery with sporadic hours, so you can be certain you'll be able to check out its incredible works along the drive.

ESSENTIAL OURIKA VALLEY

1   Leave Marrakesh by 9am, heading south on the P2017. About 43 kilometers (26mi) south of Marrakesh, stop at **La Savo'art Fer,** which features sculptures of recycled metal crafted by Abdelhaq Elyoussi, a local artist.

2   Arrive in Setti Fatma around noon, park the car, and take the short, bracing **hike** around the **waterfalls,** enjoying a brief dip if you've worked up a sweat.

3   Head to **Restaurant La Kasbah de L'Ourika** for lunch on the terrace, which has some of the best views in the valley.

4   After lunch, head back to Marrakesh, stopping by **La Paradis du Safran** on the way to learn about Morocco's most iconic spice.

Sights and Recreation

LA PARADIS DU SAFRAN

31km/19mi from Marrakesh on road P2017; tel. 0628/796 979; Wed.-Mon. 11am-7pm; 50Dh

Just a few kilometers before reaching the Ourika Valley, La Paradis du Safran is worth a short detour, especially if you won't be able to make it to Talouine during your stay in Morocco. This garden, curated by Swiss-born Christine Ferrari, is a little oasis dedicated to harvesting the extraordinary saffron flower, as well as a few other exotic fruits. The best time to visit is during October and early November when the saffron is harvested, though even outside of this season, Christine will be more than happy to explain to you the painstaking process of harvesting saffron over a deliciously floral tea. Follow the bright orange signs about 30 kilometers (18mi) outside

fresh, clear-water mountain waterfalls

of Marrakesh to find this veritable paradise.

LE SAVO'ART FER

43km/26mi from Marrakesh on road P2017, Asguine; tel. 0676/561 799; hours vary; free

One of the more interesting stops to make along the way to or from the Ourika Valley is the strange gallery of Le Savo'art Fer. The gallery features sculptures of recycled metal crafted by Abdelhaq Elyoussi, a local artist. Sculptures of recycled metal—featuring bolts, nuts, screws, car parts, tin cans, spatulas, and other discarded waste—have been gaining traction in Morocco, with several practitioners now in nearby Essaouira. The sculptures are whimsical while at the same time commenting on the state of the rusty decay of our civilization, adding a sort of melancholy to their twisting forms. One can easily imagine these figures crawling out of the local trash heap and into the living room.

✪ SETTI FATMA WATERFALLS

Distance: 2km/1.2mi
Hiking Time: 30 min
Trailhead: Across the wooden bridge crossing the Ourika River in the village of Setti Fatma, to the left side of the road as you enter the village

The last village along the road is Setti Fatma (64km/40mi, 2hr from Marrakesh), which provides for a base to hike to the Setti Fatma Waterfalls. The trailhead is well marked and lies just across the river.

Travelers should note that the hike to the waterfalls (2km/1.2mi, 30min) requires some scrambling up rock faces, though most of the hike is easy. This is a safe climb, and those in moderate physical condition shouldn't

the hike up the Setti Fatma Waterfalls

have a problem. At times the elevation might get to some who are nervous climbing heights, though the largest rock face is only three meters (10ft). There are stunning cliff faces and rocky outcrops around the waterfalls and into the nearby mountains. There is only one well-traveled path, so a guide is unnecessary. Most people do the 2-kilometer (1.2mi) circuit, though a longer circuit is available if you want to hike up all seven waterfalls. This longer circuit is best for those who really enjoy mountain hiking and being out in nature, and who are looking to really get away from the crowds.

Unfortunately, swimming isn't always available, but it's a good idea to pack your swim clothes just in case. Though much of the High Atlas region is notably conservative, locals here are used to people bathing in all sorts of attire, from diving in wearing your shorts and T-shirt, to stripping down to a bikini top. Take a look around and do whatever you feel most comfortable with.

Entertainment and Events

✪ Setti Fatma Moussem

Setti Fatma Village; four days in mid-Aug.; free

Every August a *moussem* (religious festival) for Setti Fatma takes place, typically around August 11-13, though the dates will vary. This can be a crowded, though festive, time to visit as pilgrims from around Morocco make their way to the Koubba of Setti Fatma, a local saint-like figure. Like so many of Morocco's festivals, though there are elements of religion, mostly this is a time for the community to gather. For outsiders, it's a great opportunity to see Moroccan culture at its finest, with displays of horsemanship, local music, singing and dancing, copious amounts of food, and lots of specialty drinks (nonalcoholic, of course). Locals usually find out about this festival a week ahead of time in the local markets via word-of-mouth. If you're in the region in early August, ask around to see when the festival will be held.

Food and Accommodations

Restaurant La Kasbah de l'Ourika

48km/29mi from Marrakesh on the P2017, Aghbalou; tel. 0524/484 536; daily 11am-9pm; 150dh

Restaurant La Kasbah de l'Ourika is a sprawling complex just a couple of kilometers after the turnoff for Oukaïmeden. On a chilly day, the ornate salons provide comfort, while most days, the terrace is the best seat in the valley to dine. (Those not interested in the views are best off going to one of the small cafés lining the road for an equally delicious tajine for less than half the price.)

✪ Ourika Garden Mountain Villa

50km/31mi from Marrakesh on the P2017, Aghbalou; tel. 0524/484 441; www.ourikagarden.com; 660Dh d

You can literally drink up the herb garden at the relaxing Ourika Garden Mountain Villa. Located just far enough off the main road to be immersed into the spacious terraced gardens and towering peaks surrounding the valley, this is far and away the best overnight stay one could hope for in Ourika. The traditionally built mountain retreat features lots of craggy stonework and pinewood beams around a curvy swimming pool that will take the heat off any summer afternoon. The rooms are heated by fireplace or a mechanical unit, if you

The tajines of the mountains are hearty and rich.

Grab a coffee or tea along the river.

prefer, with TV, air-conditioning, Wi-Fi, and breakfast all included with your stay. The on-site restaurant is open to travelers making a day trip in Ourika, though you will need to call at least two hours in advance. The menu features tajines, reputed as the finest in the valley, starting from 200Dh.

✪ Kasbah Bab Ourika

38km/23mi, look for signs turning off the P2017, Tnine; tel. 0668/749 547 or 0661/634 234; https://kasbahbabourika. com; 2000Dh d

If you're looking for one place to disconnect, unwind, and hide out, this is it. With immaculate gardens, breathtaking views over the valley and mountains, a swimming pool and spa, and impeccable service, this rare gem is entirely worth the price of a night's stay. Not only is the Kasbah built from ecofriendly, traditional methods with rammed earth, but with the solar array, the owners have gone to great lengths to make the Kasbah as sustainable as possible. The decoration is minimalist mixed with colorful Amazigh touches. The on-site restaurant serves local and international cuisine. But what makes this place so special is their work with the local villages: They've created or assisted a number of local initiatives, including the distillation of water, improvement of irrigation channels, and help with supplies and tutelage for the local, underserved schools. Stay here for a night or two and you'll wish you stayed longer.

Transportation

GETTING THERE

The town of Ourika lies at the junction of the P2017 and P2010 and marks the beginning of the Ourika Valley. It is easily reached by car heading southeast from Marrakesh (64km/40mi, 1.5hr). The valley continues, with the P2017 serving as the only through road until it ends about 45 minutes later (28km/17mi) at Setti Fatma.

For those willing to chance public transportation, local minivans leave from Marrakesh for Setti Fatma (2hr, 50Dh) from just outside the Jemaa el-Fnaa, near the Koutoubia Mosque, though departure times vary widely. Buses often wait until they are near full capacity to leave. For this reason, it's best to rent a car.

GETTING AROUND

The P2017 serves as the only through road, ending at Setti Fatma, the base to hike to the Setti Fatma Waterfalls. There is well-signed, guarded parking in the middle of Setti Fatma (10Dh). Once you park, you'll be on foot. Make sure to wear good walking or hiking shoes.

OUZOUD

Ouzoud, on the south end of

the Middle Atlas Mountains, is home of Morocco's longest waterfall, known throughout the country as Cascades d'Ouzoud. The spectacular waterfalls are fed by a series of small irrigation channels from the river with a wide mouth at the top of the waterfall plunges, narrowing into a picture-perfect stream of water splashing into the pools below. The pools themselves are cool, perfect to refresh after a hot early summer hike. Rainbows often form in the cascades. Alongside the waterfalls and lush valley, it all

HIGHLIGHTS

✪ **OUZOUD WATERFALLS:** Morocco's largest waterfall plunges into picturesque pools below (page 124).

✪ **BARBARY MACAQUES:** The waterfalls and forest surrounding Ouzoud are prime territory to meet these primates (page 124).

makes for a scenic getaway. The atmosphere around Ouzoud is chill, with plenty of little cafés and shady spots to relax.

ORIENTATION

It's impossible to get lost in this little village. There is a large public parking at the end of the road. From here, there's only the **one main pedestrian road** that slopes down to the waterfalls. Along the road, you'll find several **lookouts** for the falls, with the topmost viewpoints offering perhaps the better "rainbow" shots of the waterfalls. The pedestrian road ends at the bottom of the falls, at the plunge pools.

PLANNING YOUR TIME

The small village of Ouzoud is an **easy day-trip getaway** from Marrakesh, though staying a night allows for a more relaxing exploration of the area. The best time to visit by far is **spring,** from March through June. By the end of June it gets a bit **hot,** and into the summer months it can be unbearable.

From Marrakesh, it's a little less than **three hours' travel time,** whether you **drive** or take the **bus.** Though you can get to Ouzoud via public transport, it's much easier to either opt to join one of the **day-trip bus excursions** leaving from Marrakesh, such as Marrakech Excursion, or to **rent a car** for the day. For the best **photographs,** you'll want to stay until **later in the afternoon** when the sun shines directly on the waterfalls.

Great tits are just a few of the birds you can find in the region.

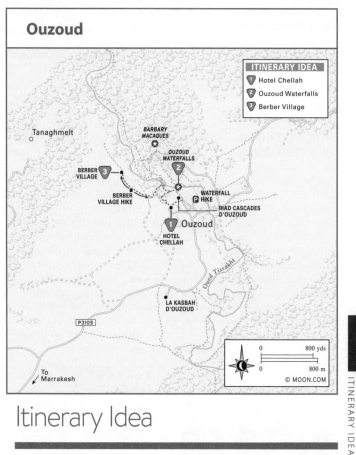

Ouzoud

ITINERARY IDEA

1. Hotel Chellah
2. Ouzoud Waterfalls
3. Berber Village

Tanaghmelt

BARBARY MACAQUES

OUZOUD WATERFALLS

BERBER VILLAGE

BERBER VILLAGE HIKE

WATERFALL HIKE

RIAD CASCADES D'OUZOUD

Ouzoud

HOTEL CHELLAH

Oued Tissakht

LA KASBAH D'OUZOUD

P3105

To Marrakesh

| 0 | 800 yds |
| 0 | 800 m |

© MOON.COM

Itinerary Idea

ESSENTIAL OUZOUD VALLEY

1 Leave Marrakesh by 9am to make sure you're at the falls before noon. Park your car at the well-marked car park and follow the pedestrian path downhill for lunch at **Hotel Chellah.**

2 Continue downhill, reaching the base of the **waterfalls** in the middle of the afternoon, and treat yourself to a little boat ride or swim.

3 Take a short hike to the **Berber Village,** returning well before dark. Drive back to Marrakesh, starting around 4-5pm, to make sure you return before nightfall.

Sights

✪ OUZOUD WATERFALLS (CASCADES D'OUZOUD)

The primary draw in the entire region are the impressive 110-meter-tall (330-ft-tall) Ouzoud Waterfalls. The waterfalls pierce through a buttress of tufa rock before plunging into a cold, clear pool of mountain water below. The mists from these pools are thought to have given rise to the name of the village, Ouzoud, which is a Tashelhit word for "mill." This is due to the impression that the mist filling the air gives off "fine flour dust," as well as the watermills that still dot the top of the waterfalls. This handful of still-functioning ancient watermills adds to the pastoral charm. Below, the rocky outcrops break the

Ouzoud Waterfalls

waterfall at several points, filling the air with a fine mist and creating a near-permanent rainbow.

At the bottom of the falls you'll find a few small boats, locally dubbed "titanics." Don't worry—despite the name, these boats are carved from the local wood and won't sink. These rowboats can take you across the water and right to the bottom of the falls for 20Dh. It's a popular diversion for both Moroccans and internationals alike. You might get a little wet, so dress accordingly. Boats travel back and forth across the pools below the waterfalls, making for some wonderful picture opportunities. Rides are typically just a few minutes, though if you wanted to go for longer, you could ask (and expect to pay a bit more).

✪ BARBARY MACAQUES

The surrounding thuya forest is a haven for a small troop of friendly Barbary macaques and eagles, hawks, and lesser kestrels, though of course the monkeys and birds should never be fed. That said, locals will likely try to offer you some nuts to feed the monkeys. If you find yourself in this situation, hold the nuts in your open hand and let the monkey climb on you to get it. Never try to pet or otherwise touch the monkeys. The best times to see the macaques are in the morning and shortly before dusk, when they're at their most active. In the mornings, they will often be atop the waterfall, drinking from the El-Abid River that feeds the powerful falls.

In the spring, you'll often find families of macaques in Ouzoud.

Sports and Recreation

HIKING

There are several well-marked hikes around the waterfalls. Most are 2-3 hours, with some leading into nearby villages where it is sometimes possible to have lunch with one of the old families from the region, making a spontaneous Amazigh cultural encounter likely. The hikes are all relatively easy. Hiring a guide or carrying a map, though somewhat helpful, isn't necessary. In the summer, heatstroke can be a real concern, so it's better to set off early in the morning. As always, you'll want to wear comfortable shoes. Because the river can overflow in parts, you might want to consider wearing waterproofs. Hiking can be had year round, though it is best in spring when the waterfall is at its strongest and the forest is in bloom.

BERBER VILLAGE HIKE

Distance: 2km/1mi round trip
Hiking Time: 45min round trip without stopping
Trailhead: Bottom of the waterfalls; path climbs up to the left past a house

This hike takes you quickly out of the waterfalls and up to a small plain. You'll find the village here, nestled against the slopes of a forested hill. The village has unique, semi-underground passages that provide an opportunity to see what villages in the area were like before modern building construction. In the spring, you will see the plain erupt in blooms with explosions of red and yellow everywhere. With the picturesque village and forest as the backdrop, it is truly idyllic. This is an easy, short hike with a bit of uphill. Inquire at the local cafés if you have trouble finding the trailhead.

Small rivulets run into the river.

numerous lookout points. In the afternoon, start looking for rainbows in the waterfalls. Within the thuya forest and occasional pomegranate tree, you'll likely see a few of the friendly Barbary macaque monkeys that have made this region their home.

An alternative to the main path for those seeking more of a hiking challenge is to cross the top of the waterfall and make your way down the donkey paths that zigzag across the far side of the waterfalls. Conversely, you could make a loop from hiking down on the main path, crossing the pools at the bottom by one of the "titanic" boats, and then come up the donkey trails on the other side.

You will likely want to budget an extra hour to explore the village.

WATERFALL HIKE

Distance: 3km/1.5mi round trip
Hiking Time: 1 hour without stopping
Trailhead: Top of the waterfalls

This is the must-do hike in Ouzoud. Alongside the trail you will find

This is an extremely easy hike down to the bottom of the waterfalls, though be warned, the return is all steep uphill. There are quite a few stairs along the hike and with the mist from the waterfalls, the stones can be slippery, particularly farther downhill. You'll likely want to spend another hour or so at the bottom of the waterfalls.

Food and Accommodations

HOTEL CHELLAH

Le Chemins de Cascades;
tel. 0523/429 180 or 0672/384 791;
www.hotelchellalouzoud.com; 250Dh d

Travelers spending just a night or two would do well to make their way down the pedestrian path to the falls and stay at Hotel Chellah. The rooms are austere, but the food is some of the best around the waterfalls. Breakfast is included with your stay. The terrace is relaxing, and the staff is friendly and very knowledgeable about the area. They'll happily direct you to some of

the better hikes you can take in the area without needing to hire a guide. Even if you don't stay the night, this is hands-down the best place for lunch. A good tajine lunch will set you back around 60Dh.

LA KASBAH D'OUZOUD

Ouzoud road; tel. 0523/429 210;
https://kasbahouzoud.com; 760Dh d

For a swell retreat, consider La Kasbah d'Ouzoud. This traditionally constructed kasbah features charming wood-beam ceilings and carved doors with tribal touches all around an open courtyard with plenty of twittering birds. The grounds include a swimming pool, garden, and lush palms. Wi-Fi, air-conditioning, and heating are all standard, and breakfast is included. Other meals are available on request. Bungalows are a bit less at 600Dh and charming in their own right. However, the kasbah is a walk up the hill, away from town by the main parking plaza.

✪ RIAD CASCADES D'OUZOUD

Chemin des moulins; tel. 0523/429 173 or 0690/425 248; www.ouzoud.com; 450Dh d, add 220Dh pp for breakfast and dinner

Perched at the top of the waterfalls is this splendid, earthy riad full of traditional charm. Using local building techniques that have been around for generations, this is the perfect place for an overnight or a little getaway from the city hustle. Quiet nights with the wind rustling in the trees of the neighboring forest, the quiet gurgle of the El-Abid River, and the occasional hoot of a woodland owl comprise the evening orchestra. Tuck in for some relaxation in the Saffron Room and enjoy sumptuous Amazigh-inspired meals in the rustic, open areas of the property.

Transportation

GETTING THERE FROM MARRAKESH

BY CAR

To get to Ouzoud from Marrakesh, take the **N8** east, following the signs for El Kelaa des Sraghna. About an hour later (67km/42mi), you'll want to take a right on the **R208** in the direction of **Azilal.** Keep following the signs for Azilal for about 1.5 hours (83km/52mi) until you see the turnoff for Ouzoud. Follow the **P3105** north for about 20 minutes (22km/13mi) until you get to the end of the road at Ouzoud.

TOUR BUSES

Tour buses make their way here from the *gare routière* in Marrakesh (3hr, 160km/99mi, 300-400Dh, depending on bus carrier) for day-trippers, though the drive from Marrakesh makes for a long day trip. An overnight stay is possible. Check with the tour bus to purchase tickets returning to Marrakesh the next day. **Marrakech Excursion** (www.marrakechexcursion.com) is one of the better-known, most reliable outfits, and offers pickup at your accommodation.

BY BUS AND *GRAND TAXI*

It is possible, though a bit complicated, to get to Ouzoud using public transportation. This option should only be taken by the most adventurous, or perhaps foolhardy, travelers. First, you'll want to board a **public bus** from Marrakesh in the direction of **Azilal.** You'll have to purchase a ticket for Azilal (40Dh), but tell the bus driver you want to get off at Ouzoud. Do not be surprised when he pulls the bus over in the middle of nowhere and tells you that this is where you get off. The driver drops you off at the start of the P3105 road that leads north (22km/13mi) to Ouzoud. Luckily, there are a number of *grands taxis* driving by on their way to Ouzoud. Generally, you will wait 15 minutes until the next one. Either pay for one seat (5Dh) or the entire taxi (40Dh).

GETTING AROUND

Outside of the village is a large parking lot for buses. Daytime and overnight parking for cars and campers is 10Dh. From the parking lot, it is a five-minute walk through the village, past cafés, restaurants, and souvenir shops, to the waterfalls.

TOUBKAL NATIONAL PARK

The most tourised national park in Morocco is the sprawling forest of the 380-square-kilometer (146-sq-mi) Toubkal National Park, just a couple of short hours into the High Atlas Mountains towering above Marrakesh's Haouz Plain, protecting the plain from the vast stretch of the Sahara. Many Moroccans venture into the High Atlas during the summer for the cool, clean air, while most Europeans and North Americans come for the incredible year-round trekking, snow sports, and the chance to mingle with the friendly locals. The

HIGHLIGHTS

✪ **EXPLORING IMLIL:** Toubkal's most famous village teems with friendly locals (page 135).

✪ **ENJOYING A MOUNTAIN RETREAT:** Cozy up for a warm night at the Imlil Lodge (page 138).

✪ **SUMMITING MOUNT TOUBKAL:** You'll want to give yourself at least two days to summit Morocco's tallest peak (page 140).

peak of Oukaïmeden is reserved for skiing and snowboarding in the winter months, with February being the best month for snow.

The biggest draw in the national park is the tallest peak in North Africa, Mount Toubkal at 4,167 meters (13,671ft), which can be summited year-round. Alongside Toubkal National Park, sometimes even within the park's boundaries, lie small towns that can provide spots of interest or places to sleep and eat for those looking to explore the park. Gateway towns are good places to store your gear while you're trekking or to spend a short weekend.

ORIENTATION

Toubkal National Park, with its proximity to Marrakesh (70km/44mi), is Morocco's most popular national park, both with locals and internationals. The park runs throughout the High Atlas, covering a wide area of nearly 100,000 hectares (247,000 acres). It is a nature lover's dream, full of diverse flora and fauna and plenty of rivers, lakes, waterfalls, cliffs, and other impressive sights to be experienced along the way. In the park, the towns of Imlil and Armed lie to the north of Mount Toubkal, while to the northeast of the park is the small ski-station town of Oukaïmeden.

PLANNING YOUR TIME

With its proximity to Marrakesh and crisp mountain weather, Toubkal National Park is a refreshing break from the heat of the city. Plan for about two hours to get between Marrakesh and Toubkal National Park. It's easy enough to spend a day hiking in the park, though you might wish you had overnighted.

This is a region with four seasons, often snowy and cold in the winter, blossoming under spring rains, warm in summer, and cooling off in the fall as the deciduous trees shed their leaves. Spring is probably the best time to visit, though there is mountainous beauty to be found in every season.

GUIDES

It is possible to do many activities in the High Atlas without a guide. However, for a really immersive experience in the Toubkal National Park, do yourself a favor and get one of the region's wonderful guides. The people leading these hikes add a cultural element to your time spent trekking in the national park that will make your time in Morocco's mountains unforgettable. The guides all speak the local lingo and know the terrain well. They

Toubkal National Park

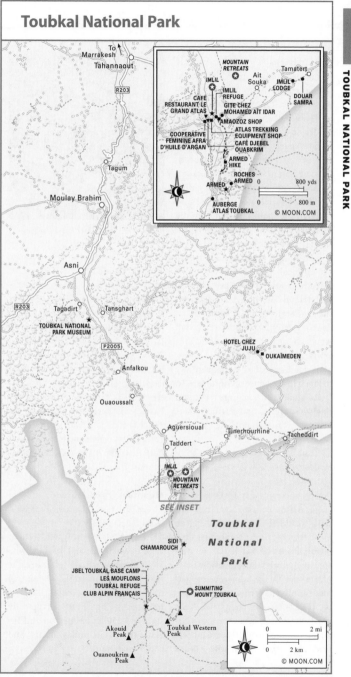

To Marrakesh
Tahannaout

R203

MOUNTAIN
RETREATS

IMLIL

Ait
Souka

Tamatert

IMLIL
LODGE

IMLIL
REFUGE

DOUAR
SAMRA

CAFÉ
RESTAURANT LE
GRAND ATLAS

GITE CHEZ
MOHAMED AÏT IDAR

AMAOZOZ SHOP

COOPERATIVE
FEMININE AFRA
D'HUILE D'ARGAN

ATLAS TREKKING
EQUIPMENT SHOP

CAFÉ DJEBEL
OUABKRIM

ARMED
HIKE

ROCHES
ARMED

ARMED

0   800 yds

0   800 m

AUBERGE
ATLAS TOUBKAL

© MOON.COM

Tagum

Moulay Brahim

Asni

R203

Tagadirt

Tansghart

TOUBKAL NATIONAL
PARK MUSEUM

P2005

Anfalkou

HOTEL CHEZ
JUJU

OUKAÏMEDEN

Ouaoussalt

Aguersioual

Tinerhourhine

Tacheddirt

Taddert

IMLIL

MOUNTAIN
RETREATS

SEE INSET

Toubkal

National

Park

SIDI
CHAMAROUCH

JBEL TOUBKAL BASE CAMP
LES MOUFLONS
TOUBKAL REFUGE
CLUB ALPIN FRANÇAIS

SUMMITING
MOUNT TOUBKAL

Akouid
Peak

Toubkal Western
Peak

Ouanoukrim
Peak

0   2 mi

0   2 km

© MOON.COM

will give you cultural insights and provide direction for trails and roads, as well as equipment, all at a reasonable cost. Additionally, guides can provide you transportation from Marrakesh, saving you the cost and hassle of renting a car to get the mountains.

Because of the complexity of the roads and occasional hazards, having a knowledgeable guide in this region is beneficial, even for experienced, die-hard mountaineers, trekkers, climbers, and bikers. With a guide, you'll have the chance to safely climb through the mountains and see the sorts of landscapes that will leave you short of breath.

The guides recommended here are all locals who know the region incredibly well. They have families and friends scattered throughout the mountain range, offering you a chance to glimpse some of the proud Amazigh history that you might otherwise miss. With a guide from the region, you'll have the best opportunity to lunch in the house of a local family.

All guides listed here are reputable, English speaking, and certified wherever certification is possible.

✪ Toubkal Peaks

tel. 0661/283 086; www.toubkal-peaks.com; 900Dh per person

For all-inclusive day treks into the High Atlas, contact Omar Jellah with Toubkal Peaks. This is the most respected tour company in the region. Prices start at 900Dh per person, including transportation from Marrakesh. Of the numerous companies running day trips and hikes into the High Atlas, this company has the most interesting hikes for every fitness level, and the guides are all certified and incredibly friendly. All-day

excursions include lunch in a traditional setting.

Guide Omar Jellah instructs on history and safety.

Toubkal Guide

tel. 0661/417 636; www.toubkalguide.com; 1,750Dh for small group

If you want to make your way deep into the mountains, get in touch with Jamal Imerhane with Toubkal Guide. He is a certified guide, well-respected by other local guides, and runs a very cozy lodge in Imlil. Most of his better excursions into the mountains are based from here. Two-day treks for Toubkal start at 1,750Dh for a small group of 2-4 people and include transportation from Marrakesh, accommodations, and all meals.

Mountain Travel Morocco

tel. 0668/760 165; www.trekkinginmorocco. com; 1,250 per person

The team at Mountain Travel Morocco is led by Mohamed and Ibrahim, who are well-respected and offer breathtaking hikes around the region. All of their guides are certified, and most speak English. Prices typically start at 1,250Dh per person and include the guide, mules, meals, and accommodations.

Itinerary Idea

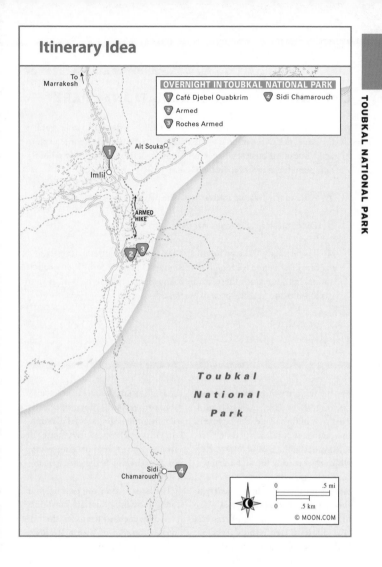

OVERNIGHT IN TOUBKAL NATIONAL PARK

1 Café Djebel Ouabkrim
2 Armed
3 Roches Armed
4 Sidi Chamarouch

To Marrakesh

Ait Souka

Imlil

ARMED HIKE

Toubkal National Park

Sidi Chamarouch

0   .5 mi
0   .5 km

© MOON.COM

Itinerary Idea

OVERNIGHT IN TOUBKAL NATIONAL PARK

1 After breakfast in Marrakesh, take the R203 road south to Imlil. Park at the large rock in the middle of the village. Give yourself an hour to explore Imlil, one of the busiest villages in the region, before tucking in for a hearty mountain lunch at Café Djebel Ouabkrim.

2 After lunch, hike up into Armed, the neighboring village.

3 Dine and sleep at Roches Armed.

4 The next day, wake up bright and early with a strong cup of coffee and big breakfast before hiking up to the modest village of Sidi Chamarouch and taking your lunch there, before following the trail all the way to your car in Imlil and heading back to Marrakesh.

Imlil   إمليل

For the majority of trekkers, the beginning of the High Atlas is Imlil. This mountain village, the largest in the region, is rural, nestled in a forested valley at the foot of Mount Adj, with a river cutting through the town, connecting it with nearby Armed and farther up the mountains, nearly to the summit of Mount Toubkal. The town has seen a number of changes geared toward eco-friendly trekking, with new guesthouses and cafés lining the main street. You're more likely to hear Tashelhit (a dialect of the indigenous Tamazight language) spoken here than you are Darija. Many people know a few words of English, particularly shop owners and hotel workers, and are happy to help. The accommodations, restaurants, and shops make this a good place to settle in for a few days. As in the rest of the High Atlas, the feel is noticeably more conservative, though perfectly friendly. Imlil begins a series of mountain villages whose primary source of income revolves around the tourist industry and, as such, they are welcoming hosts.

The large kasbah you pass on your way into town is Kasbah Tamadot, owned by Richard Branson, the billionaire founder of Virgin Records, who is famed among the locals for having this kasbah restored. The philanthropist and his mother established a foundation aiming to improve the living conditions of the women of the region. Their work can be seen throughout the valley, though there is talk locally suggesting that not all the proceeds of the cooperative next to the kasbah find their way to the women. Sadly, it is perhaps another sign of the corruption endemic in some spheres of Morocco.

ORIENTATION

Most directions around Imlil revolve around the well-signed parking lot and large rock at a bend in the road in the middle of town. Directly next to Imlil, just a couple of kilometers east up the road and after the downtown, is the area known as Tamatert, where there are a few other lodging options.

✪ SIGHTS

There is only one main road cutting up the mountainside and through the village, but it bustles with local activity. The sidewalks are uneven, but at each street corner you'll likely see something worthy of a photograph. Of particular interest are colored metal doors, which provide a great background for any composition. There are numerous cafés where you can stop in for a tea and, if it's not too cold, sit outside for some people-watching and to catch your breath. For those looking to get a taste of local village life,

Imlil village in the rain

there is perhaps no better spot in the High Atlas.

TOUBKAL NATIONAL PARK MUSEUM (Musée du Parc National de Toubkal)

tel. 0629/275 463; Mon.-Fri. 8am-noon and 3pm-6pm; 50Dh

Toubkal National Park Museum, across from the Richard Branson hotel, features displays and information on all of the naturally occurring plants and animals of Toubkal National Park, which should interest most hikers, trekkers, and naturalists visiting the region. The caretaker, who talks with you as you circle the museum, provides information in English, French, or Arabic. This service is included with admission. Signage is minimal and in Arabic and French. The hours vary quite a bit depending on the season, the weather, and, apparently, the caretaker's whims.

HIKING

Mountaineering in the High Atlas Mountains, by Des Clark, is a good guidebook for those looking to do some solo-trekking in the High Atlas. There is also one map of Toubkal done at 1:50,000 (Cordee, 2018). These are best obtained in advance, before you come to Morocco.

Armed Hike

Distance: 4km/2.5mi one-way
Hiking Time: 1-1.5hrs one-way
Trailhead: At the river on the south edge of town

For those wanting a taste of the mountains but not interested in more than a half day of hiking, this is the perfect hike. It's just enough to stretch your legs, and the views from the village of Armed out over the valley are wonderful. Even better, you can lunch in Armed before heading back down to Imlil. Follow the well-trodden mule trail that zigs and zags above the Mizane River—the path hugs the river for the entirety of the hike, so there should be no fear of getting lost—before dropping down to the bridge crossing into Armed. When you're ready, turn back toward Imlil and hike the trail in reverse.

Sidi Chamarouch

Distance: 4km/2.5mi one-way
Hiking Time: 1.5-2hrs one-way
Trailhead: Follow the mule trail along the east side of the river, toward the south end of town

Hikers looking for a bit more sport should consider continuing from Armed up to the small cluster of houses built around the *koubba,* or shrine, to Sidi Chamarouch, a historical, local, saintlike figure. Non-Muslims should not cross the concrete bridge to the *koubba.* It is considered a holy site, and many locals make yearly pilgrimages to visit the saint. The hike features mountainous terrain, largely following the river. There are bubbling waterfalls at Sidi Chamarouch, which are refreshing after a hot day. After Sidi Chamarouch, the trek flattens out into an expansive plain. You'll return the same way you came, though on the return, you'll have spectacular mountain views as you descend back to Armed.

SHOPPING

Cooperative Feminine Afra d'Huile d'Argan

Imlil Village, daily 9am-noon and 3pm-6pm

In the tiny stretch of the road that serves as the downtown of Imlil you can find the Cooperative Feminine

A woman hikes across a mountain plain.

Afra d'Huile d'Argan. This is a friendly co-op with plenty of cosmetic and alimentation oil, though as at most other cooperatives, it's impossible to tell if you're getting the "pure" argan oil. Typically, cosmetic oil is diluted, while the oil for cooking is more pure. The oil here seems to be of better quality than at many of the other cooperatives in the region.

FOOD

Cafés in Imlil serve *bissara*, lentils, tajines, and sandwiches. A typical bowl of *bissara* or lentils served with bread will run around 10Dh, while tajines typically run 30-40Dh.

Café Djebel Ouabkrim

on the corner, by the big rock, across from the parking lot; daily 10am-8pm; 35Dh

The Café Djebel Ouabkrim serves some deliciously hearty mountain tajines for 35Dh. This is about as humble of a restaurant as you'll find, and it's best for small groups looking to fill up before hiking. Tajines are made on command, with plenty of root vegetables and hunks of meat. You'll likely be waiting 30 minutes or longer for your tajine to cook, so plan on writing those postcards back home while you're taking in the mountain air.

Café Restaurant Le Grand Atlas

Imlil main road, before the parking lot; daily 8am-10pm; 40Dh

The Café Restaurant Le Grand Atlas is easily missed along the main road, across from Les Mouflons Refuge and Restaurant (not to be confused with the base camp of Mount Toubkal of the same name) before the parking lot. Breakfast is the best time to come to this little hole-in-the-wall. Pull up a seat on the small shaded terrace and

enjoy a steaming bowl of *bissara* or lentils (10Dh) while watching the kids, trekkers, and donkeys make their way up the road and into the mountains.

ACCOMMODATIONS

✪ Imlil Refuge

next to the parking lot; tel. 0661/873 771; 70Dh d

Opened in March 2015, the Imlil Refuge is one of the newer guesthouses. The lodgings are no-frills, though amenities include Wi-Fi, hot water, and a chimney to warm the cozy living room. Kitchens are open for use by guests; you just have to clean up after yourself and pay for whatever gas was used. Breakfast and dinner can be made for you at an additional cost. This is the best budget accommodation in Imlil, made better by the gracious hosts (a couple of mountaineers) and whoever else happens to be passing through on their way up or down the mountain.

Gite Chez Mohamed Aït Idar

Imlil Center, after the rock; tel. 0668/045 140; 350Dh d

When the original owner of Gite Chez Mohamed Aït Idar died, his two wives and daughters took over running it. Today, this is the only *gite* in the national park run solely by women, and it's a great budget option, particularly for single women or groups of young women traveling on a budget. There are two sets of rooms. The less expensive rooms of the *gite* are all on the ground floor and, in the winter, can be quite cold. The second floor has refurbished standard rooms with heating and en suite bathrooms, though it's not quite a budget option at 350Dh a night. Meals can be had on request.

✪ Imlil Lodge

Tamatert; tel. 0661/417 636 or 0671/157 636;
www.imlil-lodge.com; 350Dh d

The cozy Imlil Lodge is full of rocky rustic mountain charm, with Tazenakht rugs, exposed wood, and stone throughout the lodge. All rooms feature air-conditioning, Wi-Fi, and en suite bathrooms. A room with three bunk beds is perfect for small groups and families. A sprawling terrace offers views over the valley and the twin peaks of Mount Adj and Mount Toubkal. The owner, Jamal Imerhane, is a certified guide, well-respected in the region, and can lead treks or suggest routes. There's also convenient storage hikers can use to leave unneeded stuff behind, like maybe that carpet you just bought. Meals are available on request, while breakfast is included with your stay.

accommodations at Imlil Lodge

Douar Samra

Tamatert; tel. 0524/484 034 or 0636/048
559; www.douar-samra.net; 500Dh d

A self-described treehouse, the funky Douar Samra has a distinct touch, with hand-woven beige linens, bamboo shelves, and lots of exposed rock in this whimsical little guesthouse. The hot-water bottles tucked into the beds on cold nights are a nice touch, and the restaurant is one of the absolute best in Imlil, with a varied seasonal menu that includes traditional favorites, such as chicken and lemon tajine, done exquisitely well. Call ahead for reservations. This particular guesthouse is a little difficult to reach, tucked up the hill from the main road and accessible only by foot or mule, but a guide will meet you on the main road to lead you up to the guesthouse.

Armed
أرمد

A few kilometers uphill from Imlil is the sleepy mountain village of Armed (pronounced "ar-MED" and often written "Aroumd" on maps). Tucked into the folds of the High Atlas in the Ait Mizane Valley, with Mount Adj and Mount Agelzim towering overhead, Armed is the last in a series of typical Amazigh villages in the area. It's not nearly as touristed as nearby Imlil, making for a more authentic cultural experience for those looking for a base to start their High Atlas adventure. This is an excellent, preferable alternative in some ways to Imlil for trekkers and mountaineers who wish to keep away from the crowds. That said, you'll want to gear up elsewhere. There are a few small stores selling bottled water and chips, but that's about it. All accommodations offer meals throughout the day on request, with the service typically friendly as well as above and beyond.

OUKAÏMEDEN: SKIING IN AFRICA

If you've ever wanted to hit the slopes in Africa, the ski resort of Oukaïmeden in Toubkal National Park provides a golden opportunity, though with a short, and often unpredictable, season. The best time for mountain sports begins in **mid-late January,** and by the middle of March, the snows are typically melting into slush. There are **five ski lifts** with a few different routes, the longest being a 1,000-meter (3,200-ft) descent. This isn't world-class skiing, but it is a pleasant outing, and the bragging rights of slaloming African slopes shouldn't be missed by avid skiers and snowboarders.

skis for rent at Oukaïmeden

SKI PASSES AND RENTALS

Ski passes cost around 80Dh for the day. You'll find rentals on the main street in front of Club Alpin Français. Several places rent equipment, but have a look around before agreeing to rent. The quality of the equipment and the prices fluctuate highly, though you should be able to get outfitted for the day for 100-200Dh. **Ski instructors** are available for half days and full days (typically 200-300Dh). It's best to ask at **Hotel Chez Juju** for available instructors.

WHERE TO STAY

- **Club Alpin Français** (tel. 0524/319 036; 120Dh summer, 170Dh winter): The Club Alpin Français is one of the more established retreats, open year-round, catering not only to skiers and snowboarders but also to trekkers, mountaineers, and mountain bikers. The dormitory-style rooms have shared bathrooms. During the ski season it's best to avoid the weekends, as the club can be overrun with children from the local schools learning how to ski. Lodging does not include breakfast (30Dh) or other meals (100Dh). However, beer, wine, and alcohol are served, and there is air-conditioning, heating, Wi-Fi, and hot showers.

- **Hotel Chez Juju** (tel. 0524/319 005; 900Dh d): The Hotel Chez Juju offers slightly more upscale, private lodgings—some rooms have been renovated, while others are in need of a remodel. Amenities include air-conditioning, heating, TV, and Wi-Fi, and all rooms have en suite bathrooms. This hotel is expensive for what it is, but it is the most comfortable lodging in Oukaïmeden. Some of the suites feature wood paneling, and for this price range, the upgrade may be worth it. The French bistro-style restaurant is the best in town; the menu features tartiflette (potato and cheese gratin) with turkey bacon, rotisserie chicken with lemon, and duck confit (150Dh).

GETTING THERE

Oukaïmeden is easy enough to reach by car. From **Marrakesh** (79km/49mi, 1.5hr), follow the road (P2017) from the south of the city, near the Marrakesh Airport, that leads to Ourika. A well-signed turnoff from the road winds up to Oukaïmeden. Your maps may tell you it's possible to reach Oukaïmeden from Imlil, via Tamatert and then Tacheddirt in the east—unfortunately, this is not the case. Tacheddirt is the end of the road.

Grands taxis leave near **Bab er Rob** in Marrakesh (1.5hr, 79km/49mi, 60Dh), though you'll likely have to purchase the entire taxi and negotiate. A fair price is around 350Dh.

FOOD AND ACCOMMODATIONS

Auberge Atlas Toubkal

tel. 0524/485 750; 150Dh d

Before crossing the river into Armed, you'll see the rustic Auberge Atlas Toubkal across from the small dirt parking lot. The rooms here are adequate, but of good value and with en suite bathrooms. For travelers without a guide, this is quiet and easier to find than the other options up the winding pathways of Armed. Accommodations are half board, with breakfast and dinner included. It also has Wi-Fi and, thankfully, hot showers.

Roches Armed

tel. 0667/644 915; 120Dh s, 200Dh d

The Roches Armed offers views of the dominating peaks of Mount Adj and Mount Agelzim. The rooms are understated and comfortable, with plenty of heavy blankets to keep you warm. Breakfast and Wi-Fi are included with your stay. Options for half board (200Dh per person) and full board (300Dh per person) are also available. Meals are generally plucked straight from the on-site garden, making it an eco-friendly option, with vegetarian meals available on request. The friendly manager Samir can help you out with anything you need. Though he's not certified (yet!), he knows the mountains well and can guide you, or, if you want, find you an available certified guide. Prices for guided tours range from 240Dh per person and include guides, mules, and meals.

Mount Toubkal

Summiting Mount Toubkal (often called *Jbel Toubkal,* with *Jbel* meaning "mountain" in the local dialect) is one of the true peak moments of an adventure through the High Atlas (pun fully intended). At 4,167 meters (13,671ft), this is the tallest summit in Morocco and North Africa. On a clear day, you can see down the Haouz Plain to distant Marrakesh and perhaps make out the thin blue line of the Atlantic. On cloudy days, the summit generally provides outstanding views over the clouds.

✪ SUMMITING TOUBKAL

Summiting the mountain can be done year-round, though in winter months, mountain climbing gear, such as crampons and ice axes, will be necessary. In the summer all you'll need is a good pair of shoes, though the nights will likely still be very cold. It is possible to summit Toubkal from Imlil in a single day (35km/22mi, about 14hr round-trip), but keep in mind that most of the surrounding area is above 3,000 meters (nearly 10,000ft), so acute mountain sickness (AMS), commonly called altitude sickness, can be a real concern. Hurrying to the summit is a major cause of this sickness, which is why it's important to take your time. For minor symptoms, aspirin or just sucking on a candy or chewing some gum can help. For anything worse, you will want to stop, rest, and even consider abandoning your climb and descending. It's best to take a three-day climb from Imlil, to both see more

A climber pauses on the ascent to Mount Toubkal.

Because of the real danger of altitude sickness in summiting Mount Toubkal, experienced guides and trekkers in the region recommend approaching the mountain more slowly and following a trek that ascends from **Imlil** (at 1,740m/5,708ft) through a few of the more picturesque mountain valleys and villages before reaching the summit on the third day. Here is an example of a trek:

- **Day 1:** Leave Imlil after breakfast, around 9:30am, and trek up through Tizi n'Mazik pass to the village of Tamsoult (2,250m/7,381ft), where dinner and a comfortable bed await your arrival.

- **Day 2:** From Tamsoult, hike to the stunning Irhoulidene Waterfalls, have lunch, and then take mules to Aguelzim before continuing a trek to the mountain base camp (3,207m/10,522ft) to spend the night at elevation.

- **Day 3:** After breakfast, ascend Toubkal. Picnic atop the summit or descend and have lunch at the base camp before continuing back to Imlil or Armed.

Though most people are able to summit the mountain, **altitude sickness** is a real concern. Symptoms of altitude sickness include dizziness, shortness of breath, fatigue, and insomnia. The cure is easy enough and requires slowly descending below 2,450 meters (8,000ft). If it's untreated, high altitude pulmonary edema (HAPE) or high altitude cerebral edema (HACE) may occur. This is a buildup of fluid in the lungs (HAPE) or brain (HACE) and can lead to death if untreated. If you or a member of your group begins showing signs of altitude sickness, descend immediately.

of the region and allow your body to acclimate.

From Imlil, the trail heads up the Mizane Valley into Armed (1-1.5hr, 4km/2.5mi from Imlil), where it zigzags around the village, continuing to Sidi Chamarouch and finally to the Toubkal Refuge (5-6hrs, 12km/8mi from Imlil). Here, it's best to overnight and let your body adjust to the altitude. At the refuge, you'll be at around 3,200 meters (10,500ft). From here, there are two primary ascents to the Toubkal summit. The easier one, dubbed the South Cirque, takes around 2.5-3.5 hours, depending on ability levels, weather conditions, and adaptation to the altitude. The North Cirque will take you around 4.5 hours and should only be attempted by more seasoned climbers who are used to scrambling in altitude.

The trail up is a largely obvious string of donkey paths, used by locals and trekkers alike. Along the way, you'll encounter some rough rock passages and some loose scree, but outside of the winter months, when the top of the mountain is covered in snow, this is not a technical hike. Skiers and snowboarders willing to pack their equipment to the top will have a nice ride back to the base camp. Guides are not necessary, though they're highly recommended for inexperienced mountain climbers. (See page 130 for information on guides, and see below for information on equipment rental.) If going it on your own, you might consider investing in a good trekking guidebook for the region, such as *Mountaineering in the High Atlas Mountains,* by Des Clark. You can also find a large-scale survey of Toubkal mapped at 1:50,000. These are best obtained in advance, before you come to Morocco.

EQUIPMENT RENTALS

There are several places to rent equipment for summiting Mount Toubkal in Imlil, such as crampons, ice axes, sleeping bags, stoves, and rain jackets, as well as walking poles for trekkers. You'll want to make sure you're geared up before attempting the summit. The gear you will need depends largely on the time of year. In summer, you'll be able to summit with a good pair of hiking shoes, while in the winter you'll likely need crampons and ice axes.

Amaozoz Shop
Imlil Center; daily 9am-noon and 2pm-6pm

The Amaozoz Shop has rentals for climbing and mountaineering, including crampons and ice axes, for 20-50Dh a day.

Atlas Trekking Equipment Shop
Imlil Center; tel. 0668/760 165 or 0661/953 407; www.atlastrekshop.com

The Atlas Trekking Equipment Shop has all the gear you could want for 20-50Dh a day, and the staff speaks English, making requests a bit easier over the phone if you're trying to reserve gear from Marrakesh.

FOOD AND ACCOMMODATIONS

Toubkal Refuge
tel. 0661/695 463;
www.refugedutoubkal.com; 120Dh

The Toubkal Refuge run by Club Alpine Français is better known locally as Nelter, named after Louis Nelter, the French mountaineer who established this refuge as well as the nearby Lepiney ski camp. The club is dormitories only, though the food is notably a notch better than the competition. Breakfast (30Dh), lunch (50Dh), and dinner (70Dh) are all available and include tajines as well as warm vegetarian-friendly soups.

Les Mouflons
tel. 0524/449 767;
www.refugetoubkal.com/uk; 820Dh

Les Mouflons is the more comfortable of the two options, with double rooms and en suite bathrooms. Dormitories are also available (280Dh). The refuge is named after the type of deer found on the surrounding mountain slopes. The price of lodging is for two people and includes breakfast and dinner, with lunch also available on request (110Dh).

PACKING LIST FOR THE HIGH ATLAS

Nights in the High Atlas, particularly from October to March, can be surprisingly cold, with the weather often differing drastically from nearby Marrakesh. Remember to pack the following pieces to make your adventure through the High Atlas memorable for all the right reasons. If you forget to pack something, most items are available in Imlil for rent or purchase.

- Waterproof walking boots or sturdy walking shoes

- Long-sleeved shirts

- Walking/waterproof pants

- Thin fleece (summer) or thick fleece (winter)

- Lightweight waterproof jacket (summer) or warm waterproof jacket (winter)

- Warm hat and gloves (winter)

- Sunhat (styled to cover face, ears, and neck)

- Lightweight daypack

- Sleeping bag

- Sunglasses

- Insect repellent

- Sunscreen

- Flashlight and batteries

- Bathroom kit (with toilet paper, wet wipes, and antibacterial hand wash)

Transportation

GETTING THERE

The entirety of Toubkal National Park lies in the High Atlas Mountains to the south of Marrakesh. **Imlil** (2hrs, 90km/56mi) is the primary village of the park. You'll follow the **R203** south in the direction of Taroudant before turning at Asni onto the **P2005** to head into the park. This is where you'll head to start most hiking or trekking. To get to **Oukaïmeden** (2hrs, 75km/47mi) you'll follow the **P2017** southeast toward Ourika before turning up the **P2030** to head up the mountain.

IMLIL

To get to Imlil from Marrakesh, you'll take the **R203** south toward Asni (1.5hr, 77km/48mi) before turning off the main road onto the **P2005** for Imlil (15km/9mi, 25min), a quick but twisting drive. This road climbs east through the **Ait Mizane Valley.**

If you're attempting to reach Imlil by public transportation, you can take a local bus or *grand taxi* from Marrakesh to Asni. *Grands taxis* (15Dh) are always running between Imlil and Asni.

ARMED

Armed is 4 kilometers (2.5mi) uphill from Imlil (20min) and is reachable by a normal car, though **four-wheel drive** would be preferable, as it is a climb along a narrow, unpaved road that hugs the mountainside. This drive should not be attempted during the winter months. There is **free car parking** on the edge of town, down a short slope near the river on the east side, on your left, as you arrive in Armed from Imlil. Park your car and walk across the river and up through the **steep, pedestrian-only passages** of the hillside village.

There is no public transportation for Armed, though often you can ask in Imlil and transportation can be arranged for a modest fee (20Dh or so). Or, if you are staying in Armed, you can ask your accommodation to arrange for transportation.

MOUNT TOUBKAL

The best way to get to the Mount Toubkal base camp and the summit is by going to Imlil and **trekking up the mountain** from there, so plan accordingly and dress for **cold weather** at the top, no matter the time of year.

CASABLANCA

Casablanca is the beating heart

of modern Morocco. It's a Moroccan-style New York and the country's business capital, with all the hustle and bustle that entails. Casablanca can be underwhelming for travelers to Morocco, who likely think of it in light of its romantic history.

Casa, as most of the locals call it, is a unique city in Morocco, one of its few completely "new" cities. Here, you won't find any of that ancient charm of Marrakesh or Fez. However, what Casa lacks in ancient charm it makes up for in ambition. The dirty whitewashed facades of most of

HIGHLIGHTS

✪ **HASSAN II MOSQUE:** Tour the largest mosque in all of Morocco (the second largest in the world). Modern meets the traditional in this holy place, one of the few mosques non-Muslims may visit (page 152).

✪ **QUARTIER HABOUS:** This French-built, Moroccan-inspired neighborhood is one of the more pleasant shopping areas in all of Casablanca (page 153).

✪ **DINING OUT AT RICK'S CAFÉ:** You'll always have Casablanca after a night out at the best gin joint in Morocco (page 156).

the buildings betray Casa's colonial past. The city has had many names as it passed from Carthaginian to Phoenician to Roman to Portuguese to Moroccan control, but it was the French—who took control of the city under the French Protectorate era in the first half of the 20th century—who built much of what Casablanca is today.

As the economic capital of Morocco, Casa is on the cutting edge of industry and fashion. You can walk the art deco streets of Boulevard Mohammed V, shop for Gucci bags at the new Morocco Mall, and visit the impressive Hassan II Mosque (one of the few mosques non-Muslims can enter in Morocco). For foodies, the booming business and international clientele has been a major boon, with Casablanca sporting some of the finest and most diverse dining in all of Morocco. Treat yourself to dinner at a five-star restaurant before heading out to a night at Rick's Café to hear some great jazz and the nightly staple, "As Time Goes By."

ORIENTATION

Like any sprawling metropolis, Casablanca can be a bit difficult to figure out, though unlike many other Moroccan cities, it is well signed, so GPS-assisted maps typically work very well. The city hugs the Atlantic Coast and has some long (though not necessarily clean) stretches of coastline, and it hosts one of the busiest seaports in Morocco. The city is somewhat divided into "old" and "new" like many Moroccan cities, with the "old" city being the Moroccan **medina** and the "new" being the rest of the urban sprawl of the **Ville Nouvelle.** The small, grubby medina forms a sort of focal point of the city, near the **marina** and the **Hassan II Mosque.** A wide, busy thoroughfare, **Boulevard de la Corniche,** begins at the Hassan II Mosque and continues southwest. Along the southern end of the boulevard is the connection with the tram at Aïn Diab, which can take you back into the city. When the sun is out, as it often is in Casablanca, this can be a pleasant walk.

Boulevard Sidi Mohamed Ben Abdellah runs east from the Hassan II Mosque along the busy marina and industrial port to the seaside, passing the neglected outer walls of the medina, where you can find **Rick's Café,** before arriving at the convenient **Casa Port train station.**

The vibrant **Place des Nations Unies,** on the other side of the medina from Hassan II Mosque, is the real heart of Casablanca. Cafés and restaurants surround the square, with pedestrian-friendly streets to explore. This neighborhood is one of the better-preserved art deco neighborhoods in the world, though to be frank, it's in need of a good scrub.

Farther south from the Place des Nations Unies is the central **Park of the Arab League (Parc de la Ligue Arabe).** The park is usually busy with picnickers and families, as well as pockets of homeless, and isn't unlike New York's Central Park or London's Hyde Park. This is where the majority of museums, theaters, and restaurants can be found, as well as a few of the more architecturally interesting buildings, such as the **Palais de Justice** and the **Cathédrale Sacré Coeur.** To the west of the park you'll find the **U.S. Consulate.** To the southeast is the trendy **Quartier Habous,** with its more upscale Moroccan markets and bazaars burgeoning beneath stone arches.

PLANNING YOUR TIME

For many travelers coming from North America, Casablanca is the port of arrival, with Casablanca's **Mohamed V International Airport** serving the majority of flights in and out of the country. Airplanes generally arrive in the morning and early afternoon, making it possible to continue straight on to other destinations, like Marrakesh, by train, and arrive in time for dinner.

However, Casablanca can be a good place to get acclimated and rest after a long flight, or to spend some time before flying back home for travelers with early morning departing

inside the impressive Hassan II Mosque

Casablanca

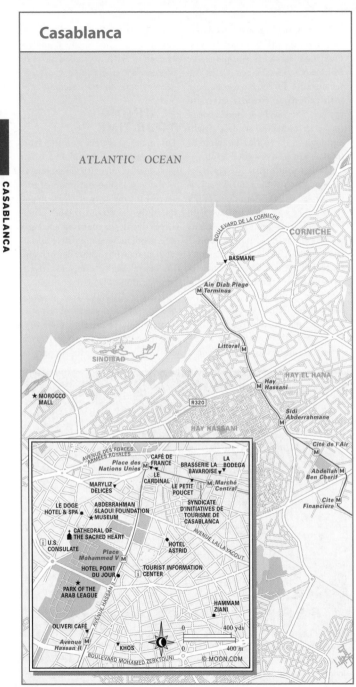

ATLANTIC OCEAN

BOULEVARD DE LA CORNICHE

CORNICHE

BASMANE

Ain Diab Plage
Terminus

Littoral

SINDIBAD

HAY EL HANA

Hay
Hassani

MOROCCO
MALL

R320

Sidi
Abderrahmane

HAY HASSANI

Cité de l'Air

Abdellah
Ben Cherif

AVENUE DES FORCES
ARMÉES ROYALES

Place des
Nations Unies

CAFÉ DE
FRANCE

BRASSERIE LA
BAVAROISE

LA
BODEGA

Cité
Financière

LE
CARDINAL

MARYLIZ
DELICES

LE PETIT
POUCET

Marché
Central

LE DOGE
HOTEL & SPA

ABDERRAHMAN
SLAOUI FOUNDATION
MUSEUM

SYNDICATE
D'INITIATIVES DE
TOURISME DE
CASABLANCA

CATHEDRAL OF
THE SACRED HEART

U.S.
CONSULATE

HOTEL
ASTRID

AVENUE LALLA YACOUT

Place
Mohammed V

HOTEL POINT
DU JOUR

TOURIST INFORMATION
CENTER

PARK OF THE
ARAB LEAGUE

HAMMAM
ZIANI

OLIVERI CAFÉ

AVENUE HASSAN II

Avenue
Hassan II

KHOS

BOULEVARD MOHAMED ZERKTOUNI

0   400 yds

0   400 m

© MOON.COM

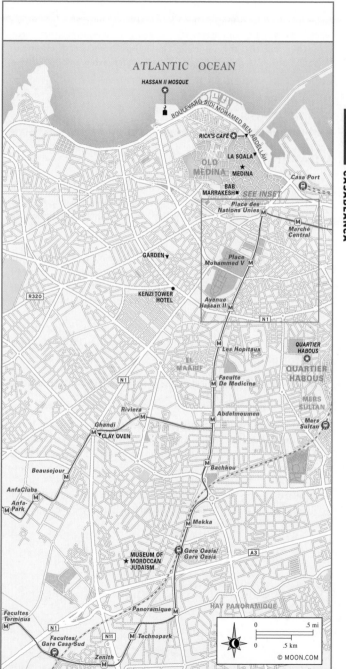

ATLANTIC OCEAN

HASSAN II MOSQUE ★

BOULEVARD SIDI MOHAMED BEN ABDELLAH

RICK'S CAFÉ ▼

LA SQALA ★

OLD MEDINA
MEDINA ★

Casa Port 🚉

BAB MARRAKESH ■

SEE INSET

Place des Nations Unies

Marché Central

GARDEN ▼

Place Mohammed V Ⓜ

KENZI TOWER HOTEL ●

Avenue Hassan II Ⓜ

R320

N1

Ⓜ

Les Hôpitaux

QUARTIER HABOUS ★

EL MAARIF

QUARTIER HABOUS

Faculté De Medicine Ⓜ

N1

MERS SULTAN

Riviera Ⓜ

Abdelmoumen

Mers Sultan 🚉

Ghandi Ⓜ
▼ CLAY OVEN

Beausejour Ⓜ

Bachkou Ⓜ

AnfaClubs Ⓜ
Anfa-Park Ⓜ

Mekka Ⓜ

Gare Oasis/ 🚉 Gare Oasis

A3

MUSEUM OF MOROCCAN JUDAISM ★

Facultes Terminus Ⓜ

Panoramique Ⓜ

HAY PANORAMIQUE

N1

N11

Technopark Ⓜ

Facultes/ Gare Casa Sud 🚉

Zenith Ⓜ

0 .5 mi
0 .5 km
© MOON.COM

flights. In a half day before or after a flight, you can easily tour the Hassan II Mosque and visit the Quartier Habous, two of the city's biggest attractions. Those who love urban jungles could consider more time here, given the sheer number of accommodations and restaurants.

Itinerary Idea

A DAY IN CASABLANCA

1 After arrival, either from Marrakesh or the airport, hop off the train at Casa Port directly from the airport and take the tram to Ligue Arabe to get settled in at the nearby Hotel Point du Jour, a simple, centrally located hotel right in the middle of Casablanca.

2 Once you've freshened up, hop in a taxi or enjoy the 40-minute walk past the Parc de la Ligue Arabe and the impressive art deco Sacred Heart Cathedral to the massive Hassan II Mosque. Join the first possible tour (Sat.-Thurs., nearly every hour 9am-4pm) to see inside this true modern wonder of architecture.

3 Stop by Basmane and enjoy a relaxing lunch in an ornate Moroccan salon.

4 After lunch, walk north along the waterfront corniche and take in the afternoon sun.

5 Hop on the tram or take a *petit taxi* back to your hotel to change into your nicest outfit. Then, consider diving into Casablanca's medina. Easy access into the medina from the main square is found near the old clock tower.

6 For dinner, you have to eat at Rick's Café. Just make sure to check the dress code and reserve in advance. Sip on a well-deserved cocktail in the bar after dinner. Of all the gin joints...

Itinerary Idea

ATLANTIC
OCEAN

OLD MEDINA

CORNICHE

R320

N1

EL MAARIF

N1

A DAY IN CASABLANCA

1. Ligue Arabe and Hotel Point du Jour
2. Hassan II Mosque
3. Basmane
4. Corniche
5. Medina
6. Rick's Café and Bar

0   0.5 mi
0   0.5 km

© MOON.COM

To
Casablanca Mohammed V
International Airport

Sights

MEDINA

The old medina is relatively small, and an exit is never more than a few minutes away. This is a largely pedestrian-only zone, though plenty of scooters zoom about, adding to the chaos. Bab Marrakesh, across from the Place des Nations Unies near the clock tower, is the best entrance. Shuffle through lively fruit and vegetable sellers before plunging into the narrow, mazelike streets of the medina. The outward-facing balconies are reminiscent of the medina of Tangier. Somewhat surprisingly, this medina is not nearly as touristed as other medinas in Morocco, giving it an authentic, albeit grungy, air.

VILLE NOUVELLE

Casablanca is the largest city in Morocco, and nearly all of it is in the enormous Ville Nouvelle. The protectorate-era boulevards surrounding the medina feature some of the nicest architecture in the city. With the new tram, Boulevard Mohammed V has been transformed into a car-free zone. This is a spot for walking around the neighborhood on a tour of the art deco past of Casablanca. Observe the detail of the wrought-iron work, the strange arabesques adorning many of the buildings, and the quintessential funk of the signage.

A bit farther southeast lies the **Quartier Habous**, a chic alternative to the medina shops. Along the coast are different developments, such as the **Hassan II Mosque**, the **corniche**, and the **Morocco Mall**.

✪ HASSAN II MOSQUE

Blvd. de la Corniche; guided tours Sat.-Thurs. 9am, 10am, 11am, 2pm, and 4pm, depending on prayer times; 120Dh, students 60Dh

The Hassan II Mosque is a staggering achievement of modern architecture by Frenchman Michel Pinseau that towers over the crashing waves of the Atlantic Ocean. It is the second-largest religious building in the world, after the Masjid al-Haram mosque in Mecca, and has the capacity for over

Couples hang out at the fountains of Hassan II Mosque.

80,000 worshippers. The mosque was constructed in a flurry of activity beginning in 1986 and finishing in 1993, after local workers toiled day and night. Six thousand Moroccan master crafters were involved in the building, using

after sunset in the old medina

their skills with *zellij* tile work, wood carving, and ornate stucco work to bring the overwhelming sense of the gracious to its expansive halls. Here, the traditional blends with the modern. Non-Muslims are allowed to enter as part of a one-hour tour with English-speaking guides available, while the doors open at prayer times for Muslims and for longer Friday services.

CATHEDRAL OF THE SACRED HEART (Cathédrale Sacré Coeur)

Rue d'Algiers, on the edge of the Parc de la Ligue Arabe

The Cathedral of the Sacred Heart is a former Roman Catholic church built during the French protectorate era in the 1930s. It has recently been used for the occasional exposition but has otherwise been left for the birds—quite literally. Pigeons live high up the towering art deco columns. The church ceased holding services after Moroccan independence in 1956 and now serves as a cultural center. A guardian who usually watches over during the day will let you enter for free if you ask nicely. The interior, with its ornate stucco and stained glass, is somewhat interesting, though for most, a view of the neo-Gothic exterior will suffice.

ABDERRAHMAN SLAOUI FOUNDATION MUSEUM (Musée de la Fondation Abderrahman Slaoui)

12 Rue de Parc; tel. 0522/206 217; www. musee-as.ma; Tues.-Sat. 10am-6pm; 30Dh

The often overlooked Abderrahman Slaoui Foundation Museum houses a wonderful collection of art deco posters (*affiches*) from old publicity for Morocco, done by the French to increase tourism. Posters include originals of the infamous *La Belle Fatma* and *Venez au Maroc,* which promoted a racial stereotype of Morocco. The museum is well worth the price of admission for those who are intrigued by these art deco masterpieces. It also houses a collection of 19th- and 20th-century Moroccan jewelry, including some ornate headpieces, and paintings by Mohamed Ben Ali R'bati, known for his daily scenes of Tangier shortly after the turn of the 20th century. Information for the museum is only in French.

✪ QUARTIER HABOUS

Blvd. Sidi Mohamed Ben Abdellah

Sometimes called the "new medina," the Quartier Habous is something of an anomaly. The French constructed this medina to combat the overcrowding in the old medina and throughout the rest of the city in the 1930s. Though modeled on the design of Moroccan medinas, it incorporated modern plumbing and obeyed city planning ordinances and public health regulations in its construction. For a long time, Habous was neglected, though a

Cathedral of the Sacred Heart

shopping in the Quartier Habous

revival effort recently took place and really cleaned up its streets. Shopping-wise, if Casablanca's medina proves to be a bit too much for the senses, head to Quartier Habous. Now there are traditional crafts and bazaars, making this a less-authentic experience than shopping in the dusty souks of Marrakesh or Fez, though the relaxing atmosphere and general cleanliness are in some ways more desirable.

MUSEUM OF MOROCCAN JUDAISM
(Musée de Judaïsme Marocain)

81 Rue Chasseur Jules Gros, Oasis; tel. 0522/994 940; www.jewishmuseumcasa. com; summer Mon.-Fri. 10am-6pm, Sun. 11am-3pm, winter Mon.-Fri. 10am-5pm, Sun. 11am-3pm; 40Dh

A bit east from the city center in the neighborhood of Oasis is the only known Jewish museum in an Islamic country, the Museum of Moroccan Judaism. The museum highlights the link of Morocco with its long, and proud, Jewish past. Religious texts, traditional garments, and sacramental artifacts make up much of the collection, with connections to the various mellahs (Jewish quarters) around Morocco. Much of the information is in French, though English versions

are available—just ask. The museum is within walking distance from the Oasis train station.

MOROCCO MALL

Blvd. de la Corniche; tel. 0801/001 230; daily 10am-9pm

It might seem a little strange to come all the way to Casablanca only to head to the mall, but this is what the hip, trendy, and petit bourgeois of Morocco are doing. The Morocco Mall, at the end of the Aïn Diab beach, is a modern architectural treat. Opened in 2011, this is the largest indoor mall in Africa, with a curvy design by architect Davide Padoa that incorporates elements of the ocean that borders it. The outdoor musical fountain lights up at night, its classical score emphasizing all the high-end retailers found here, such as Fendi and Gucci, as well as the more quotidian brand names, such as American Eagle and Starbucks. There is an Adventureland for kids, a three-story aquarium with an elevator plunging into its midst (Sun.-Thurs. 10am-9pm, Fri.-Sat. 10am-11pm, 50Dh), and a contemporary take on the Moroccan souk. The attached IMAX movie theater shows 3D movies and English-language films on Thursdays.

PARK OF THE ARAB LEAGUE
(Parc de la Ligue Arabe)

Bordering Place Mohammed V is the Park of the Arab League. This is the widest green space in Casablanca, and after the crush of the city, it's the perfect place for a picnic. As in large public parks in other cities, there are some homeless people, though they keep largely to themselves. Around the park are some of the best examples of the colonial-era art deco French construction.

Sports and Recreation

HAMMAMS

Casablanca has high-end hammams and spas dotted throughout the city, each offering an experience not unlike what you might find back home. For a more authentic Moroccan hammam experience, you'll want to check out the offerings in the medieval medinas of Fez and Marrakesh.

Hammam Ziani

59 Rue Abou Rakrak, Benjdia; tel. 0522/319 695; www.hammamziani.ma; 50Dh

Hammam Ziani offers a reasonable experience for a reasonable price, including a body scrub (20Dh) that will leave you feeling fresh and invigorated. This is about as authentic of a hammam experience as you can find in Casablanca. A vapor bath will relax you, while the humid heat activates your blood circulation and relaxes muscles.

Le Doge Hotel & Spa

9 Rue de Docteur Veyre; tel. 0522/467 800; http://hotelledoge.com; 500Dh

The on-site spa at Le Doge Hotel & Spa is one of the most luxurious spas in Casablanca and includes a refined traditional hammam as well as a hot tub, steam room, and rooms for manicures, pedicures, facials, and other treatments. Post- or pre-trip pampering here is highly recommended.

Food

Casablanca has one of the best food scenes in Morocco, which is to be expected given that it is the business hub of the country. Restaurants offer everything from traditional Moroccan dishes to French *haute cuisine*. Most restaurants still don't have a nonsmoking section, so this can be a problem for travelers sensitive to cigarette smoke.

MEDINA
La Sqala

129 Rue Allah Ben Abdellah off Blvd. des Almohades; tel. 0522/260 960; daily 9am-11pm; 90Dh

If you're wandering the medina, ask around for La Sqala, a café and restaurant housed in the middle of the ruins of the old Portuguese fortress. For first-timers to Morocco, this is a great place to get familiar with different types of Moroccan cuisine, including the famous tajine, though the pumpkin soup and meat-filled pastries are not something to miss out on for those

There's a lot of white linen service in Casablanca.

155

looking to dig into a tasty traditional Moroccan dish. Service can be a little bit slow, but this just gives you more time to take in the setting—eclectic traditional with a touch of modern. Take a look at the old black-and-white photos of Casablanca on display for a real sense of history. Breakfast is also served with an array of Moroccan crêpes, honey, confiture, and eggs, a spread fit for a king for less than 50Dh.

✪ Rick's Café

248 Rue Sour Jdid; tel. 0522/274 207;
www.rickscafe.ma; daily noon-3pm
and 6:30pm-1am; 300Dh

A stop in Casablanca is somehow incomplete without hearing Sam croon "As Time Goes By" at Rick's Café—or rather, Issam, as the piano player is known in this Hollywood-come-to-life restaurant and bar. For those in love with the movie and wanting a dash of romance, Rick's Café does a wonderful job of re-creating the world of Bogie and Bergman. The menu features fresh vegetables and fish selected from the local markets and expertly thrown together. Goat cheese salads featuring perfectly ripe figs and seared swordfish steaks are menu staples. The rooftop terrace has views over the port, though likely you'll want to spend time in the gallant interior of this remarkable replica. Be sure to pack your fancy shoes, as the dress code is strictly enforced, and even with a reservation, you'll likely be turned away at the door if you're wearing sneakers and a baggy sweatshirt. Gentlemen will want to wear a button-down and slacks, and ladies should put on their

American-Moroccan fusion at Rick's Café

fanciest threads! Of course, if dinner doesn't suit your palate, you could always just belly up to one of the finest gin joints in Morocco at the expansive bar.

CORNICHE
Basmane

corner of Blvd. de l'Océan Atlantique and
Blvd. de la Corniche; tel. 0522/797 532;
www.basmane-restaurant.com;
daily 7pm-midnight; 300Dh

If you're looking for a little belly dancing to go with your tajine, Basmane has just the spin for you. Set inside a traditional Moroccan house full of ornate stucco and complex zellij work, Moroccan tajines and heaps of couscous are served alongside the nightly entertainment, a parade of professional belly dancers who gyrate around the room, bringing the local male clientele to a near faint. Food is bland, but that's not the main draw anyway. It's popular with internationals and locals alike, both men and women, looking for something fantastical.

For most travelers, the local bars and nightclubs of Casablanca are places to be avoided. For the most part, the bars around here are of the "smoky dive bar" variety, feature seedy all-male clientele, and are home to rampant prostitution. That's not to say you can't have a nice drink, but just be aware. There's always the bar at Rick's Café.

TIPS AND SAFETY

Nightclubs are generally the realm of the less savory characters of Casablanca, and they're incredibly expensive to boot. Most large-scale hotels in Casablanca have their own nightclubs. If you absolutely have to get out, you could try **the nightclub in your hotel;** this way you can avoid being stranded somewhere late at night in the city or a host of other possible problems. The party never starts in Morocco until after **midnight,** with ladies and gentlemen often showing more skin than in most places in the United States or Europe.

If you are traveling out, be sure to **taxi** back and forth, as these are the hours to avoid walking the streets. However, be aware that in some neighborhoods, taxis can be notoriously difficult to find late at night.

If nightlife is your thing, the more internationally friendly environs of **Agadir** and **Marrakesh** are more genial to late-night fêtes

CASABLANCA
FOOD

VILLE NOUVELLE

Café de France

Pl. des Nations Unies on Ave. Hassan II;
tel. 0522/472 820; daily sunrise-11pm; 20Dh
Café de France is the best spot in town for people-watching, on the patio beneath the arcade, though you might have to fight off a few street vendors. This is a good haunt for literary types looking for a little inspiration as they watch the people from Casa breeze by across the busiest plaza in the city. For a thick hot chocolate worthy of its name, ask for a *chocolat fondant* (22Dh).

La Bodega

123 Rue Allal Ben Abdellah; tel. 0522/541
842 or 0522/312 203; www.restopro.ma/
bodega; daily noon-4pm and 7pm-1am;
150Dh
La Bodega has a full bar, though at a price, including the most expensive bottle of Budweiser you'll likely ever have. Tapas start at 60Dh. The best deal is the "express midi" menu at 100Dh, which is large enough to serve two and includes a starter, main, and dessert. This is the place to go to throw

a bit of an *olé* zest into your stay in Casablanca or if you have a hankering for some great Ibérico ham.

Oliveri Café

Pl. Mohammed V on Ave. Hassan II;
tel. 0522/982 898; www.oliveri.ma;
daily 8am-10pm; 25Dh
If you're spending the day at the Park of the Arab League, the nearby Oliveri Café is a 1950s-styled ice cream parlor café, with a long wood bar and leather-backed chairs completing the look. This is a great stop for the kids, or the kid inside you, for an ice cream, sorbet, or milkshake. You might find a few of these cafés sprinkled around Casablanca. It's becoming a local tradition of sorts.

Maryliz Delices

53 Ave. Hassan I; tel. 0522/471 282;
daily 7am-9pm; 20Dh
Tucked off the Place des Nations Unies, Maryliz Delices features some of the most delicious pastries in town, including buttery croissants and spinach quiche, for a quick pick-me-up to take to the park or to the beach.

Clay Oven

245 Boulevard Ghandi; tel. 0522/992 133;
daily noon-3pm and 7pm-11pm; 160Dh

Casablanca has seen a surge in Indian restaurants, with an up-and-coming Indian population finding homes in and around Casa. Aptly placed right on Boulevard Ghandi, Clay Oven leads the way for those craving food with a bit more kick. Come for the butter chicken with naan bread and jeera rice with flavors that will take you straight back to Mumbai; stay for the good vibes and enclosed outdoor terrace.

Le Cardinal

11 Blvd. Mohammed V; tel. 0522/221 560;
daily noon-10pm; 95Dh

The popular Le Cardinal is a French-style brasserie, though with surprisingly great service, which somehow takes away from the Parisian-style dining (though perhaps in a good way). The restaurant is small and often full of smokers. Entrecôte (steak) with grilled mushrooms and a gratin of spinach and freshly caught fish highlight the menu, though to be clear, you're coming here for the ambiance more than anything.

Brasserie la Bavaroise

133 Ave. Allal Ben Abdellah;
tel. 0522/311 760; Mon.-Sat. noon-3pm
and 7:30pm-11:30pm; 250Dh

Just off the Boulevard Mohammed V, behind the Marché Central, the Brasserie la Bavaroise has a well-earned reputation for serving the best steaks in Morocco. The beef is sourced from locally grown, groomed, and herb-fed cattle indigenous to the Atlas Mountains. Entrecôte, New York, and T-bone steaks are all grilled to perfection in these rich confines. With oysters from Dakhla in the Western Sahara and fish caught right off the

sizzling shrimp at Clay Oven

coast, this is the long-established classic steakhouse of Casablanca. Meat lovers should not miss out.

✪ Garden

corner of Rue Mahmoud Akkad and Rue Commisaire Ladeuil; tel. 0522/200 333; www.garden.ma; daily 11am-11pm; 70Dh

If you're feeling a little heavy from the tajines and couscous, or if you're a vegetarian or vegan looking for a break, rejoice and head to Garden for a wide selection of salads, bagel sandwiches, and fresh juices. The few rope swing chairs will channel your inner child, while the good vibes will leave you feeling light, energetic, and ready to explore. The nonsmoking atmosphere is a welcomed retreat from the smoke-heavy restaurants in the city. Salads are always fresh, picked from local ingredients and the nearby markets, and you can customize your salad on the spot.

Khos

44 Rue Annoussour; tel. 0522/273 716; www.khos.ma; Mon.-Fri. 8:30am-5pm, Sun. 10am-3:30pm; 40Dh

Another wonderful stop for a quick soup and salad is Khos, close to the Park of the Arab League, near the hospital. The fresh salads and delicious soups on offer, all served in an incredibly hygienic atmosphere, are a good change-up from the heavier meals generally found around Casablanca. The Sunday brunch is worth a look if Saturday was a long night out.

Le Petit Poucet

86 Blvd. Mohammed V; tel. 0522/490 060; daily noon-11pm; 80Dh

Of the dive bars, perhaps the most interesting is Le Petit Poucet, famed for a number of French patrons, but most of all for Antoine de Saint-Exupéry, the author of *The Little Prince*, who stopped here often between flights as he was working for the French postal service as a pilot. Its long history of famous patrons also includes Albert Camus and Edith Piaf. The bar is typical of Moroccan bars, with generally male clientele and hard drinkers, though foreign females are welcomed—a completely authentic experience, if a bit edgy for most. It's the sort of place that might become your local hangout if you lived in Casa.

Accommodations

Accommodations can be had in Casablanca at virtually every price point imaginable, though decent accommodations at budget prices are difficult to find. Most of the budget options cater more toward illicit activities, such as prostitution, than they do toward travelers. Of all the cities in Morocco, Casablanca is perhaps the best choice for stretching your budget, not necessarily for what is offered so much as for the lack of availability of other types of accommodations. For the best deals, make sure to book online a few weeks ahead of time.

VILLE NOUVELLE
UNDER 400DH
Hotel Astrid

12 Rue 6 Novembre; tel. 0522/277 803; 300Dh d

One of the better deals in the city is

Hotel Astrid. The simple rooms have Wi-Fi, though it's often a bit slow, and en suite bathrooms. A generally clean hotel, though definitely in need of some renovation work, like all other budget hotels found throughout Morocco. This particular hotel suffers from problems with moisture during the winter. Those sensitive to molds should avoid the hotel in the cold months. The location near Place Mohammed V makes it centrally located and good for exploration. Breakfast will set you back an extra 35Dh.

400-800DH
✪ HOTEL POINT DU JOUR

10 Rue du Lieutenautberger; tel. 0522/279 207; www.hotelpointdujour.ma; 400Dh d

A centrally located two-star hotel with five-star service. Redouane, the manager, has done a great job hiring some of the most helpful, friendly staff in all of Casablanca. They can help you get around town and will even look after you if you've caught the traveler's flu. The hotel itself has been renovated, though the water pressure isn't the greatest and the Wi-Fi not the most robust. Breakfast is a good value, though you should look elsewhere for lunch or dinner. The elevator is a bonus if you have sore feet from walking around. Request a room opposite the road for a quieter night. Perhaps not the most romantic spot, though comfy and as welcoming for single travelers as it is for families.

OVER 800DH
Kenzi Tower Hotel

Twin Center, Blvd. Zerktouni; tel. 0522/978 000; www.kenzi-hotels.com; 1,200Dh d

Even if you don't stay at the opulent Kenzi Tower Hotel, it's worth a visit to the top-floor Sky Bar 28 (daily 9am-1am) for panoramic views over Casablanca. Located in one tower of the Twin Center, the hotel has prompt, professional service. The ventilation system is good enough that, for the most part, cigarette smoke goes unnoticed. The beds are downy plush, and rooms have floor-to-ceiling windows that make the most of the view. There is a buffet breakfast and lunch, as well as the independent gastronomic restaurant Sens, though meals are not included with your stay. A full-service spa, business center, fitness room, and swimming pool make this a luxurious splurge.

✪ Le Doge Hotel & Spa

9 Rue de Docteur Veyre; tel. 0522/467 800; http://hotelledoge.com; 1,700Dh d

If boutique hotels are your thing, Le Doge Hotel & Spa is wonderfully maintained with Jacuzzi-size tubs, rich wood furniture, plush beds, and art deco-period touches sprinkled throughout the hotel. The on-site spa is one of the most luxurious in the city. The salon is a private library with plenty of comfy seats to curl up with a book around the fireplace, while the fifth-floor garden terrace provides plenty of green space to catch some rays. The pampering available at Le Doge is well worth it.

Information and Services

VISITOR INFORMATION

Tourist Information Center (Délégation Régionale du Tourisme de Casablanca)

60 Ave. Hassan II; tel. 0522/206 266; www.visitcasablanca.ma; Mon.-Thurs. 9am-12:30pm and 2:30pm-6:30pm, Fri.-Sat. 9am-12:30pm and 3pm-6:30pm

The Tourist Information Center, right at Place Mohammed V, has some maps and updated information about city events, particularly about the numerous festivals and gallery showings.

Syndicate d'Initiatives de Tourisme de Casablanca

98 Blvd. Mohammed V; tel. 0522/221 524; Mon.-Fri. 8:30am-4:30pm

The Syndicate d'Initiatives de Tourisme de Casablanca also carries free information on events and happenings, though sometimes the brochures are a bit outdated. Malika is usually behind the desk. She speaks some English, is very friendly, and can help you find your way around Casa.

U.S. Consulate

8 Blvd. Moulay Youssef; tel. 0522/264 550; appointment only

U.S. citizens who need consular services or assistance, such as in the case of a lost or stolen passport, should contact the U.S. Consulate in Casablanca. The **U.S. Embassy** (tel. 0537/637 200) in Rabat is largely diplomatic. For emergencies, contact the **American Citizen Services hotline** (tel. 0522/642 099, Mon.-Fri. 8am-5pm, tel. 0661/131 939 after hours).

SAFETY

Casablanca is a relatively safe city, though with the booming population and shantytowns ringing the city, prostitution, drug use, and petty crimes remain high. Since a terrorist attack in 2003, the only one in recent memory, security has been beefed up to protect the economic interest of the country and the safety of its people. The new tram track provides safe, secure passage across different neighborhoods of the city, and police patrol the streets around the clock. Still, care should be taken with walking late at night because, as in most metropolitan cities, muggings are known to happen.

POST OFFICES AND COURIER SERVICES

There are several post offices scattered around Casablanca, including Place Mohammed V, Boulevard Mohammed V, and Place Zallaqa. Post offices keep the same hours (Mon.-Fri. 9am-4:30pm, Sat. 9:30am-noon, with abbreviated hours during Ramadan).

MONEY

Cash machines are ubiquitous around Casablanca, though they only distribute 100- and 200-dirham notes.

At the Place des Nations Unies tram stop you'll find a handy **Attijarwafa Bank** (Mon.-Fri. 8:15am-3:45pm, Ramadan 9:15am-2:30pm) and **Wafacash Currency Exchange** with **Western Union** (Mon.-Fri. 8am-7pm and Sat. 9am-4pm) as well as the Banque Populaire (Mon.-Fri. 8:15am-4:30pm) and BMCI (Mon.-Fri. 8:15am-6:30pm, Sat.-Sun. 9am-6pm, Ramadan 9am-5pm). Right on Place Mohammed V there is a Bank Al-Maghrib (Mon.-Fri. 8:30am-3pm).

For travelers checks, foreign currency exchanges, and other services, it's best to use BMCE. The most convenient location for most travelers is across from the Cathédrale Sacré Coeur. Near the Hassan II Mosque you can find BMCE, Al Barid, and Banque Populaire (as well as a post office) on Rue Sanhaja.

HOSPITALS, CLINICS, AND PHARMACIES

If necessary, head directly for Hospital Dar Salaam (728 Blvd. Modibo Keita, tel. 0522/851 414) for emergency services. There are pharmacies seemingly on every street in Casablanca. All keep posted hours for off-hour pharmacies. The Grande Pharmacie Commerciale (Pl. des Nations Unies, Mon.-Fri. 9am-12:30pm and 3:30pm-8pm, Sat. 9am-1pm) is one of the more conveniently located pharmacies, just off the Place des Nations Unies in the heart of the city.

Transportation

GETTING THERE
BY PLANE
Mohammed V International Airport
Nouasseur, about 30min south of Casablanca via the A7 or N9; tel. 0522/539 040; www.casablanca-airport.com

The airport train connects directly with Casa Voyageurs and Casa Port, the main train stations in Casablanca. Trains leave the airport every hour daily 3:55am-11:45pm (30min, 19 daily, 2nd/1st-class 43Dh/64Dh). You will find the station downstairs from the arrivals hall. This is the most convenient way in and out of the airport, especially after a long flight if you don't want to haggle for a taxi. If you're staying in Casablanca, consider debarking at the l'Oasis stop to connect with the tram.

Taxis are always available to shuttle travelers into the city (300Dh) and will be found just outside the arrivals gate, though you'll likely have to haggle your fare. At night, the prices

are raised substantially (500Dh) and you should always try to bargain if you have the energy.

BY TRAIN
Casablanca is a train hub. ONCF (tel. 0890/203 040, www.oncf.ma) operates two major train lines. The first follows the coast from Tangier to Marrakesh (this line gave rise to the popular Marrakesh Express) and the second crosses the country northeast through Meknes and Fez before ending at distant Oujda at the eastern border with Algeria.

Casa Voyageurs Train Station
at the eastern end of Blvd. Mohammed V

Trains connecting with Marrakesh (3.5hr, 9 daily, 87Dh/150Dh) leave and arrive from the newly remodeled Casa Voyageurs train station in Casablanca. In Marrakesh, you will of course want to catch the train at the Marrakesh train station in Gueliz.

The Casa Voyageurs Train Station connects the tram with the rail.

BY CAR

Casablanca is well-connected by the tolled autoroutes. Tolls vary according to type of automobile and where you'll enter/exit the tolled route. In principle, it's a good idea to travel with 400Dh just for tolls, though you'll likely not use it all. From Marrakesh, follow the A1 autoroute north for 245km/153mi, about three hours.

BY BUS

The most convenient and nicest buses servicing the Marrakesh-Casablanca route are run by CTM (www.ctm.ma). There are over 20 buses scheduled every day, with the "Premium" and "Comfort Plus" options being good for those wanting Wi-Fi on their journey. In Marrakesh, the CTM station (rue Abou Bakr Seddiq, tel. 0800/090 030) is two short blocks from the train station. In Casablanca, the most convenient CTM station (rue Leo l'Africain, tel. 0800/090 030) is a short walk east from the Place des Nations Unies. The ride to or from Marrakesh takes about 4 hours (80Dh, premium available).

GETTING AROUND

BY TRAM

The clean, new, eco-friendly tram line (tel. 0522/998 383, www.casatramway. ma) is the cleanest way to get around town. The tram will take you near most major destinations. It runs daily 5:30am-10:30pm, with trains passing every 15 minutes or so. Fares are 7Dh per trip (plus 1Dh for a rechargeable card that you can use for up to 10 trips). Purchase a ticket at any tram stop using the ATM-looking machines. Change and credit cards are accepted (no paper bills), and instructions on the machine are available in English, though stops along the tram are only signed with their French and Arabic names. The tram connects with the main train stations near Casa Port and Casa Voyageurs, making train connections around the country, as well as to and from the airport, fairly easy.

BY PETIT TAXI

The notorious red *petits taxis* of Casablanca are generally the quickest way around town, though taxi drivers are aggressive, both in driving and business. They often try to charge foreigners 3-4 times the going rate. Ask the taxi to use the counter. As with other taxis around Morocco, prices go up by 50 percent at night. If you're having trouble getting drivers to use the counter, even the "rip-off" rates are generally not exorbitant, with rides costing 50-100Dh.

BY CAR

If you have a car, Casablanca is a place to park it and leave it for a few days. Navigating the city with its intense 24-hour traffic, aggressive drivers, and road signs that are not at all obvious to the uninitiated (or even to the initiated) is best avoided. Most hotels have guarded parking available, and street parking is generally safe, though likely you'll be asked to tip 5Dh or so to the guardian.

ESSAOUIRA

Though no longer the sleepy vil-

lage it once was, Essaouira has maintained its
diversity, its love for art, and its popularity with
the hippie crowd. There's a little something for
everyone, and for most people traveling through
this region, this city itself is a real highlight. The
distinct cry of seagulls descending on the fishing boats entering the port, the chipped paint and
weathered stone, the quiet mornings and lively
evenings—these are just a few of the memories
travelers come away with. With an abundance of
great restaurants and warm, temperate weather

HIGHLIGHTS

✪ **WALKING THE RAMPARTS:** The Portuguese-built oceanfront ramparts of Essaouira make for a romantic sunset walk (page 171).

✪ **WINDSURFING:** Few places in the world have a more consistent breeze for windsurfing (page 175).

✪ **COOKING CLASSES:** Learn more about Moroccan cuisine with a local chef, who will explain the spices and techniques that make it so extraordinary (page 176).

nearly year-round, within an easy three-hour drive from Marrakesh, Essaouira is great for a day trip or overnight from the Red City.

Within the old medina, you can feel history emanate from the walls that give shape to the city. These walls were first built under Portuguese rule in the 16th century, when Essaouira was known as Mogador. It wasn't until the 1960s and the more recent Arabization of Morocco that Mogador became commonly known by its Arabic name: Essaouira.

Essaouira has a long history with evidence of inhabitance from the 5th century BC, when the Carthaginians were spreading up and down the coastline of Morocco. At the beginning of the 16th century, when the region came under Portuguese rule, Mogador prospered as a major fishing port, as well as a strategic military post. For a time, like Salé to the north, Mogador was known for its trade in sugar and molasses, though it was the pirate trades and slavery that brought in the most wealth.

During the reign of Mohammed III in the 18th century, Mogador was transformed as the sultan oversaw a vast plan to reinforce the walls, add to the fortification of the city, and direct trade from Marrakesh through the port. The Jewish community was encouraged to relocate here for business. Nearly 40 percent of the population at this time was Jewish, as evidenced today by the large mellah, with stone carvings of the Star of David over many doors, the many synagogues, and the immense Jewish cemetery.

Today, Essaouira is better known as the Windy City for the near-constant wind that cuts over the beach. It might be better called "Windsurfer City," as this pastime for locals and Europeans has come to define the beachfront south of the fortified walls.

There is a real international feel to the city, despite the medieval surroundings, and a touch of mass tourism. However, this isn't such a bad thing, particularly when looking for a nice place to go out and eat. If anything, Essaouira is replete with great restaurants catering to international tourism. But above all, it is the clean salt air, a crisp respite after a few days in Marrakesh, the heat of the desert, or the clutter of Casablanca, that is perhaps the most alluring.

ORIENTATION

Essaouira is easy to navigate. Its medina is less mazelike and quite a bit

ESSAOUIRA IN POP CULTURE

Essaouira first memorably popped into the consciousness of Hollywood in 1952 with a selection of memorable scenes filmed by the renowned Orson Welles in his adaptation of Shakespeare's *Othello.* Since then, Essaouira has been featured in Terry Gilliam's cult classic *Time Bandits* as well as Ridley Scott's *Gladiator* and *The Kingdom of Heaven,* in which it was transformed into Jerusalem. More recently it has served as the background to the popular series *Game of Thrones,* in which it was thrust into the more imaginary realms of Astapor and King's Landing, as well as in the last installment of the *John Wick* action-movie trilogy.

By the 1960s, Essaouira's place on Morocco's hippie trail was firmly established, with local musicians joining with visiting musicians, such as **Cat Stevens,** to create fusion music that had never before been heard. Today, all around Morocco and throughout the world, you can now jam to **Gnawa-Blues,** a type of fusion arising from this era. Popular myth has it that **Jimi Hendrix** composed "Castles Made of Sand" while chillaxing on the beaches of Essaouira. The fact that Hendrix wrote "Castles Made of Sand" two years before he actually visited Essaouira hasn't stopped this myth from becoming something of a local legend, facts be damned!

smaller than most of the others around Morocco. It's very safe (unless you count the occasional bellicose shopkeeper) and is a wonderful medina to explore, with plenty of nooks and crannies as well as unique shops that provide delightful surprises.

The medina is surrounded by 18th-century walls and divided roughly into the following neighborhoods: the Kasbah, Bani Antar, the Mellah, Bouakhir, Chbanat, and Ahl Agadir. The kasbah is in the southwest of the city and is the area just around the tall citadel that watches over the harbor. Sometimes this is further divided into the "old" kasbah toward the north and the "new" kasbah on the southernmost

a city gate leading into the old medina

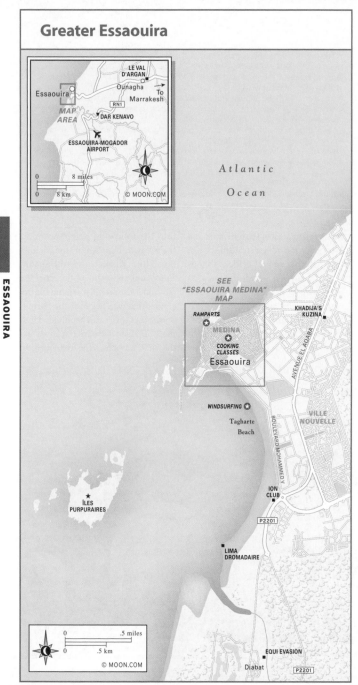

Greater Essaouira

LE VAL
D'ARGAN

Essaouira

Ounagha
To
Marrakesh

RN1

MAP
AREA

DAR KENAVO

ESSAOUIRA-MOGADOR
AIRPORT

0   8 miles
0   8 km

© MOON.COM

Atlantic

Ocean

SEE
"ESSAOUIRA MEDINA"
MAP

RAMPARTS

KHADIJA'S
KUZINA

MEDINA

COOKING
CLASSES

Essaouira

AVENUE EL AQABA

WINDSURFING

Tagharte
Beach

VILLE
NOUVELLE

BOULEVARD MOHAMMED V

ION
CLUB

ÎLES
PURPURAIRES

P2201

LIMA
DROMADAIRE

0   .5 miles
0   .5 km

© MOON.COM

EQUI EVASION

Diabat

P2201

corner of the medina. From the kasbah, you can easily walk along the ramparts or out of the medina to the port. Following the ramparts to the north, the neighborhood of **Bani Antar** to the northwest has many cafés and restaurants. The **mellah**, like the kasbah, is sometimes divided into "old" and "new." It runs adjacent to Bani Antar between the main thoroughfares of Avenue Sidi Mohamed Ben Abdellah and Avenue d'Istiqal—which turns into Avenue Mohamed Zerktouni before exiting through the north gate, **Bab Doukkala.** There are *riads* in the mellah as well as the heart of the medina, Souk Laghzal. The largely residential neighborhoods of **Bouakhir, Chbanat,** and **Ahl Agadir** lie to the east, farthest away from the ocean. There are a few larger *riads* here, and the streets of Rue Chbanate and Rue Mohammed el Qori host a number of shops. **Bab Marrakesh** is a popular exit to the east, along Rue Mohammed El Qori, and where most buses pick up and drop off.

Beyond Bab Marrakesh, the **Ville Nouvelle** cradles the old medina of Essaouira, stretching inland as well as north and south along the coast. Just off the coast, to the west, you'll see the **Îles Purpuraires** resting in the water.

PLANNING YOUR TIME

Essaouira is about a **three-hour drive** from Marrakesh. **Buses** leave frequently from around the Marrakesh train station. You'll want to leave on the earliest possible bus to maximize your time in Essaouira. You could easily tour the city in **half a day,** leaving another half day or so for an **activity** or **long lunch** at any one of Essaouira's delectable restaurants. It's perhaps best to plan an **overnight** to really get the most from Essaouira and leave some time for the **beach.**

Itinerary Idea

OVERNIGHT IN ESSAOUIRA

1 After arriving in Essaouira on the early morning bus from Marrakesh, drop your bags off at the **Chill Art Hostel,** tucked away in a quiet corner of the medina, and tap into the town's hippie vibe.

2 For lunch, you'll want to head to **Yoo Healthy Food** for a vitamin-soaked pick-me-up.

3 Spend the afternoon and evening wandering the **medina,** ducking into the odd art gallery, touring the little streets, and checking out the artisans dotting the old town.

4 Have a light dinner at **Triskala.** Enjoy a fresh salad and some vegetarian- or vegan-friendly Moroccan fare.

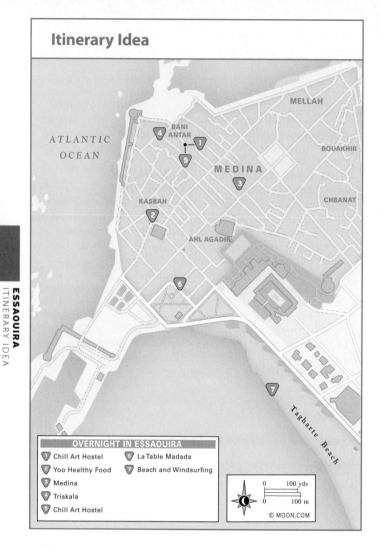

Itinerary Idea

MELLAH

ATLANTIC
OCEAN

BANI
ANTAR

4

1

5

MEDINA

BOUAKHIR

3

KASBAH

CHBANAT

2

AHL AGADIR

6

7

Tagharte Beach

OVERNIGHT IN ESSAOUIRA

1 Chill Art Hostel   **5** La Table Madada

2 Yoo Healthy Food   **7** Beach and Windsurfing

3 Medina

4 Triskala

5 Chill Art Hostel

0   100 yds

0   100 m

© MOON.COM

5 That night, chill at the **hostel** and make a new friend or two on the rooftop terrace.

6 The next day, enjoy breakfast at the hostel before heading to a cooking class at **La Table Madada.** You'll tour through the local market before making your own Moroccan lunch.

7 Spend the afternoon on the **beach,** soaking up some rays or trying your hand at **windsurfing.** Taking an early evening bus back to Marrakesh to arrive in time for a late dinner.

Essaouira Medina

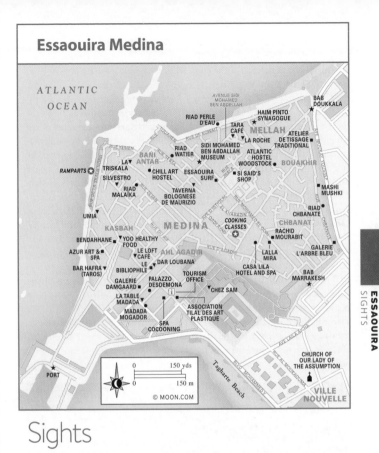

ATLANTIC OCEAN

AVENUE SIDI MOHAMED BEN ABDELLAH

BAB DOUKKALA

RIAD PERLE D'EAU

HAIM PINTO SYNAGOGUE

TARA CAFÉ

MELLAH

LA ROCHE

ATELIER DE TISSAGE TRADITIONAL

RUE YEMEN

RIAD WATIER

SIDI MOHAMED BEN ABDALLAH MUSEUM

ATLANTIC HOSTEL WOODSTOCK

BOUAKHIR

BANI ANTAR

LA

RAMPARTS

TRISKALA

CHILL ART HOSTEL

ESSAOUIRA SURF

SI SAID'S SHOP

MASHI MUSHKI

SILVESTRO

RIAD MALAÏKA

TAVERNA BOLOGNESE DE MAURIZIO

RIAD CHBANATE

UMIA

KASBAH

MEDINA

CHBANAT

COOKING CLASSES

RACHID MOURABIT

BENDAHHANE

YOO HEALTHY FOOD

AZUR ART & SPA

LE LOFT CAFÉ

AHL AGADIR

LALLA MIRA

GALERIE L'ARBRE BLEU

BAR HAFRA (TAROS)

BIBLIOPHILE

LE DAR LOUBANA

CASA CILA HOTEL AND SPA

BAB MARRAKESH

GALERIE DAMGAARD

PALAZZO DESDEMONA

TOURISM OFFICE

LA TABLE MADADA

CHEZ SAM

MADADA MOGADOR

SPA COCOONING

ASSOCIATION TILAL DES ART PLASTIQUE

PORT

0   150 yds
0   150 m

© MOON.COM

Tagharte Beach

BLVD MOHAMMED

CHURCH OF OUR LADY OF THE ASSUMPTION

AVE LALLA AICHA

VILLE NOUVELLE

Sights

Though Essaouira is known more for its artists, activities like windsurfing, and events such as the Gnawa Music Festival, there are still several sights worth visiting during your stay.

MEDINA
✪ RAMPARTS

The ramparts are thick, protective stone walls that surround the old city of Essaouira. They were first built by the Portuguese in the 16th century, though it was the work of Mohammed III—who had enlisted the service of a French engineer, Théodore Cornut,

as well as a few other European architects and technicians—in the 18th century that gave Essaouira the medina and fortress for which it is known today. The ramparts include the harbor fortifications as well as the citadel watching over it, built by Ahmed el-Inglizi, or Ahmed the English, an Englishman of note who converted to Islam and spent much of his life in the pirate capitals of Salé and Essaouira. The most popular walk along the ramparts takes you up a flight of stairs to the Skala de la Ville (a walkway atop the ramparts) and a row of Dutch cannons that were purchased by Mohammed III and installed for defense of the city. *Game of Thrones* fans might remember Daenerys meeting her loyal army of Unsullied for the first time along these ramparts and at the Skala de la Ville. From atop these ramparts, the Îles Purpuraires and Mogador Island can easily be viewed to the south. A meditative sunset walk is something of a rite of passage here.

MELLAH

A walk through the mellah will put you in touch with several aspects of the history and culture of Essaouira. In the 18th century, the Jewish population made up nearly half of the city's populace. This is evidenced today by a large number of synagogues, the expansive Jewish cemetery, and the Stars of David engraved above many of the doors in this neighborhood.

SIDI MOHAMED BEN ABDELLAH MUSEUM

Rue Laâlouj; tel. 0524/472 300; daily 10am-6pm; 70Dh

Located in the mellah in a traditional 19th-century mansion along one of the big pedestrian thoroughfares of the medina, this is perhaps the only museum worth visiting in Essaouira. The museum is named after the founder of the city, Mohamed Ben Abdellah, and displays various historical artifacts, including ancient pottery, coins, and jewelry relevant to local history. Signage is only in French and Arabic, though there is an English handout that provides a bit more information on the history of the museum and its collection.

HAIM PINTO SYNAGOGUE

Rue Mellah; tel. 0676/048 352; daily 10am-6pm; 20Dh (suggested donation)

Joseph Sebag, proudly the last Jew in

The ramparts of Essaouira have backdropped many film and TV productions.

Morocco is proud of its Jewish culture.

Essaouira, has been the custodian of this Sephardic synagogue for years. He is usually around throughout the day to give a short tour, though he is not an official tour guide, and explain a bit about the Jewish history in Morocco and in Essaouira specifically. In the synagogue you'll find a photography exhibition that celebrates the Jewish history of Essaouira, while there is also all the necessary holy equipment for completing Jewish prayers, with separate salons for the men and women. On the ground floor you can also see the rabbi's quarters, left exactly as the last rabbi, Haim Pinto, for whom the synagogue has now taken its name, left it years ago.

VILLE NOUVELLE
CHURCH OF OUR LADY OF THE ASSUMPTION
Just outside **Bab Marrakesh** lies the Church of Our Lady of the Assumption (Église Notre Dame de l'Assomption). This is one of the very few churches in Morocco whose bells ring on Sunday for the call to service. You can hear them at 10am sharp every Sunday, marking the beginning of service. Construction began on the church in 1939. Weddings can be arranged at the church, and travelers on their way through Essaouira typically make up most of the congregation. This art deco church is seldom touristed. For those looking for a Christian service, it is a welcome respite and one of the few going strong in Morocco.

PORT
The famed port of Essaouira is a bustling place of activity, filled with fishers cleaning their nets and boats, getting ready to set sail, coming back with the day's catch, and calling back and forth about the good fishing spots of the day, the state of the ocean, and the coming weather. Flocks of seagulls cry overhead, plunge into the water, and scurry on the old wood docks. Cats lurk about, keeping to the shadows, sometimes lounging in the sun, hoping for some fresh fish from a worker who will take pity on them. This is a good place for a morning stroll.

ÎLES PURPURAIRES
The Îles Purpuraires (Purple Islands) are easily seen just off the beach of Essaouira. Though there are a couple of notable ruins, including an old prison and a mosque, the island has been left strictly for the birds. There is no access to the islands, outside of officially sponsored, government-endorsed studies.

Birders will want to make a trip around the islands for some wonderful migratory bird-watching, with plenty of teals and coots. The real treat, though, are the Eleanora's falcons. They breed here in late summer/early autumn in breeding colonies before continuing on their route to their winter homes on Madagascar, the opposite corner of the continent. The falcon feeds primarily on smaller migratory birds. It was recently discovered that this impressive hunter will capture its prey live before imprisoning it in small rock crevices to eat later.

Local fishers can take you around the islands. The boat ride is memorable, though it can be costly depending on how good your bargaining skills are. Expect to pay at least 200Dh to be taken around the uninhabited main island, Mogador, and 400Dh or more for a half-day out.

Sports and Recreation

HAMMAMS

As usual in Morocco, if visiting one of the local hammams in the old medina, just don't forget an orange to eat while you are relaxing in the cooling room. Ask your lodging where the nearest hammam is and, by all accounts, avoid Hammam Mounia. There are serious questions of hygiene and perhaps other less-than-savory goings on happening at this address.

Azur Art & Spa

15 Rue Khalid Ben Walid, Pl. Moulay Hassan; tel. 0524/785 794, www.azur-essaouira.com; reservations only

The Azur Art & Spa offers the full Moroccan hammam experience, with a scrub of soap (*rhassoul*) and steam room starting at a reasonable 120Dh. Massages, facials, manicures, pedicures, waxing, and other options are available. For an upscale hammam

the long stretch of beach outside of the city

experience, this is maybe the best option for value in Essaouira.

Lalla Mira

14 Rue d'Algerie; tel. 0524/475 046; daily 9:30am-7pm

Lalla Mira, the oldest traditional hammam in Essaouira, though it has been remodeled, is still a bit dingy. You'll find it attached to the *riad* by the same name. The retrofitting of this hammam included solar thermal equipment, making it the first hammam in Morocco heated exclusively by solar power. From the natural *tadelahkt* walls and polished green clay tiles, you wouldn't know that this was once a hammam used historically by slaves. Today, the hammam is popular with tourists and locals alike, with a full exfoliation treatment with argan oil for 180Dh. Massages are also available, though given on plastic mats on the floor, so totally skippable. Reservations are recommended for women and required for men. If you're looking for a local experience, it's expensive for what it is. Better hammams can be found easily in Marrakesh and Fez.

Spa Cocooning

2 Rue Mohamed Ben Massoud; tel. 0524/783 035; http://spacocooning.com/contact; daily 9:30am-7pm

If money is no object or you don't mind splurging for a little self-care, make a beeline for Spa Cocooning. Aziza, Fatima, Sara, Souad, and the rest of the team will make sure you leave with your skin baby soft and your bones and muscles feeling like warm, fuzzy jelly. Go all out with the full hammam treatment with black soap scrubs and exfoliation, followed by a nice tea in the relaxing room before diving in for a full body massage. They use only the best Moroccan cosmetics, all 100 percent natural and great for your skin. Budget 400Dh or more for an unforgettable spa experience.

The winds are nearly always perfect for windsurfing.

✪ WINDSURFING, KITESURFING, AND SURFING

If you're looking to learn how to **windsurf**, the long beach strip just south of Essaouira is the place to do it. Year-round, the geography of the land practically ensures a stiff breeze perfect for windsurfers. Beachside companies have updated, well-maintained equipment and offer lessons for beginners and long loops for advanced windsurfers. However, January and February can sometimes see lesser winds, great for beachgoers but a possible disappointment for those counting on a little wind to scoot around the surf. For slightly less expensive options, head a few kilometers south of Essaouira to the beachfront town of Sidi Kaouki.

Ion Club

Blvd. Mohammed V; tel. 0524/783 934; www.oceanvagabond.com

Windsurfing, kitesurfing, and surfing instruction is available for all age groups and levels throughout the year at the internationally renowned Ion Club. Lessons start at 1,100Dh for a two-hour lesson, all equipment included. Instructors speak English, French, Spanish, and Arabic. The gear is the newest available, including brands such as Triwave, Freewave, and Gecko. For those staying at Ion Club, free clinics are available.

Essaouira Surf

30 Avenue Sidi Mohamed Ben Abdellah;
tel. 0645/742 030; www.essaouirasurf.com

If you're looking to expand your horizons, the team at Essaouira Surf has gear to really get you in the air. Instructors speak English and are well equipped for beginner windsurfers, kitesurfers, and surfers to explore what they can do on the waves and with the wind. Instruction is available starting at around 1,000Dh for gear and lesson. Those who are serious about learning might consider one of the 2-7 night packages that include accommodations, breakfast, transportation in and out of Agadir or Marrakesh, and instruction and equipment starting at 1,700Dh.

CAMEL TREKKING AND HORSE RIDING

If you just can't shake the dream of riding a camel on a secluded strip of beach, then there are several companies based in Essaoiura that can make this dream come true for you.

Lima Dromadaire

tel. 0668/189 220;
www.limadromadaire.com

Lima Dromadaire is the company of choice, with long treks along the beach and friendly professionals who will do their best to make you comfortable atop the relatively uncomfortable

hump of a dromedary. Mostafa will happily show you the region of Essaouira, and overnight bivouac excursions are also available. Prices start at 150Dh for a short, one-hour ride. Children under five ride free with a paying adult.

Equi Evasion

tel. 0666/780 561; www.equievasion.com

Finding yourself drawn to dromedaries but hooked on horses? Equi Evasion has both for you to ride. Rides can be arranged for as little as one hour (150Dh) and include safety helmets. Also available are half-day rides that include picnics and six-day treks that include stays in Bedouin tents along the Atlantic Coast. This is a great way to explore the region in harmony.

☼ COOKING CLASSES

In the last few years, cooking classes have increased in popularity, with many travelers interested in learning how to make their own tajine, couscous, and other Moroccan specialties. This is a great opportunity to really taste the culture and learn how to bring a piece of it home with you.

Khadija's Kuzina

Avenue Allal Al Fassi, across the street from Pharmaice Bouhaira; tel. 0670/071 232; 300Dh

Khadija's Kuzina offers intimate Moroccan cooking classes inside the family home of Khadija. It's a cheerful environment to talk about and understand Moroccan culture and people better through its cuisine. The menu is completely customizable and can be catered to any dietary needs. Even better, Khadija and her husband, Lahoussaine, have been working with the Peace Corps since 2003. Not only do they host volunteers, but they have a passion for cross-cultural exchange that is evident throughout their work and life. Best for couples, friends, and families, and those looking for something a bit more than just learning how to cook a delicious meal.

La Table Madada

7 Rue Youssef el Fassil; tel. 0524/472 106;
www.lateliermadada.com; 500Dh

La Table Madada offers one of the most humorous, engaging cooking classes around, with Chef Mouna always telling you to "cut smaller" as you dice and slice the ingredients necessary for your own delicious tajine lunch. This cooking class includes a trip to the local souk to purchase vegetables, meat, spices, and other necessities. This is a great insider's look at Moroccan souks, and it provides a reference for how much things should cost. Those with a sweet tooth might want to consider the shorter Moroccan pastry workshop (220Dh) in the afternoon. Instruction is in English with French and Arabic also available.

WINE TASTING
Le Val d'Argan

Route de Marrakesh, Ounagha;
tel. 0524/783 467; www.valdargan.com;
open daily 11am-5pm; 100Dh

One of the better wine-tasting experiences in Morocco, though a step behind Napa Valley and the better wine regions of France. Located just off the road linking Marrakesh with Essaouira, this is a stop that's best coupled with lunch and a proper *degustation*. Dine just off the pool of the attached boutique hotel, Ryad des Vignes, among centuries-old olive trees. Plates are traditional Moroccan paired specifically for the wines. In the warmer months, go for the Gazelle Rose, a beautifully pink rosé with notes of fresh-picked raspberries and tart grapefruit. In the colder winter months, cozy up with one of the rich, deep reds, like the Orian Rouge.

Entertainment and Events

ARTISTS AND GALLERIES

Artists, both national and international, have long felt an affinity for Essaouira. Though the atmosphere of Essaouira is changing, there are still numerous painters, sculptors, and other artists who call Essaouira home. You'll find them in the bazaars lining Avenue Sidi Mohamed Ben Abdellah and tucked into the various little streets of the medina.

Association Tilal des Art Plastique

4 Rue du Caire; tel. 0524/475 424;
daily 8:30am-12:30pm and 2:30pm-7pm

Association Tilal des Art Plastique features work by female Moroccan artist Najia Kerairate, a Moroccan sculptor and painter specializing in the avant garde, as well as other artists. Art Plastique is sponsored by l'Association des Arts Plastiques d'Essaouira and is recognized by UNICEF for its contribution to disadvantaged youth.

WHAT'S COOKING IN MOROCCO

Morocco is a veritable melting pot of different cultures. People from around the Mediterranean, Africa, and the Middle East have influenced its most notable dishes, creating a cuisine that is unparalleled in its use of sweet and salty spicing. Here are a few of the dishes that you can expect to eat while in Morocco or make for yourself in one of the popular cooking courses you can find in most cities.

STARTERS

- *Zaalouk:* a salad that is generally served as a starter alongside several other salads (listed below). *Zaalouk* is made using roasted eggplant, tomatoes, and spices. This is a staple of Moroccan restaurants throughout the country.

- *Chakchouka:* a traditional Moroccan salad using fresh chopped tomatoes, onions, grilled peppers, and generous amounts of olive oil. This is perhaps the most common fresh (non-cooked) salad you'll find throughout the country.

SOUPS

- *Bissara* (also known as *bisr* in the north): a rich vegan-friendly fava bean soup. It usually is made up of boiled and mashed fava beans and served with cumin, red paprika, hot chili spice, and olive oil. A popular dish with sailors and fishermen who praise its positive effect on the lungs.

- *Harira:* a thick tomato soup filled with chickpeas and often beef or lamb stock. Sometimes, you'll find *harira* with rice and lentils as well. This soup is typically served throughout the month of Ramadan to break the day of fasting, though you can find it in restaurants year-round.

MAINS

- **Couscous:** Though known throughout North Africa, couscous remains the national dish of Morocco. It's a small, hand-rolled pasta that is traditionally served on

Perhaps a bit too on the cutting edge for some, though most should appreciate what this program does for the local youth community.

Azur Art & Spa

15 Rue Khalid Ben Walid, Pl. Moulay Hassan; tel. 0524/785 794, www.azur-spa-essaouira.com/en; reservation recommended

With local artists on display, Azur Art & Spa is well worth a visit. A permanent collection rests downstairs, while upstairs you can sip on a tea and look at some of the new paintings, photos, and sculptures being exhibited. Contact for reservations. This is a great place to get to know a few of the local artists and their works.

Bendahhane

3 Rue El Hajjali; tel. 0661/347 262; www.bendahhane.com; Tues.-Sat. 10am-1pm and 3pm-6pm

Curated by Abdel Bendahhane, the gallery seeks to build bridges between artists and the public. Bendahhane tends toward pointillism, expressionism, and brutalist art. There is a wide spectrum of local talent on display. For those on a tight budget, but who still want some original art from Essaouira, check into the limited prints and art cards available.

Galerie Damgaard

Ave. Oqba Ibn Nafiaa; tel. 0524/784 446; www.galeriedamgaard.com; Tues.-Sat. 10am-1pm and 3pm-6pm

Friday afternoons. Meat, often beef or lamb, will often be served with the couscous, though having the dish with only vegetables is an option.

- **B'stilla:** A specialty from Fez, this elaborate pie is an intriguing mix of salty and sweet. Traditionally, this was made with pigeon meat, though these days chicken and seafood are often used. The filling is marinated and cooked in spices, then topped with a layer of toasted ground almonds and cinnamon before being wrapped in a filo dough.

- **Tajine:** Named after the conic-shaped pottery in which it was traditionally cooked and served, tajine is perhaps the most-known dish throughout the country. The tajine is a slow-cooked stew that uses a combination of spices and generally includes root vegetables, such as potatoes and carrots. Tajines can use chicken, beef, lamb, goat, fish, or zucchini and eggplant as central elements.

DESSERTS

Moroccans are famed for their sweet tooth, and it's easy to see why! The country produces some of the world's sweetest oranges and dates. Perhaps the most common dessert served is a simple plate of sliced oranges drizzled with orange blossom water and honey, or a bowl of dates. However, there are a number of popular cookies and sweet biscuits that are also served. Here are a few:

- **Shebakia:** a pretzel of deep-fried sesame dough, drizzled with organic honey. There are entire shops dedicated to the art of perfecting the *shebakia*. Sales of this treat spike tremendously during the holy month of Ramadan.

- **Briouates:** These can be both savory and sweet. The sweet version is a deep-fried triangle-shaped dough packed with almond paste and orange blossom water and dipped in sticky, delicious honey.

- **Corne de gazelles:** delicate, soft, crescent-shaped cookies that look a bit like gazelle horns—thus the name. Like *briouates*, these delicacies are stuffed with almond paste and a touch of orange blossom water and often sprinkled with sesame seeds or toasted almonds.

Many local artists have spent some time being exhibited in the Galerie Damgaard, a gallery dedicated to showcasing the talent of artists from Essaouira since its inception in 1988. If you're in the market or curious about what the most contemporary artists in and around this corner of Morocco are putting on canvas, this is the place to stop.

Rachid Mourabit

115 Rue Mohammed El Qori; daily, hours vary

Rachid Mourabit, an Essaouira native, creates sculptures from pieces of recycled metal, such as old cans, pieces from car engines, and greasy parts that you might find buried in your uncle's garage. He fuses these pieces together into whimsical forms, such as insect-looking musicians or comedic personas. The end product is clunky and robotic and maintains a sense of naive humor and ingenious charm. Rachid enjoys his work and enjoys every sale he makes. Prices will not hurt the

Argan oil is a local specialty.

179

Since 1998, Essaouira has devoted a portion of its energies to transforming its little labyrinth of streets and wide beaches to rhythmic drumbeats of Gnawa musicians. Every May, over the course of four nights, a festival atmosphere envelops the city as it fills with thousands of music lovers. The free festival has concerts throughout the city on five stages: **Place Moulay Hassan, Beach Stage, Dar Souiri, Borj Bab Marrakesh,** and **Issaoua Zaouia.** Place Moulay Hassan and the Beach Stage typically host the biggest names in Gnawa and other headliners, free of admission charge, while Dar Souiri is the only paid entrance for more intimate performances. Borj Bab Marrakesh is a new stage, strictly for the Gnawa fusion, and features some of the most interesting musical performances throughout the festival, while Issaoua Zaouia keeps the Gnawa spirit alive with its all-night trance (*hadras*) performed by local musicians. This is Woodstock, Moroccanized.

Gnawa music can trace its roots to Sub-Saharan Africa, though Morocco and Algeria are the modern bastions of this ritual music that combines prayers, chants, and poetry with rhythm. Often, songs can continue for hours as the *mâalems* (primary singers) find themselves in the music, connecting and weaving their chants with the rhythm of the group. Though the more spiritual form of Gnawa music can still be heard privately and maintains its sacred energy, the Gnawa as it is practiced at the festival is more secular and more fusion-inspired. The artists performing open up Gnawa music to collaborations with jazz, reggae, and hip-hop, though the more natural collaborations happen with blues musicians, as both musical styles emphasize the third, fifth, and sometimes the seventh of the scale. Here's a quick run-down of the main instruments:

- **Krakeb:** a large iron castanet-type rhythm instrument that produces the essential *kerketoo* rhythm

- **Hajoui:** a rustic base lute that creates swaying, lilting chords

pocketbook, starting at 100Dh or less for your very own small, twisted souvenir of Essaouira.

FESTIVALS AND EVENTS

Gnawa Music Festival

www.festival-gnaoua.net; May; free

Though its focus is on Gnawa music, the largely free annual Gnawa Music Festival includes rock, jazz, and reggae music. Dubbed the "Moroccan Woodstock," this four-day music festival held every May will leave even the most diehard music enthusiasts gasping for breath at the end. The festival now attracts nearly half a million visitors, making accommodations expensive and difficult to come by, not to mention the logistical problems with transportation in the region.

Andalusian Music Festival

Oct.; free

Generally overshadowed by the Gnawa Music Festival, the less-popular Andalusian Music Festival is no less interesting, with days full of music performed by well-known groups from around Morocco and Spain. Oftentimes, musicians get together,

Moroccan music is known for its trance-like effect.

improvising around town, creating new rhythms and melodies, fusing contemporary music composition with the more structured music of *al-Andalus.* Typically held at the end of October, this is a festival worth attending for those who love music but are willing to skip the crowds.

Shopping

A lot of the shopping is found along **Avenue d'Istiqlal** and **Avenue Sidi Mohamed Ben Abdellah,** though a detour down **Rue Chbanate** in the mellah and farther away from most of the touristed strips of the medina is well worthwhile, in terms of both price and interesting boutiques. On this strip, there are a number of shops of interest, each doing something a bit different than the standard tourist fare.

Just inside Bab Marrakesh, **Rue Mohammed El Qori** is another shopping strip, with plenty of popular *hanoots* (small stores) selling everything from laundry soap to bottled water, mixed in with a few specialized tourist shops and bazaars.

TRADITIONAL GOODS AND HANDICRAFTS
Atelier de Tissage Traditional
4 Bis Rue Ziane; tel. 0663/150 648;
daily, hours vary
Atelier de Tissage Traditional, run by Abderrahim Hachetouf, has a selection of handmade blankets, towels, and scarves as well as some traditional carpets. Prices are honest and Abderrahim himself is friendly, charming, and willing to help you find just the right material or fit. He operates from two locations in Essaouira, this one on Rue Ziane and another at 31 Bis Rue Chbanate along the strip of boutique shops. To get to the second

location, enter Bab Doukkala into the medina and take your first left. About 60 meters (200ft) down you'll find his other shop full of blankets, scarves, and cotton poufs.

carpets for sale in the medina

BOUTIQUES AND FASHION
Mashi Mushki
94 Rue Chbanate; daily 1pm-6pm,
though hours vary
Mashi Mushki features funky designs alongside small paintings by local artists and replicas of vintage Moroccan record covers. Some of the proceeds benefit the Project 91 charity across the street. This is a good place to get a handmade silk scarf to keep your

neck warm on those chilly Essaouira nights. The name is a play on the popular Moroccan phrase *mashi mushkil,* meaning "no problems."

JEWELRY
Galerie l'Arbre Bleu
233 Rue Chbanate; Mon.-Sat. 10am-1pm and 3pm-7pm

Pop in for a little infusion tea and do some shopping at the Galerie l'Arbre Bleu, a boutique café featuring locally made and recycled jewelry as well as the paintings of local favorite Monique Favière. The jewelry makes for fun accent pieces.

bags for sale in the medina

BOOKSTORES
Le Bibliophile
24 Rue de Rif; daily 10:30am-1pm and 3pm-7pm

Le Bibliophile has the best selection of English-language books around and focuses on classic titles, though a fair amount of genre and pulp fiction can be had. If you need a beach read, this is the place to go, though it's not only books on offer. Mohamed, the owner, has a thing for vintage vinyl and old postcards, which you'll also find in quantity.

SPICES
Si Said's shop
199 Marché aux Épices; daily, hours vary

If spices are your thing, stop by Si Said's shop in the spice market. He has honest prices that are standard for the region and most of Morocco. You'll find that elusive Taliouine saffron and, if you're lucky, a "royal tea," a special Moroccan tea made of a combination of 15 spices. This is a great place to stock up on valuable spices before heading home. Look for Said's shop and the spice market hidden behind the fish market.

Food

More than perhaps any other city in Morocco, Essaouira is a foodie's paradise. With a number of traditional Moroccan restaurants, international restaurants, street eats, fusion foods, and fresh seafood, the one thing for certain is that your taste buds will come away from Essaouira absolutely delighted. Nearly all of the restaurants cater to the international crowd and international tastes. You'll find

the dining in Essaouira overall more comfortable than just about any other corner of Morocco, with a number of options for nearly every budget and every palate.

A good selection of Moroccan street food is typically available outside of **Bab Doukkala,** including spicy chickpeas, snail soup, popcorn, grilled corn, and other seasonal treats. Most plates are 5-10Dh and make for a festive atmosphere, particularly at night before taking a stroll around the medina. For those looking for tasty street eats or to pinch pennies, this is a great option.

Seafood lovers can head to the port for huge plates of sardines, rouget (red mullet), shrimp, langoustine, and crab, though the callers working at the little fish shacks can be aggressive in trying to twist your arm into a meal. Plates start at around 100Dh (though you can always bargain) and are big enough for two to share. A large picnic area makes this a good spot for an afternoon lunch.

VILLE NOUVELLE
SEAFOOD
Chez Sam
Essaouira port; tel. 0544/476 513;
daily noon-3pm and 7pm-11pm; 200Dh
For a less stressful lunch or dinner, Chez Sam offers up fresh fish culled straight off the docks every day. Good portions are deliciously prepared in this rustic port restaurant with a terrace that juts out over the water. The better dishes involve simpler preparation, which allows the fresh seafood to really stand out. This popular spot is often crowded, so come early. Reservations are recommended.

MEDINA
MOROCCAN
⭐ La Roche
Place Taraa; tel. 0524/472 716;
Sun.-Fri. noon-11pm; 80Dh
Located on a small square just out of the Jewish Quarter, La Roche entertains a surprisingly eclectic, international menu served up by Chef Amina. Though the staple couscous and tajines can be found (and are delicious), many travelers looking for a break from heavier Moroccan fare could

spices for sale in the medina

ESSAOUIRA
FOOD

183

look toward the selection of soups or even dive into Amina's club sandwich. The apple fritter (*beignet des pommes*) is a big hit with kids, while others might consider stopping in for a quick fresh-squeezed juice. For lunches, arrive before 1pm to make sure you get your choice of everything from the menu, as stock is limited.

Tara Café
Place Taraa; tel. 0653/602 019;
daily 9am-midnight; 30Dh

If La Roche is too full, pop across the street to Tara Café. This friendly out-of-the-way place is a great stop for a quick coffee, tea, or even a Moroccan salad or tajine for lunch. Though the menu isn't quite as varied as some of the other options, its location right on the Plaza Taraa, in the mellah at the end of Avenue Sidi Mohamed Ben Abdellah, ensures a quieter lunch affair. A nice spot to meet friendly locals. Wi-Fi is available.

VEGETARIAN AND VEGAN
✪ Yoo Healthy Food
8A Rue Ibn Roch; tel. 0601/524 609;
Mon.-Sat. 10am-10pm, Sun. 1pm-10pm; 70Dh

Vegans rejoice! This little shack tucked down an alley, cozy and clean, has a diverse menu that features all vegetarian and vegan food, including soy-based and lentil-based veggie burgers. For a quick pick-me-up, splurge on one of a number of slow-pressed fresh juices. Frozen yogurt is also an option, as well as the Shrek, a hearty milkshake loaded with bananas, chocolate, and cinnamon. Seating is limited, so it's best to eat a little early or late. If hummus, grilled veggies, salads, or a bunch of gluten-free options sound like they might hit the spot, you can't do any better.

✪ La Triskala
Rue Touahen; tel. 0524/476 371
or 0655/585 131; Tues.-Sat. 11am-7pm; 80Dh

Another great vegetarian option is La Triskala, which has a quirky vibe with photos of Bob Dylan, Jimi Hendrix, and others decorating the walls. The owners strive to be eco-friendly and serve only locally produced goods. The menu changes every day and depends on the freshest ingredients from the local souk—get the frothy cilantro gazpacho if it's available. If you're coming for dinner, it's best to show up early during the busy season, as they often run out of some of the more popular items. No wine or beer is available, but there is no corkage fee, so you can bring your own.

ITALIAN
Silvestro
70, Rue Laalouj; tel. 0524/473 555;
daily 7pm-11pm; 120Dh

Climb the grungy stairs to Silvestro, but don't let the stairs turn you off! Inside you'll find an explosion of flowered wallpaper and Moroccan stucco work set against a soft jazzy background. The menu offers up a fine choice of Italian classics like *penne arrabbiate* (spicy pasta), made with homemade pasta, and some killer gnocchi. Pizzas are all wood-fired, and the seafood and mushrooms are fresh. There's a selection of wines and liquors, and it's nonsmoking.

Taverna Bolognese da Maurizio
7 Rue Youssef Ben Tachfine 7;
tel. 0655/360 347; daily 7pm-11pm; 120Dh

If you're looking for a *tagliatelle alla bolognese* to fill that Italian craving, or maybe you just want a taste of something a bit more familiar than Moroccan fare, head to Maurizio's fine Italian diner. With a menu filled with some of his favorites from back home, including traditional recipes straight from Maurizio's hometown of Bologna, the only real disappointment is that the house wine isn't Italian (it's expensive to import), but it is Moroccan. Fortunately, Moroccan red wine shares a lot of the same body and properties as its Italian cousin.

FRENCH
La Table Madada
7 Rue Youssef el Fassi; tel. 0524/475 512;
www.latablemadada.com;
Wed.-Mon. 7:15pm-11pm; 250Dh

For an upscale, French-style dinner, pull up your chair under the stone arches of La Table Madada. The menu features some classic cuisine with a touch of local flavor, such as the spider crab and avocado tartare with a hint of argan oil and tiger prawns served with *charmoula* and Taliouine saffron rice. The bar has a full array of cocktails and a list of wines from France and Morocco. Tapas (35Dh) are also served, making the bar a wonderful place to stop in before heading out somewhere else for dinner. Cooking classes are available during the day.

Le Loft Café, Resto and Galerie
5 Rue Hajjali; tel. 0524/476 389 or
0638/949 793; Wed.-Mon. 9am-10:30pm;
120Dh

It's okay to hold lofty expectations when walking through the front doors of the Loft Café, Resto and Galerie. This is a particularly well-done concept café that blends vintage design and local art with one of the freshest menus around. Everything is seasonal, usually bought that day, with options for vegetarians. Some of the house favorites include spinach-cheese rolls and a mouthwatering saffron-vanilla crème brûlée.

✪ Umia
22 bis Skala St.; tel. 0524/783 395;
Tues.-Sun. noon-3pm and 7pm-late; 250Dh

For delicate, delicious French-Moroccan fusion, this is perhaps the best address in the country. Candlelit and intimate, it is wonderful for couples looking for a special-occasion dinner or friends looking to sip on some full-bodied, cozy reds together. Fresh seafood is the highlight of the menu, as expected, and with the chef using local products, such as the locally sourced Taliouine saffron, with a deft French touch, it's easy to see why this is a foodie favorite. Go for the clam starter and consider the saffron cream monkfish as your main, but make sure to leave room for the oozy delicious chocolate soufflé.

AROUND ESSAOUIRA
FRENCH
Dar Kenavo
Douar Bouzama, Km13 Idaougard;
tel. 0524/474 835; daily noon-3pm and
7pm-10pm; 120Dh

A few kilometers outside of Essaouira is the fantastic spread of Dar Kenavo. The organic, seasonal menu has possibilities to entertain anyone's dietary needs. With a wonderful garden and a heated pool, it's a bit more upscale, with three-course lunches and dinners, but for diners looking for something a bit different, a night at Dar Kenavo fits the bill in spades. Most ingredients are plucked straight from the on-site garden. If you're looking for a delicious break from the beach crowds, a break from the wind, or just want to spend an afternoon poolside, call them ASAP. Reservations are required.

Bars and Nightlife

Notably more subdued than Marrakesh, the nightlife in Essaouira is more relaxed than it is vibrant. Many of the (overpriced) beach bars will close up by 8pm, while the others around town generally have last call well before midnight, unless there are festivals happening... in which case, Essaouira wakes up and never really seems to sleep.

MEDINA
Bar Hafra (Taros)
Ruette Layach; tel. 0524/476 407;
daily noon-late

For a truly local experience, you couldn't ask for a better watering hole. Local fishermen and port workers sip suds and trade stories. Beers are the cheapest in town and internationals are welcomed, though some might be put off by the often raucous crowd, particularly if a football (soccer) match is on TV, while others will feel right at home. It's best to come here on a Friday or Saturday before 9pm when it's still possible to get a table. If there are no tables, feel free to squeeze up to the bar. Tapas are served (20Dh and up). Occasionally,

buskers will stop by and play for tips, adding to the festive tableau.

Dar Loubana
24 Rue du Rif; tel. 0524/476 296;
daily noon-11pm

The casual, beautiful patio of Dar Loubana features traditional live Gnawa music every Saturday night, which is worth seeing if you're not heading out to the Sahara. Outside of dinner hours, you can still make good use of the patio. Lunch is a relatively okay deal, with traditional Moroccan tajines starting at 80Dh, but happy hour is where it's at, with Moroccan-style tapas (10-40Dh) served daily 6:30pm-7:30pm and a selection of beer and Moroccan wine at standard prices.

La Table Madada
7 Rue Youssef el Fassi; tel. 0524/475 512;
www.latablemadada.com; Wed.-Mon.
7:15pm-11pm

Tapas (35Dh) are served at the bar, making this spot a wonderful place to stop in before heading out for dinner or afterward for a nightcap. Good for wine lovers and those in need of a stiff cocktail, it's also a great place for couples or friends looking to have a chat.

Accommodations

There are plenty of great options in Essaouira for travelers of all budget types, making this a good time to scrimp and save on your journey or really splurge—however your wallet sees fit.

MEDINA
UNDER 400DH
Atlantic Hostel Woodstock
34 Rue Ellabanna; tel. 0629/652 268; 50Dh
for a dorm bed, 240Dh d

For a clean, friendly hostel experience,

Atlantic Hostel Woodstock caters to the many students and backpackers who come through Essaouira. Divided into two buildings (Atlantic and Woodstock) right next to each other, this hostel has slowly built a reputation for being one of the better ones in Morocco, with a quiet night of sleep the norm. For travelers on a tight budget, it's sometimes possible to sleep on the roof, weather allowing, for even less. This is a good place to meet fellow travelers and maybe make a new friend. Woodstock is typically quieter, while Atlantic has the kitchen and much of the socializing. Both buildings offer dorms and private rooms. Coffee, tea, breakfast, and kitchen access cost extra (usually 10Dh). Free Wi-Fi is available in the foyer.

☻ Chill Art Hostel

21, Rue Abderrahamane Eddakhil; tel. 0600/150 138; 95Dh for a dorm bed, 260Dh d

As chill as its name implies and easily the best hostel in Essaouira, if not in the whole country. Its location in the heart of the Essaouira medina, coupled with the vibrant, arty vibe, make this a great place for musicians, students, artists, backpackers, and travelers looking to connect with like-minded people. Housed in a converted traditional *riad,* the hostel is run by Pierre and Elena, each married to Moroccan partners. A scrumptious breakfast is served every day at 10am (30Dh), and always includes a creative egg dish, such as spicy eggplant omelets, with a sweet finish (think caramel-drizzled croissants). Hearty dinners are served at 8pm (50Dh). The kitchen is open for everyone to use. You'll probably make a lot of nice friends out there, as Cat Stevens sings in the background. This is a nonsmoking property except for one corner on the rooftop terrace.

The property sleeps around 35 people, which makes finding a bed at the last minute a definite possibility.

400-800DH
Palazzo Desdemona

Rue Youssef El Fassy; tel. 0524/472 227; www.palazzodesdemona.com; 500Dh d

The Palazzo Desdemona is an exceptional bargain in the medina. The rooms are wonderfully decorated with tribal rugs, canopy beds, and authentic Amazigh wood doors. The feeling is more upscale, but for half the price of more luxe hotels, and the rate includes breakfast. Rooms are spacious and clean and include working fireplaces for those cold winter nights. Panoramic views from the terrace overlook the ramparts, medina, port, beachfront, and nearby garden. It is basic, without air-conditioning or heating, but a good value nonetheless, and you'll be surprised at how you don't need all the mod-cons for a great night of sleep.

☻ Riad Malaïka

17 Derb Zayan; tel. 0524/784 908; www.riad-malaika.com; 750Dh d

For warm, friendly lodging, look no further than Riad Malaïka. Conveniently located in the heart of the medina, just off the main thoroughfare, this renovated *riad* has kept just enough historic detail to make it interesting, including the retro tile work leading to the rooftop terrace. The service and food are top-notch, and the staff have cleanliness on their minds, as a quick tour of the bottom-floor kitchen will attest. The rooms are cozy with plush beds, perfect for a quiet night of much-needed sleep. Wi-Fi, heating, and breakfast are all included. If you have any questions about Essaouira or the region, do not hesitate to ask. This is one of the few locally owned and run *riads* in Essaouira, and one of the best locally run *riads* in the entire country. All of the staff are proud of this and extremely knowledgeable about the area.

Casa Lila Hotel and Spa

Rue Mohammed el Qori; tel. 0524/475 545; 800Dh d

If you're looking for a great spa experience with your stay, the Casa Lila Hotel and Spa is a wonderful option. The spa treatments are available at the on-site Espace Bien-Être. The rooms all have themes of different spices, making a stay in paprika-, saffron-, or anise-accented bedding something of a novelty. The staff is friendly and helpful, though it's best to make use of your French or Arabic, as little English is spoken. As long as you're okay with this, there is nothing else you could ask for in this price range. Well located with all the amenities.

OVER 800DH
✪ Riad Watier

16 Rue Ceuta; tel. 0524/476 204; www.ryad-watier-maroc.com; 900Dh d

One of the best-lit traditional *riads* in the medina is Riad Watier. This unique *riad* sports a couple of patios, which give a lot of natural light to the large, airy rooms, decorated with various paintings and sculptures from local artists. Larger rooms are available for families, and babysitting is even available. The owner lives on-site and will see to your every need. If you want to feel a bit pampered, this is the place. Argan oil massages are available, along with a traditional, private hammam for your spa needs. Breakfast is delicious, and the traditional Moroccan tajines and other choices available for dinner are exquisite. The minimum

stay is two nights, though most travelers leave wishing they had booked a longer stay.

Madada Mogador

7 Rue Youssef el Fassi; tel. 0524/475 512; www.latablemadada.com; 1,200Dh d

The team at Madada Mogador has put together a charming, traditional *riad* full of creamy beiges, rustic sands, and deep browns with torch lighting that instantly puts you at ease. This is a place for those looking to unwind. Large terraces give out to views over the ocean, and plenty of the rooms are big enough to really spread out. All rooms have air-conditioning, heating, and Wi-Fi and include a delicious breakfast of traditional Moroccan crepes (*miloui*) as well as homemade jams and jellies. Massages are available, which is just the thing when complemented by ocean views. The staff is friendly, and the attached restaurant, La Table Madada, is one of the best in town. Standard rooms, however, don't feature views. If you're already splurging, spend the extra 200Dh a night for views out over the Atlantic. You won't regret it.

✪ Riad Chbanate

179 Rue Chbanate; tel. 0524/783 334 or 0668/034 757; www.riadchbanate.com; 1,600Dh d

One of the best high-end *riads* in the city is Riad Chbanate. Tucked into the back of the medina, just off the main shopping road leading from Bab Chbanate, this expansive *riad* has some fun designs, including a rope swing in one of the suites and wide bathtubs big enough for two. The ground-floor restaurant offers fine dining by candlelight. Breakfast, included with the room, is a veritable culinary experience with *viennoiseries* (pastries), fresh bread, Moroccan-style crêpes, and fresh orange juice. The terrace is private, with views out over Essaouira and the ocean, perfect for a little sun-tanning away from the crowds.

Riad Perle d'Eau

64 Rue du Kowaït; tel. 0661/601 955; www.riad-essaouira-perledeau.com; 1,800Dh d

With coffee and tea served in your room and a real French-style breakfast, there is a lot to like about this hidden gem of a *riad*. The attention to detail is impeccable. For those looking for something with a bit more of a European flair, tuck in for your stay here. However, to really take advantage of the property, book one of the three rooftop suites to fully enjoy the sea views. This is becoming quite a popular getaway for the European jet-setting crowd, so be sure to reserve well in advance. Guests should also check out the on-site spa for some real pampering. Air-conditioning, heating, and speedy Wi-Fi are all included. Best for couples.

Information and Services

Cash machines are concentrated around Place Moulay Hassan in the south of the medina, near the port, including Banque Populaire, Attijarwafi Bank, and Crédit du Maroc. For emergencies, the Sidi Mohamed Ben Abdellah Hospital is outside of Bab Marrakesh, just across the parking lot. Pharmacies are sprinkled throughout the medina and the Ville Nouvelle.

Tourism Office

10 Rue du Caire; tel. 0524/783 532; daily 10am-6pm

The friendly Tourism Office (Delegation Provinciale du Tourisme) is directly attached to Morocco's ministry of tourism and handicrafts. It has updated maps of the city and hours for many of the museums and galleries.

Transportation

GETTING THERE
BY CAR

The route to Essaouira from Marrakesh is straightforward, just along the newly widened National Road 8 (N8), which turns into the R207 (178km/111mi, 2.5hr).

Grands taxis commonly run to/from Marrakesh (2.5hr, 177km/110mi, 90Dh).

BY BUS

CTM (tel. 0800/0900 30, www.ctm.ma) runs buses between Essaouira and Marrakesh (2.5hr, 2 daily, 75Dh).

Supratours (tel. 0524/888 566 or 0524/885 632, www.oncf.ma) operates the buses affiliated with the national train line, ONCF. Buses depart directly from the Marrakesh train station to Essaouira (3hr, 6 daily, 120Dh) and are the most convenient way to get from Marrakesh to Essaouira for those traveling by train. The 9am bus leaving from Marrakesh is a "Comfort Plus" bus, with Wi-Fi, an on-board toilet, and a bit more leg room, and costs only 30Dh more. The "Comfort Plus" leaving Essaouira for Marrakesh departs at 5pm. If budget and schedule allow, the upgrade is worth it.

GETTING AROUND

Most travelers seldom use a taxi around Essaouira, preferring to walk to and from the beach by foot. If you're pressed for time, *petits taxis* are a great way to get around the different entrance points of the medina, with most trips costing 15-20Dh. Otherwise, Essaouira is a place for walkers. It is relatively flat without any discernible hills, though sometimes along the beach the wind will pick up and blow sand around. Be sure to bring something to cover your face, perhaps one of those blue Toureg wraps, as the sand can really sting.

AGADIR AND TAGHAZOUTE

Agadir is the bustling capital of

southern Morocco. It is a city of over 500,000 and one of the fastest-growing cities in Morocco. If you're looking for a traditional or authentic Moroccan experience, this is not the place. There are typically over 340 days of sunshine a year, making the vibe almost Californian, the perfect weather to enjoy the 6-kilometer-long (4-mile-long) beach. This used to be one of the favorite cities of King Mohammed VI, who came here occasionally to jet ski. The extra attention from the king shows, with new construction and a neat

HIGHLIGHTS

✪ **SUNSETS:** Curl your toes in the sand and watch the sun set from Banana Beach (page 203).

✪ **SURFING:** Ride a wave with one of Taghazoute's popular surf camps (page 203).

✪ **YOGA:** Wake up, align your chakras, and take in the sunrise while breathing in ocean air (page 204).

waterfront boulevard. These days, Europeans come to Agadir in search of sun. Though it has the most pleasant city beach in all of Morocco—and women travelers will be happy to sport their swimsuits without the extra attention given them in most other Moroccan cities—the tourism here has more of a packaged-holiday feel, akin to Cabo San Lucas in Mexico or Majorca in Spain.

Located just a short 20-minute drive north of Agadir, Taghazoute (often: Taghazout) is a fast-growing little village that hugs the Atlantic coastline and, like its big sister to the south, has sunny weather basically year round. Since 2015 or so, the stretch of beach just south of Taghazoute has been under development. This once barren beach is now a haven of beach resorts, somewhat reminiscent of resorts found on Hawaii or the Canary Islands, the evident overspill of Agadir. Though Taghazoute is already seeing a lot of growth from these developments, its heart is still a fisher and surfer town, always in tune with the waves.

Surfers from around Europe, plus a few in-the-know Australians, Canadians, and Americans, make their way here to catch a wave, making Taghazoute a surprisingly international destination with a super-chill beachside vibe. This is a cheaper, more laid-back alternative to Agadir, with a number of yoga and surf retreats becoming increasingly popular. Taghazoute has become a great place to unwind, catch a wave, and meet up with people from around the world. A word of warning for beachgoers: The beach right next to town with the fishing boats is generally not the cleanest. It's better to head out to the adjacent Banana Beach, just south of town near the resorts.

ORIENTATION

Taghazoute and Agadir lie southwest of Marrakesh via the tolled A7 autoroute. The two are within a 30-minute drive (12km/8mi) of one another on the N1 road, which hugs the Atlantic Coast, with Taghazoute to the north.

AGADIR

Most of the restaurants, hotels, and nightlife hug the stretch of beach south of the port. This neighborhood is aptly named **Secteur Touristique** and sports the wide, wonderful Rue la Plage, a largely pedestrian-only boulevard that is lit up at night with restaurants and pleasant cafés. The **port** is a lively diversion around 10am and just

Agadir and Taghazoute

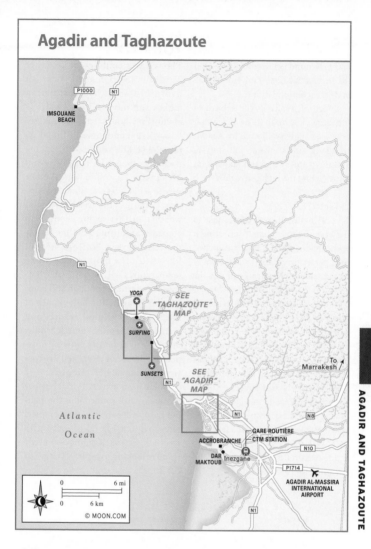

before nightfall when fishermen bring in the fresh catch.

South of the Secteur Touristique, following either Boulevard de l'Oued Sous or Boulevard du 20 Août, is the **Founty** neighborhood, which has several large beachfront hotels and all-inclusive resorts. Much of the rest of Agadir spreads inland and is largely referred to as **Nouveau Talborjt** (New

Fortress or New City), though in reality it is several distinct neighborhoods. **Abattoir** continues on the other side of the Avenue Hassan II from the beach, along Avenue Abderrahim Bouabid, and hosts the largest daily souk in the region, **Souk el Had,** as well as the *gare routière* for *grands taxis* and buses. **Boutchakat,** also on the east side of Avenue Hassan II, north of Abattoir, has several eateries as well as the Catholic Church of Saint Anne. Around here you will also find the Industrial Zone and most of the budget accommodations.

South of Agadir is the suburb of Inezgane, a town in its own right but now seemingly swallowed by Agadir. Inezgane offers several golf courses and the primary bus and taxi station for traveling through the region.

TAGHAZOUTE

The N1 national road passes just to the east of Taghazoute, connecting it with Agadir, while a small, unnamed road passes through the small town of Taghazoute itself. Locals call this the "Road to Essaouira." This is the major artery and connects with the N1 to the north and south of Taghazoute at well-marked roundabouts. From this road are a few smaller turnoffs, though most of the accommodations and restaurants are easily found along this main strip. There is a beach just outside of town, Taghazoute Beach, used by local fishermen. This is usually not the cleanest beach. Banana Beach, just a few minutes' walk to the south, on the way to the new resorts, is typically cleaner and friendlier for beach activities.

PLANNING YOUR TIME

Though you could come to either Agadir or Taghazoute for a day, an overnight in either destination makes the most sense. Agadir is about three hours from Marrakesh, with Taghazoute an additional 30 minutes (23km/14mi) north, making it a bit of a long drive to go there and back in one day. You'll want to make sure to see at least one sunset or sunrise. Because of the great year-round weather in this region, you could consider an outing here no matter the time of year. Wintertime will likely see a few more storms, while temperatures will be noticeably hotter in the summer, though still comfortable. During the holy month of Ramadan, nearly all resorts and restaurants keep the same schedule, making this region an enticing prospect for those not interested in experiencing Ramadan in Morocco.

There is an international airport in Agadir with connections throughout Europe. It can make a lot of travel sense to fly into Marrakesh and catch a return flight from Agadir, particularly if you're looking to explore Morocco's coastline.

Itinerary Idea

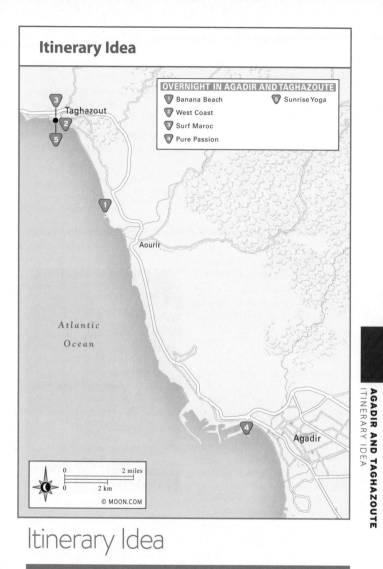

Itinerary Idea

OVERNIGHT IN AGADIR AND TAGHAZOUTE

1 After arriving in Taghazoute, drop off your bags at your accommodation, change into your swimsuit, and head straight out to **Banana Beach** to enjoy the rest of the morning.

2 For lunch, head to **West Coast** for a deliciously healthy poke bowl.

3 In the afternoon, head back to the beach for a surf lesson at **Surf Maroc.**

4 Tuck in for some fine sunset dining at **Pure Passion** in nearby Agadir. Consider a night cap on the rooftop terrace before heading to bed.

5 The next morning, wake up early for some **sunrise yoga,** and head back to Surf Maroc to take advantage of their excellent café before hitting the road back to Marrakesh.

Agadir

SIGHTS

There are few buildings or sights of cultural or historic importance in Agadir. Most people come for the long, gorgeous stretch of beach, the sunny weather, and the nightlife.

KASBAH

on the tall north hill 7km outside of the city center; free

There isn't much left of Moulay Abdallah al-Ghalib's old kasbah, but there are some outstanding views over Agadir. The old fortified city is best reached by taxi (20-30Dh or more, depending on how well you can bargain and if the taxi will wait for you to descend), though it is possible to walk to the top of the steep hill. The fortress itself was constructed around 1570 and well situated to protect the harbor, keep watch over the territory, and keep the granary stores. A first earthquake destroyed the city in 1731. The Dutch helped to rebuild, and because of this the inscription that appears under the kasbah gate reads in Arabic and Dutch: "Fear and honor your king." Now,

A shoemaker plies his trade in a market in Agadir.

numerous street vendors and faux guides will try to direct your attention here, for a price. It might be worth paying 40-50Dh to discover a bit more about the history of this kasbah and see the fault line of the Great Leap Day Earthquake of 1960. Camels are available for a short ride and photo op (20-50Dh).

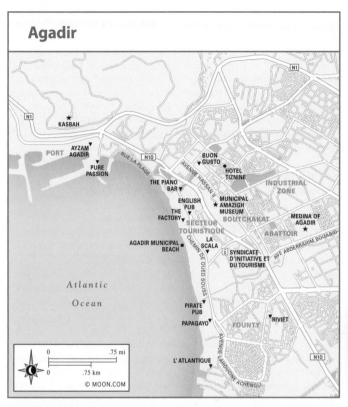

Agadir

KASBAH

PORT

AYZAM AGADIR

PURE PASSION

N1

N10

RUE LA PLAGE

AVENUE HASSAN II

BUON GUSTO

HOTEL TIZNINE

THE PIANO BAR

ENGLISH PUB

THE FACTORY

SECTEUR TOURISTIQUE

MUNICIPAL AMAZIGH MUSEUM

BOUTCHAKAT

INDUSTRIAL ZONE

MEDINA OF AGADIR

ABATTOIR

AGADIR MUNICIPAL BEACH

CHEMIN DE OUED SOUSS

LA SCALA

SYNDICATE D'INITIATIVE ET DU TOURISME

AVE ABDERRAHIM BOUABID

Atlantic

Ocean

PIRATE PUB

PAPAGAYO

FOUNTY

RIVIET

AVENUE AHROUINE ACHENGLI

L'ATLANTIQUE

N10

0   .75 mi
0   .75 km

© MOON.COM

MUNICIPAL AMAZIGH MUSEUM

Ave. Hassan II, Passage Aït Souss; tel. 0528/821 632; Mon.-Sat. 9:30am-1pm and 2pm-5:30pm; 20Dh

Dive into the history of the region at the Municipal Amazigh Museum (Musée Municipal du Patrimoine Amazighe), which has a small collection of Amazigh wood, pottery, and carpets from the Souss, Massa, and Draa regions that reveal the aspects of daily life in these environs just around Agadir. Myriad displays show the art of spinning pottery, weaving carpets, and carving the intricate wood designs seen all around. There are some English materials available, though the vast majority is in French and Arabic.

Several eateries nearby make this an attractive stop to escape the heat, learn about the region, and then stop for lunch.

MEDINA OF AGADIR

Aéroport Militaire Bensergao; tel. 0528/280 253 or 0661/396 261; daily 9am-6pm; 40Dh

The Medina of Agadir hosts a variety of artisans. Many of them take Tuesday off, though the medina is still open. Here you can find quality Moroccan slippers, jewelry, textiles, mosaic tables, and carved wood as well as a café where you can rest your feet. While you're there, check out Chez Azzab Med's shop (#Z1-57, tel. 0667/019 115). He has a great selection of silver jewelry for good prices, though you can always try to bargain down a bit. The shopping atmosphere is more laid-back than elsewhere in Morocco and, as far as replica outdoor medinas go, it is something of a novelty. Taxis will bring you from downtown Agadir (50Dh), though you might want to pay extra to have them wait for you, as finding a ride to leave can be a hassle.

BEACHES

The reason why Agadir is arguably the most touristed city in Morocco begins and ends pretty much at the **beachfront** and its long beachfront promenade. Moroccans and Europeans flock here for the long stretch of beach and the year-round sun. This long promenade, well-lit at night and full of people from around the world, is perhaps the best developed stretch of beach in Morocco. You can ride a camel along the beach, relax beneath a sunshade on a rented beach chair sipping on a cocktail, and then take in the sunset. Many of the younger local boys come out to play soccer on stretches of the beach, and women and men jog and power-walk at the edge of the surf. Farther out in the ocean, beginning and more experienced surfers try to catch waves, and children splash in the warm water, with trained lifeguards just a shout away throughout the daytime. Trade in your shoes for flip-flops for a day or, if it suits you, just go barefoot and sink your toes deep in the warm sand. This is as Hawaii as Morocco gets.

AGADIR MUNICIPAL BEACH

One of Morocco's nicest municipal beaches is in the resort town of Agadir and has a 5-kilometer (3-mile) stretch of sand that rivals the best beaches of San Diego. Though there is some surf, this is more a beach for sunbathing, swimming, and sand sports. You'll likely want to drive here (20min from Taghazoute). Beach chairs and umbrellas are for rent at a reasonable cost all along the beach. You could dine at any one of the beachfront restaurants, head just off the beach to quench your thirst at the **English Pub,** or dig in with the locals at a fish shack just off the port.

SPORTS AND RECREATION

TREE CLIMBING
Accrobranche

N1 at Ave. de l'Embouchure de l'Oued Souss; tel. 0546/153 579 or 0654/591 972; daily 9am-sunset; from 100Dh

If you fancy a climb in some trees, head to Accrobranche. Located in the Founty neighborhood near the golf courses, this challenging rope course will take you into the trees on five climbs over suspended rope bridges and up into the foliage. Each climb seems to be more daunting than the last. Staff are all well trained and the equipment is kept up to date. This is popular for a half-day excursion with children and wannabe children.

CAMEL TREKKING

Those who can't resist the idea of taking a camel ride have a few options around town. Atop the hill at the north end of the town at the old kasbah are usually several camels you can take for a short jaunt and photo op (20-50Dh), though the more interesting option is to book a two-hour camel tour that will take you completely around Agadir, past the Royal Palace, through Bird Valley, and down to the beach just in time for sunset. Two hours on a camel will leave you sore, perhaps just in time for that hammam and massage you've been putting off.

For a more bespoke, private experience, contact **Amodou Cheval** (tel. 0670/341 510, http://amodoucheval. com, 300Dh).

FOOD

There are plenty of restaurant options in Agadir that diverge from traditional Moroccan cuisine. Here you'll be able to find everything from sushi to French haute cuisine. After a long voyage through Morocco dominated by tajines and heaping plates of couscous, the variety is greatly appreciated. From snack stands to five-star meals, there is something for every price range.

Seafood lovers should stop by the fishing port and its barbecues, open all day long. Sit and enjoy a freshly grilled seafood lunch with Moroccan round bread, olives, and mint tea for 40Dh. What's served is what has been caught that day. Be careful of the touts, though. They will try to steer you toward options where you might spend 3-4 times as much.

SEAFOOD
Ayzam Agadir
Agadir port; tel. 0528/380 838; Sun.-Fri. 11:30am-10:30pm, Sat. 11:30am-11pm; 50Dh
A reliable option in the port is Ayzam Agadir for no-nonsense grilled fish and fried calamari. A fantastic place for families with young kids, as the large fish tanks and constant activity tend to keep the kids occupied. Before or after lunch, make your way down the slipway and check out the boats. The cacophony is half of the fun of eating at the port.

L'Atlantique
Sofitel Agadir Thalassa Hotel, Baie des Palmiers; tel. 0528/849 200 or 0528/388 000; Mon.-Fri. 11:30am-2pm and 7pm-11pm; 450Dh
L'Atlantique is perhaps the best seafood restaurant around. The tables are all lit by chandeliers with hanging glass bobbles reminiscent of Chihuly's work. Service is immaculate, as are the white linens, outdoor lounge, and open grill. Food is sourced daily from the local catch, and the menu includes many gluten-free dishes. Those not wanting cigarette smoke interfering with their meal are advised to dine outside.

ASIAN FUSION
Riviet
28 Residence Khalij Annakhil; tel. 0528/232 233, www.riviet.ma; daily 11am-11pm; 90Dh
There are a few Thai, Chinese, and Japanese restaurants around Agadir. Riviet is largely a sushi house, though some Thai-style noodles and soups are also available. The decor inside is self-styled Asian—clean lines with lots of red and black, and Shanghai fonts decorating the walls. If you're craving some sushi, dive in here for the *maki* rolls and sashimi. You won't be disappointed, except maybe by the service. It can be a little slow, even for Morocco. Free delivery is available anywhere in Agadir, making a night in or sushi on your beachside patio a definite possibility.

ITALIAN
✪ Buon Gusto
42 Galerie Faiz, Pl. Cinema Rialto; tel. 0528/844 861; daily 11:30am-midnight; 70Dh
The super-popular Buon Gusto is known around town for its delicious wood-fired pizzas. The atmosphere is cozy (it's a pretty small restaurant), though bright and modern, while the little plants dotting the alleyway

give it a homey touch, but you're really coming here for the Napoli pizza. Takeaway is available. When you need to get your Italian on or quiet the kids down, head here. The free garlic bread is a nice touch.

STEAKHOUSES
✪ Pure Passion
Complexe Marina; tel. 0528/840 120; noon-3pm and 7pm-11pm; 300Dh

If upscale is your thing, make a beeline for Pure Passion, with fantastic views over the bay and marina, attentive staff, chefs that prepare your filet perfectly to instruction, and generous portions. From the amuse-bouche through courses of succulent crab croquettes, lamb with honey and thyme sauce, buttery monkfish, or perhaps the chateaubriand, your senses will be swimming, which seems appropriate given the location.

La Scala
Rue de l'Oued Souss, Complexe Tamlelt; tel. 0528/846 773; Tues.-Sun. noon-3pm and 7pm-midnight; 250Dh

For a candlelit dinner, think about heading to La Scala. The service is top-notch and the setting is charming, with an outdoor patio that makes the most of its location away from the beach, with warm lighting that sets the mood for a little romance under the stars. If it's too cold out for the patio, come early to avoid the possibility of a cigarette-smoking neighbor. The menu features some of the best steaks in the city as well as scallops in a rich Taliouine saffron sauce.

BARS AND NIGHTLIFE

Agadir is famed for its nightlife, and it's easy to see why. Europeans flock here for the summer sun, often dancing well into the morning hours.

Most nightclubs are open year-round every night starting around 10pm or 11pm, though the party often doesn't get started until well after midnight. Hours change slightly according to season, as does the cover charge. Gentlemen can expect to pay 100-200Dh for a cover charge, while ladies often get in free. Dress codes are laid-back, as is the general atmosphere.

Singles should be wary. The club scene is fertile ground for Agadir's prostitutes, both female and male. Sex tourism, unfortunately, is one of the dark draws for many Europeans and Middle Easterners to this part of Morocco.

Many of the midrange hotels have their own nightclubs, an option for those not wanting to venture far from home or deal with late-night taxis. It's not unusual to walk from club to club looking for the right scene for the night. Most of them are within the Secteur Touristique, making this a fun, easy late-night parade with the possibility to unwind on the beach and catch a sunrise after dancing the night away.

If low-key is more your thing than a booming club scene, there are a few bars to choose from, but be warned: drinking in Morocco is not cheap. Most drinks run 40-80Dh. The bars tend to be fairly quiet in the off-season, though still busy during the weekends and holidays. Most large hotels have full bars with large terraces to lounge on and enjoy a tequila sunrise at sunset.

Papagayo
Chemin des Dune; tel. 0528/845 400; 10pm-late; drinks about 100Dh

This long-standing favorite often has international DJs spinning the latest mixes from Europe, adding to the late-night crazy vibe of this 1,500-person club. You would be forgiven if you thought you were spending your night starring in a music video. Hired dancers populate the club most nights, gyrating and grinding to the newest beats while a veritable techno-laser show blazes across the dance floor. Like all nightclubs, a night out at Papagayo comes at a price. Drinks are typically 100Dh, so pace yourself.

The Factory

Hotel Tafoukt, Blvd. du 20 Août, across from the English Pub; tel. 0528/221 314; www.lafactory.ma; 10pm-late; drinks about 100Dh

The Factory is a popular alternative to Papagayo, with specialized nights in techno, house, funk, and trance, with the occasional Moroccan Chaabi music thrown in just for local flavor. The atmosphere here is more of a nightclub feel than a music video, with fewer of the more undesirable elements and with more students studying abroad and young people on vacation having fun. Ladies' night is typically a great deal, with ladies getting free entry and free drinks starting at midnight.

English Pub

Blvd. du 20 Août; tel. 0528/847 390; daily noon-1am

Of the local bars, the best of the bunch is the English Pub, which shows live sports, serves draft beer, and has karaoke every night. The pub food on offer, including English-style fish-and-chips (120Dh), hits the spot after a long night out. The variety of vegetarian-friendly options is attractive, and the large terrace is great for mingling and people-watching. Beers are a bit more expensive than at some other bars

around town, though the atmosphere is a little less divey.

Pirate Pub

4 Front de mer; tel. 0661/265 563; daily noon-1am

To sip on some suds and maybe snack while enjoying the beach, the Pirate Pub fits the bill nicely. With friendly service right along the beachfront and Moroccan and pub-style classics, this is one of the new favorites for those looking to chillax. The inside can get pretty smoky rather quickly and is mostly for drinking. Outside, just a few yards away from the beach, is where it's at.

The Piano Bar

Blvd. du 20 Août; tel. 0618/774 246; daily noon-2am; drinks about 100Dh

Women traveling alone looking to unwind and not be hassled should consider the Piano Bar in the Anezi Tower Hotel. The atmosphere includes lounge-style piano music (of course), friendly staff, and distance from the sport-fanatic crowd that seems to saturate other bars. Drinks are decently priced and competently cocktailed. Leather chairs and ornate cedarwood ceilings add to the Rick's Café vibe of this place. The outdoor pool makes for wonderful outdoor seating if there are too many smokers inside.

ACCOMMODATIONS

UNDER 400DH

Most of the real budget options in Agadir are well away from the beach and littered throughout the new city.

✪ Hotel Tiznine

3 Rue Drarga; tel. 0528/843 925; 90Dh d

Hotel Tiznine in Nouveau Talborjt is refreshingly nonsmoking. Rooms are clean, though sterile, with drab tile work and no real charm to speak of. However, for the price, this is unbeatable. There are shared bathrooms (or you can ask for a room with an en suite bathroom for a bit more), and guests staying for longer periods are granted access to the upstairs kitchen. There's no breakfast served, though there are plenty of spots nearby to grab a good breakfast.

OVER 800DH

Several large resort hotels in Agadir are along the beachfront and in the Founty district, each a true five-star experience, with custom architecture, cozy beds, and service befitting the cost. For those in search of a "regular" high-end hotel, these are worth looking into, particularly online as you can find some good deals, though they're soulless and lacking any sort of local charm.

✪ Dar Maktoub

Chemin l'Oued Souss, Founty; tel. 0528/337 500; www.darmaktoub.com; 900Dh d

If you're looking for a real retreat away from the resort crowds, head to Dar Maktoub, in the Founty neighborhood just a few minutes south of the Secteur Touristique of Agadir, nestled between golf courses. This sprawling guesthouse is tucked away into well-manicured grounds, replete with bougainvillea, aloe, daisies, and hundreds of other plants, and features a private pool, restaurant, Wi-Fi, and friendly staff that will see to your needs. The rooms all feature top-of-the-line beds and cozy linens with plenty of charm. Breakfast is included, and other meals are available on demand. Guests will likely want to have their own transportation to reach the nearby beaches, restaurants, and other sites and activities around the city, though taxis are always available and can be arranged by the guesthouse staff.

INFORMATION AND SERVICES

British travelers should contact their consulate in Agadir (www.british-consulate.net/uk/United-Kingdom-Consular-Assistance-Agadir, tel. 0528/841 219) for any emergencies.

Syndicate d'Initiative et du Tourisme

Blvd. Mohammed V; tel. 0528/840 307; www.visitagadir.com; daily 10am-5pm

For updated information on any local performing arts, including plays, concerts, and dance performances, check with the Syndicate d'Initiative et du Tourisme. There is information online and at the tourism office about local pharmacies, doctors, and bus schedules, plus a handy map of Agadir, though the office itself is often closed.

Taghazoute

Taghazoute is perhaps the most beach-friendly environ in all of Morocco, making it equally comfortable for men and women.

BEACHES

TAGHAZOUTE BEACH

This easy-to-access beach is downhill from town. Distinguished by its continued use of fishermen and their dinghy boats, this can be an extremely photogenic location, though better beach activities are found on other nearby beaches.

a quiet moment on Taghazoute Beach

⍟ BANANA BEACH

Popularized a bit with the nearby resorts, this strip of beach guarantees surfable swells pretty much every day of the year. The bay is surrounded by a tall rockface, which protects it from a lot of the stronger winds that can occasionally cut through the area. For most beachgoers, this is the beach to plant your parasol. You can walk to Banana Beach by a quick climb over the rocks at the south edge of Taghazoute Beach or cut through the south end of town. It's a 10-minute walk from the center

of Taghazoute. For lunch, you could consider packing a picnic or heading up to the **Sol House Resort** for lunch by the pool.

IMSOUANE BEACH

Farther up the coastline, heading north toward Essaouira, is the little fishing village of **Imsouane** (1.5hr, 80km from Taghazoute). This is another surfer spot, though out of the way for travelers without a car. Other than surfing and lounging on the beach, there's not much else to do. This was once an old Amazigh fishing village, and fishing still is an important part of the local economy, though the numerous surf shops, restaurants, and cafés catering to surfers attest to the growth of surfing tourism.

⍟ WINDSURFING, KITESURFING, AND SURFING

Surf Maroc

Centre Ville; tel. 0528/200 230;
www.surfmaroc.com; lessons from 250Dh,
equipment rental from 200Dh

For English speakers, Surf Maroc

Taghazoute is Morocco's surf capital.

Imsouane Beach, a surfer's dream

is perhaps the best all-around option around Taghazoute. They have a great selection of well-kept boards and offer lessons for all levels. They can also arrange surf trips up and down the coastline and generally know the best surf spots on any given day. Solo female travelers or small groups of women should check out the girls-only surf program. The atmosphere is all surfer-friendly, with people helping each other out to give rides up and down the coastline and catch waves together, no matter the nationality. Two-hour coaching sessions start at 250Dh and include coach, board, and wetsuit. Additional (more expensive) options include transportation to other beaches as well as lunch. Board and wetsuit rental is 200Dh a day.

Surf Camp Taghazout

Centre Ville; tel. 0665/611 288;
www.surfcamptaghazout.com; lessons
from 300Dh, retreats from 450Dh
If you are planning your surfing trip ahead of time, Surf Camp Taghazout offers a full range of services and can not only help with surfing equipment and lessons but also has all-inclusive surfing retreats from the bargain-basement price of 450Dh, including accommodations, wetsuits, boards, meals, yoga classes, and surf instruction, as well as trips around the area and pickup from the Agadir *gare routière*.

✪ YOGA

Amouage

Centre Ville, on the main road; https://
surfmaroc.com/en/location/amouage; 120Dh
per class, packages available
Though it seems like most accommodations in Taghazoute have caught on to the fact that many people would like yoga classes, the classes at Amouage, with the perfect setting on the rooftop garden, overlooking the Atlantic Ocean, is still the bar to which other places aspire. Because of this, the evening classes can fill up quickly. For the absolute best yoga experience, book the sunrise yoga with fewer participants. The instructors all speak excellent English.

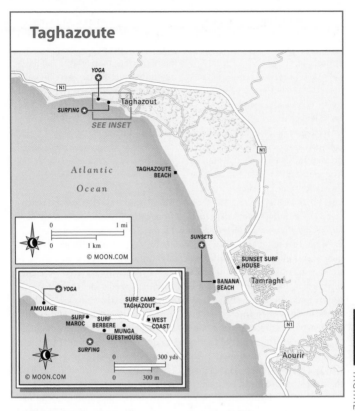

Taghazoute

YOGA

N1

SURFING

Taghazout

SEE INSET

Atlantic
Ocean

TAGHAZOUTE
BEACH

N1

0   1 mi
0   1 km
© MOON.COM

SUNSETS

SUNSET SURF
HOUSE

BANANA
BEACH

Tamraght

N1

Aourir

Inset:

YOGA

AMOUAGE

SURF CAMP
TAGHAZOUT

SURF
MAROC

SURF
BERBERE

MUNGA
GUESTHOUSE

WEST
COAST

SURFING

0   300 yds
0   300 m
© MOON.COM

FOOD AND ACCOMMODATIONS

There are a number of *grillades* and snack shops lining the main street, alongside more surf shops than you can count. These can do in a pinch, but the real value is in the hotels. Each of them have an in-house café or restaurant, generally offering up some fantastic fare, much of it more sensitive than other places in Morocco to food allergies or preferences. Gluten-free, vegan, and vegetarian are par for the course. For breakfast, don't shy away from asking for that avocado toast you know you've been craving. Many of the accommodations in Taghazoute have excellent on-site restaurants.

West Coast

Centre Ville, on the main road; tel. 0618/458 129; Thurs.-Tues. 10am-10pm; 100Dh

You know that poke bowl you've been craving? This is the place to get it. This charming, ramshackle beach café features a light, fresh menu full of quinoa goodness. The service is friendly to a fault, with Khadija and the rest of her staff happy to field whatever request or question you might have. The menu is seasonal, highlighting lots of local greens, fruit, and nuts, making it a fantastic stop for vegans, vegetarians, or gluten-free eaters. You can make your own poke bowl from the assortment of ingredients or opt for one on the menu. After

205

a slog of heavy Moroccan eating, this can lighten your load considerably.

Amouage

Centre Ville, on the main road; tel. 0622/082 726 or 0658/60 065; https://surfmaroc. com/en/location/amouage; 800Dh

For a longer sunny getaway, travelers interested in bespoke customized accommodations and experiences would do well to take a look at Amouage. The specialty of this stylish designer-lover's boutique hotel lies in the week-long itineraries it puts together for its clients. Beginning surfers, in particular, can benefit tremendously from the daily instruction of Mehdi, the kind, patient surf guru. Yogis can meditate to their chakras' content on the rooftop garden floor, while the spacious rooms make the most of the ocean views, as does the infinity pool. For breakfast and dinner, guests can eat together on sharing tables to participate in the relaxed communal vibe that is a different sort of experience than the standard hotel. Each day of the week offers a different set menu with a selection of dishes, though they can cater to any dietary needs. The restaurant is only for guests of Amouage.

Sunset Surf House

Centre Ville, on the main road; tel. 0622/082 726 or 0658/60 065; https://sunsetsurfhouse.com; email: info@ sunsetsurfhouse.com; restaurant open daily 9am-10pm; 120Dh, 150Dh dorm-style bed

Perhaps the best cheeseburger in town, which might be just the thing after a long day out on the water while you're sipping on some suds on the rooftop terrace. Like the other properties, yoga and surf instruction are available in a variety of packages. This is more for the hostel crowd and for students

traveling on a budget. Bathrooms are shared. A clean kitchen is available to make your meals, and the dorms are more spacious than others. You'll feel the difference, particularly if you're coming from Marrakesh. Popular with European surfers.

✪ Surf Maroc

Centre Ville, on the main road overlooking the water; tel. 0528/200 230; http://surfmaroc.com; daily 9am-7pm; café 120Dh, 450Dh d

Travelers interested in a good beachfront café will want to check out Surf Maroc. This is a favorite spot for surfers to stay as well as other travelers looking for clean, friendly accommodations with waterfront views. On offer are surf classes and oceanfront yoga. Surf rentals are available on-site. In addition to the simple hotel rooms, private seaside villas are available for around 1,000Dh a night. For groups splitting costs, this is a good option. That said, the café is the real draw, with its wide oceanside windows, menu full of smoothies (try the vitamin booster with fresh-squeezed orange juice and carrots), and fresh catches coming in from the fishermen below. The free Wi-Fi is cool, but the fact they are fighting against plastic waste and have a clean on-site water tap is perhaps cooler.

Surf Maroc has been expanding in recent years, opening more amazing properties, from the villas mentioned above to Amouage, their more upscale, yoga-focused boutique hotel. On their website, this property, their first, is now being referred to as "Taghazoute Villa," but in real life, you'll still see "Surf Maroc" written on the outside wall. Regardless of what you call it, it's a wonderful place to stay in Taghazoute.

Surf Berbere

Centre Ville, on the main road overlooking the water; tel. 0528/200 290; 200Dh dorm-style bed

Similar but a bit rougher around the edges is Surf Berbere. The rooms are no-frills, though the views out over the water are breathtaking. It's a good option for students and backpackers, though there are cheaper options farther into town, off the water. The only option is sleeping in a room with eight bunk beds, which can be a way to cut down on costs. This might be attractive for some, though still not as inexpensive as one might imagine. The surf camp feel is intoxicating for those who have a love for the water. Rooms include breakfast.

✪ Munga Guesthouse

17 Rue Ilwite; tel. 0528/200 202 or 0698/680 680; www.mungaguesthouse. com; 1,000Dh d

Perfectly funky, Munga is something of a mix between a traditional B&B and cutting-edge art hotel. None of the 15 rooms or any of the common spaces are alike. Here, it's all salvaged wood and recycled materials. Multiple terraces offer up some of the best sunset viewing along the coast. The overall vibe is cozy, chic, arty, and chill. If you're looking to spend some time getting away from it all, this is the sort of getaway experience you imagine. Come for the surf and sun, but stay for the people. Not all rooms have views, so be sure to request a room with a view overlooking the water (preferably with a private balcony, of course). You'll find two dining options. Downstairs is a bit more simple and good for a quick catch of the day, though you'll want to make your way upstairs for rooftop dining and a glass of white to sip with your sunset. If you're really splurging, go for the magnum suite. It's a real treat for a real getaway.

INFORMATION AND SERVICES

Cafe Mouja in Surf Maroc is the best spot for free Wi-Fi and to meet locals and other travelers.

Surfers will want to check out www.surf-forecast.com before arrival to find the best waves in the region, though you can rely on the local hotels as they are all up-to-date with local conditions. If you're going out surfing by yourself, it's a good idea to let people know of your whereabouts, just in case.

For emergencies, you can contact the fire department or ambulance by dialing 150 from any Moroccan phone, while the police can be reached at 190.

Transportation

Agadir and Taghazoute are 20 minutes away from each other by car.

GETTING THERE

AGADIR

By Car

By car, Agadir is easily reached via National Road 1 (N1) from Marrakesh (243km/151mi, 2.5hr).

The roads are pleasant to drive, though extreme caution should be used when driving at night.

By Bus

The primary gare routière is in Inezgane, just south of Agadir hugging the N1. Here, you can also find the CTM station (94 Ave. Mokhtar Soussi). There is another *gare routière* across the street from Souk el-Had in Agadir with a few *grands taxis* and local buses, though it is a bit far from the beach and run-down. However, if you're commuting to or from Taghazoute, this station can make the most sense. From either station, take a *petit taxi* into town (around 20Dh).

CTM (tel. 0800/0900 30, www.ctm.ma) runs buses from here to Marrakesh (3hr, 16 daily, 120Dh).

Supratours (tel. 0524/888 566 or 0524/885 632, www.oncf.ma) operates the buses affiliated with the national train line, ONCF. Buses run from the Marrakesh train station to Agadir (3hr, 12 daily, 120Dh) and are the most convenient way to get from Marrakesh to Agadir for those traveling by train.

By Plane

Many direct flights arrive from Europe to the Agadir Al-Massira International Airport (20km/14mi east of Agadir, tel. 0528/839 112, www.agadir-airport.com). From the airport you can take a *grand taxi* directly to your hotel (30min, 220Dh, entire taxi only). Those wanting to skip Agadir could arrive at the airport and head directly for Taghazoute.

TAGHAZOUTE
By Car

From Marrakesh (3.5hrs, 281km/175mi), you should consider a rental car, though this isn't absolutely necessary. The drive is easy enough from Marrakesh. You follow the A7 tolled freeway toward Agadir. In Agadir, you turn north on the N1 following the signs for Taghazoute, about 20 minutes away. You will find plenty of street parking in Taghazoute.

By *Grand Taxi*

From Agadir, *grands taxis* run back and forth to Taghazoute (20min, 20km/12mi, 15Dh).

GETTING AROUND
AGADIR

The ubiquitous *petits taxis* are the choice of travel for most getting around the city. Taxis are friendly and metered, and drivers know most of the major hotels and restaurants, but it is always good to have a map (either on your phone or paper) to show the driver. An average taxi ride will cost 7-20Dh, a relative steal. Otherwise, with wide sidewalks, pedestrian-friendly boulevards, and year-round sun, Agadir is one of the more pleasant cities to walk around.

TAGHAZOUTE

Once in town, all you'll need are flip-flops, a bathing suit, and a towel.

OUARZAZATE AND AÏT BEN HADDOU

Originally built by the French
during the protectorate era in 1928 as a military installation, Ouarzazate serves as the gateway to the desert for most travelers today. Ouarzazate comes from the Tashelhit expression *aourz nfzat,* or "ankle of Zat Mountain." Located where the Ouarzazate and Dades Rivers join to form the head of the Draa River, Ouarzazate has become the chief town and administrative capital of the region. The massive production of *Lawrence of Arabia* in the 1960s gave rise to the film studios here and Ouarzazate's new nickname, the

HIGHLIGHTS

⭐ **ATLAS FILM STUDIOS:** Ouarzazate is known as the "Hollywood of Africa" for good reason, and if you can only visit one studio, make it this one, which was the backdrop for many an epic (page 212).

⭐ **AÏT BEN HADDOU:** This quintessential kasbah should be on every traveler's bucket list (page 215).

⭐ **GETTING PAMPERED IN A HAMMAM:** Whether splurging on a spa worthy of the rich and famous or mingling with locals in the public bath, a hammam is the best way to wash off the dust of the desert (page 216).

"Hollywood of Africa." Many movies and TV series are shot here throughout the year, giving Ouarzazate a particular buzz of big-name directors, busy camera crews, and movie stars.

ORIENTATION

The Taourirt Kasbah has been given some restoration efforts by UNESCO, and next to it lies a relatively unexplored old medina. There are a few bazaars in the medina, along with cafés and *riads*. The small Cinema Museum of Ouarzazate and the Ensemble Artisanal are across the street from the kasbah. Otherwise, there are the two movie studios (Atlas and CLA) along the road to Marrakesh. Aït Ben Haddou is just over 30 kilometers (20mi) west of the town. Lodging is possible in the *ksar,* and can be a nice alternative from a city—plus, you'll be treated to incredible sunrises.

PLANNING YOUR TIME

One day in Ouarzazate is enough for most travelers before continuing on to the region's more scenic locations, including the numerous palm groves, ancient kasbahs, winding gorges, villages constructed from ocher-colored earth, and the majestic Sahara Desert. Most travelers will want to make their way to nearby Aït Ben Haddou, the most interesting *ksar* (connected series of fortresses) in the area, to wander around and take photos for a half day at least. You could consider Aït Ben Haddou and Ouarzazate as an overnight trip from Marrakesh without continuing to the Sahara. However, once you've made it this far, you'll likely feel the irresistible pull of the great sand sea. Thus, this stop is best seen as a layover between Marrakesh and the desert.

Itinerary Idea

OVERNIGHT IN OUARZAZATE

1 Leave from Marrakesh after breakfast to arrive in Ouarzazate by lunchtime for a meal at **Accord Majeur,** keeping an eye out for Hollywood royalty.

2 In the afternoon, tour **Atlas** and **CLA Film Studios** and learn all about films shot here.

3 Explore the mazelike **Taourirt Kasbah,** built in the 19th century.

4 Head over to browse the local goods and handicrafts on sale at **Ensemble Artisanal.**

5 Have dinner at **Le Petit Riad** before tucking in for the night.

6 The next day, enjoy your breakfast by the Le Petit Riad's pool and, if time allows, take a dip. Head to the **Aït Ben Haddou** kasbah and spend the morning discovering this ancient city. Lunch in one of the cafés at the kasbah before driving back over the pass to Marrakesh.

downtown Ouarzazate looking toward the High Atlas Mountains

Ouarzazate and Aït Ben Haddou

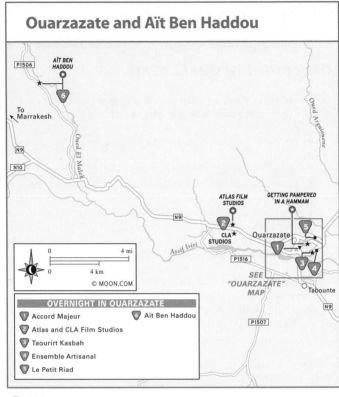

OVERNIGHT IN OUARZAZATE

1. Accord Majeur
2. Atlas and CLA Film Studios
3. Taourirt Kasbah
4. Ensemble Artisanal
5. Le Petit Riad
6. Aït Ben Haddou

© MOON.COM

Sights

✪ ATLAS FILM STUDIOS

Rte. de Marrakesh Tamassinte;
tel. 0524/882 166; Oct.-Feb. daily
8:15am-5:45pm, Mar.-Sept. daily
8:15am-6:45pm; adult 50Dh, child 40Dh

If you're going to visit one studio, Atlas Film Studios is the one. Movie sets here have been used for films such as *Gladiator, King Tut, Cleopatra,* and *Exodus.* Tours, approximately one hour, are available in English, though not really necessary. The many highlights for film buffs include the set of "old Tangier," used for many medina shots in movies, and the gaudy Egyptian throne room used in *Asterix & Obelix.* Tours are not usually available during film shoots. In the distance from the back lot, you can see the looming castle structure from nearby CLA Studios set against the snowcapped backdrop of the High Atlas. Be sure to have your camera ready. Action!

CLA STUDIOS

Rte. de Marrakesh Tamassinte;
tel. 0544/882 053; www.cla-studios.com;
daily 8am-6:30pm; adult 50Dh, child 30Dh,
under 12 free

Ouarzazate

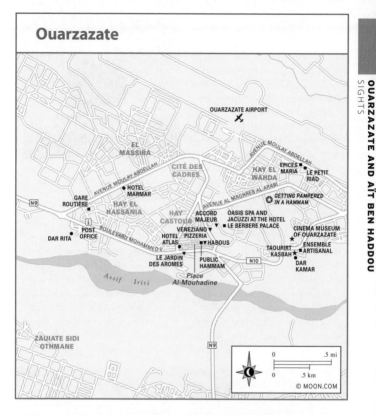

OUARZAZATE AIRPORT

AVENUE MOULAY ABDELLAH

EL MASSIRA

CITÉ DES CADRES

HAY EL WAHDA

EPICES MARIA

LE PETIT RIAD

AVENUE MOULAY ABDELLAH

GARE ROUTIÈRE

N9

HOTEL MARMAR

HAY EL HASSANIA

AVENUE AL MAGHREB AL ARABI

GETTING PAMPERED IN A HAMMAM

POST OFFICE

DAR RITA

BOULEVARD MOHAMMED V

HAY CASTOUR

ACCORD MAJEUR

VENEZIANO

HOTEL PIZZERIA ATLAS

HABOUS

OASIS SPA AND JACUZZI AT THE HOTEL LE BERBERE PALACE

CINEMA MUSEUM OF OUARZAZATE

ENSEMBLE ARTISANAL

LE JARDIN DES AROMES

PUBLIC HAMMAM

Place Al-Mouhadine

N10

TAOURIRT KASBAH

DAR KAMAR

Assif   Iriri

ZAOUIATE SIDI OTHMANE

N9

0   .5 mi
0   .5 km

© MOON.COM

The nearby CLA Studios offer a chance to visit the site of the city of Astapor from the popular *Game of Thrones* series (or if you prefer, the castle from *Kingdom of Heaven*). There are no English-language tours available. However, you do have free run of the castle and can climb up and down the vast set, examine the catapult, and picture yourself alongside your favorite Hollywood star as you act out scenes from *Troy, Gladiator, Lawrence of Arabia,* and other movies. You will want a car to take you out to the Astapor set and to the set of *Journey to Mecca,* now falling into ruin. The road is bumpy and should not be traveled if it's a rainy day unless you have four-wheel drive.

TAOURIRT KASBAH

Ave. Mohammed V; tel. 0666/940 302; daily 8am-6pm; 10Dh

The 19th-century Taourirt Kasbah has been partially renovated, though perhaps not for the better. Many rooms in the mazelike fortress of Taourirt have been reinforced with concrete and tiles not typical of the era. Still, it's worth the price of entry if this is the only kasbah you are going to see. Guides compete for customers, so you might find them fighting over you; a few speak English, and having a guide will make the tour infinitely more interesting, so it's worth hiring one. Guides will explain the history of the inner sanctum; the process of constructing the traditional *tataoui* ceiling, a sort of thrush-reinforced ceiling, still visible in some parts; and the history of the notorious Pasha of Marrakesh, El Glaoui, who had control of this region and the camel trade over the Sahara in the early part of the 20th century. The going rate for a guide is 70Dh, which will include a 30- to 60-minute tour of the kasbah and, if you choose, the small medina within the kasbah walls. If you're on the tall side, be sure to watch your head. There are numerous short ceilings that can give you a surprising bump.

CINEMA MUSEUM OF OUARZAZATE (Musée du Cinéma de Ouarzazate)

Ave. Mohammed V; tel. 0524/882 166; daily 8am-5:30pm, closed Fri. noon-2pm; 30Dh

For cinema buffs, the Cinema Museum of Ouarzazate, just across the street from the Taourirt Kasbah, is a

Ouarzazate is known as the "Hollywood of Africa" for its large movie studios and productions.

great look into the history of the various landmark movies and TV series that have been filmed in and around Ouarzazate. Discover how the local film industry began with *Lawrence of Arabia,* and learn about the progression of the industry through today and the outlook toward the future. Props from movies such as *Asterix & Obelix* and *Kingdom* can be found here. It's not nearly as interesting as a visit to

a fake Hollywood castle that has appeared in countless films

crossing the river to Aït Ben Haddou

either of the studios, but it can be a pleasant diversion in the middle of town to escape the afternoon heat.

TOP EXPERIENCE

✪ AÏT BEN HADDOU

Just 32 kilometers (20mi) west of Ouarzazate lies the *ksar* of Aït Ben Haddou, one of the most impressive in all of Morocco. If you could only see one *ksar* in Morocco, this would be the one. Set alongside a palm-lined hillside with the towering, oft snowcapped High Atlas Mountains serving as the backdrop, this crumbling series of six joined kasbahs and nearly 50 palaces has been a UNESCO World Heritage Site since 1987. Though the seasonal rains perpetually damage the buildings, the oldest of which date back to the 17th century, a nominal entrance fee to the *ksar* (10Dh) goes toward restoration efforts and maintenance.

For many years, Aït Ben Haddou was one of the great economic and cultural crossroads of the region and served travelers after their long journey through the desert along the caravan road to Marrakesh. Today, it is perhaps most famous as a filming location for a number of movies. *Gladiator, The Mummy, Kingdom of Heaven, Prince of Persia,* and many, many other movies have used Aït Ben Haddou as a setting for their sprawling epics. Its sheer size, the winding medina roads, the clay brick walls, and the lingering calm that descends on travelers once they enter the gates to the sprawling *ksar* are all part of the magic. Be sure to pack an extra battery for your camera. It's irresistible not to take as many photos as possible of this photogenic gem.

Getting across the river to the *ksar* can be a challenge for some. There are sandbags in the river, which generally runs low enough that you can step across the sandbags to the entrance. A new footbridge built farther upstream runs across to the town gate farther uphill. Those staying in the calm confines of Aït Ben Haddou should keep this in mind, as cars cannot cross, and you'll have to carry across the river whatever you don't want to leave in the car.

Across the river from the *ksar* is a newer town that has sprung up in recent years, with hotels, cafés, and shops catering to tourists.

Getting There

If you're driving to Aït Ben Haddou, head west from Ouarzazate via the N9 before following the signs for the turn-off on P1506 (30min, 32km/20mi).

Travelers without their own vehicles will have to come from Ouarzazate. The *gare routière* in Ouarzazate is just off Avenue Moulay Abdellah and is the primary hub for *grands taxis* and buses. *Grands taxis* regularly head to Aït Ben Haddou (30min, 32km/20mi, 100Dh, entire taxi only). There is a smaller *grand taxi* stop just off Place Al-Mouhadine, where you can also hire taxis to take you to Aït Ben Haddou.

Around Aït Ben Haddou, there are several places to park along the main road. The *ksar* is accessible only by foot.

Sports and Recreation

✪ HAMMAMS

The perfect end to a taxing, sweaty, sand-filled journey through the desert is a relaxing, steamy hammam. Take a moment to wash the sand out of every nook and cranny and, while you're at it, pamper yourself a bit. Ouarzazate has several Moroccan hammams, ranging from high-end luxury to something less elaborate but still relaxing.

Oasis Spa and Jacuzzi at the Hotel Le Berbere Palace

Rue El Mansour Addahbi; tel. 0524/883 105; daily 10am-8pm by appointment only; 150Dh

Oasis Spa and Jacuzzi at the Hotel Le Berbere Palace offers the type of scrubbing, exfoliation, and massage meant to make you feel like Hollywood royalty. This is the epitome of luxury. You could easily imagine Gwyneth Paltrow or Keira Knightley emerging from the steam clouding the Moroccan *zellij*,

taking a moment to indulge in some self-care after a long day of shooting.

Epices Maria

1579 Ave. Moulay Abdellah; tel. 0524/883 776; Sat.-Thurs. 10am-8pm by appointment only; 150Dh

The less elaborate Epices Maria, next to Le Petit Riad, offers a chance to have the sand of the desert scrubbed off you with traditional Moroccan soaps and essential herbs. For those of us not necessarily comfortable rubbing elbows (or knees, for that matter) with Hollywood royalty, this is a more humble place for mere mortals.

Public Hammam

Pl. Al Mouhadine; 10Dh

Another option is the newly built public hammam near the Patisserie Habouss, where you can mingle with locals. For those looking for an authentic experience, this is where you can go to hear all the women trading the latest tales and the men talking up the latest football (soccer) match. Don't worry if you don't have soap—they sell it at the door. You will want to remember a pair of flip-flops and a towel, though.

Shopping

Ensemble Artisanal

Ave. Mohammed V; daily 9:30am-12:30pm and 1:30pm-6pm

Worth a glimpse is the Ensemble Artisanal, where you can find local crafts on display for a fair price, including inlaid daggers, Amazigh carpets, and lamps of all shapes and sizes. Of particular note is Said's shop. Said is one of the few remaining stoneworkers handcrafting traditional tribal Tashelhit designs of the High Atlas, alongside some more commercial pieces, in white and black alabaster. Said's pieces range from something to tuck into your pocket to much larger objects that will have to be carefully wrapped and shipped back home.

Food

For breakfast, lunch, or a light snack, head to Place Al-Mouhadine, which has numerous indistinguishable cafés and food joints. The meals are all pretty standard, but these are great spots for grabbing a little sun while people-watching on the sprawling patio that feeds out onto the plaza.

FAST FOOD
Habous

Place Al-Mouhadine; daily 7am-9pm; 35Dh

Popular with locals and travelers, this Ouarzazate staple serves up a lunch menu with a variety of fast-food style plates, like burgers and chips (fries) and pizzas. These are good in a pinch, and the service is usually fantastic. If your accommodations don't offer breakfast, consider making this your breakfast stop. Sip on a coffee and nibble on a pastry while doing a little late-morning people-watching... just like the locals.

ITALIAN
Veneziano Pizzeria

Ave. Moulay Rachid; tel. 0524/887 676; daily noon-9:30pm; 40Dh

Veneziano Pizzeria serves up standard, if not a little disappointing, Moroccan-style pizzas, salads, and tajines. Stick with the thin-crust pizzas. Varieties include a spin on the Hawaiian pizza, with salami substituted for ham, and the Pizza Américaine, with seasoned ground beef, mushrooms, and cheese. Vegetarian options are available, as is Wi-Fi. It's well located close to Place Al-Mouhadine, across from the large Banque Populaire.

FINE DINING
✪ Accord Majeur

Rue El Mansour Addahbi; in front of
the Berbere Palace; tel. 0524/882 473;
Mon.-Sat. 11am-10pm; 200Dh

If you're looking to brush shoulders with the Hollywood crowd and nibble on delicious French cuisine, Accord Majeur is the place to be. Expect crowd favorites such as escargot and duck confit alongside seared salmon or grilled haddock covered with saffron-butter sauce. Though the food is delish, the real draw is the setting, replete with the film industry crowd chatting about the day's shoot in the warm, Moroccan-chic salon. The French bistro vibe and a fully stocked bar serve as the backdrop to your own Hollywood dream. Reservations are recommended for dinner; the restaurant will fill up at night, especially if there is a film shoot in town, and there often is. Best for couples and those looking for a break from Moroccan fare.

MOROCCAN
Le Jardin des Aromes

69 Ave. Mohamed V; tel. 0524/888 802;
Tues.-Sun. noon-2:30pm and 7pm-midnight;
200Dh

While you might think of stopping in exclusively for the fantastical decor—a blend of lush gardens and Arabian kitsch, like something described in the pen of Sir Richard Burton—that would be missing the main attraction. And what is the attraction of this new up-and-coming player in desert cuisine? The food, of course! Come here for crispy vegetarian *bastilla* (vegetable pie), perfectly spiced *meshoui* (roast lamb), and a mosaic of Moroccan salads. Service is friendly, as expected. Great for couples and families.

Accommodations

Accommodations in Ouarzazate range from pensions and auberges to larger hotels catering to tour groups and smaller boutique hotels located in quaint (though nearly impossible to locate) neighborhoods dotted around the downtown. They all have their good and bad qualities. Similar to Casablanca, Ouarzazate functions more as a travel hub for the area than as a destination in its own right. There are more interesting and picturesque accommodations available in towns around Ouarzazate, particularly in Aït Ben Haddou, the Dades and Todra Gorges, and the oases of Skoura and Zagora.

100-250DH
Hotel Atlas

13 Rue de Marche, just off Pl. Al-Mouhadine;
tel. 0524/887 745; 50Dh s, 180Dh d

For travelers on a shoestring budget, the brightly painted Hotel Atlas has simple, functional rooms. It's a good spot for student groups and backpackers. The front desk is friendly and knowledgeable about the area. The location, right off the Place Al-Mouhadine, is ideal for exploration and close to many cafés and snack places. Bathrooms are generally shared. Hot showers are 10Dh.

room with a view into the city

Hotel Marmar

16 Ave. Le Prince Moulay Abdellah; tel. 0524/888 887; www.hotel-marmar.com; 160Dh s, 250Dh d

Just a short walk from the *gare routière,* Hotel Marmar is the cleanest, though perhaps most characterless, option in Ouarzazate. The helpful, knowledgeable staff will gladly call for taxis and arrange transportation for you to continue your journey. The café downstairs is handy for a quick breakfast and freshly squeezed orange juice. If you're just arriving and the hotel isn't full, it is sometimes possible to negotiate prices.

OVER 500DH

Dar Rita

39 Rue de la Mosquée, Hay Tassoumaât; tel. 0654/164 726; www.darrita.com; 550Dh d

If off-the-beaten-track-in-a-big-city is your thing, consider the guesthouse Dar Rita, in the midst of the Tassoumaât neighborhood, a popular neighborhood in Ouarzazate a bit far from the main square and sights. Consider having someone meet you to take you to the guesthouse, as it is buried in a short maze of unnamed

streets that can be daunting to navigate for the uninitiated. The decor is a bit cluttered, but it retains a sort of family charm. The staff is friendly to a fault, Wi-Fi is available, and breakfast is included.

✪ Le Petit Riad

1581/1582 Hay Al Wahda; tel. 0524/885 950; www.petitriad.com; 650Dh d

Le Petit Riad is a charming house on the edge of the Al Wahda neighborhood southeast of the airport along Avenue Moulay Abdellah. Though taxis are possible from this location, it is better if you have your own car. The newly constructed house has lots of artistic charm, featuring adaptations of tribal Amazigh motifs, comfortable beds, an outdoor patio garden with a pool, and lots of space to spread out. Fatima, the owner, was the first licensed female guide in southern Morocco and will happily point you in the direction of some of the more interesting spots in and around Ouarzazate. Dinner here shouldn't be missed, whether dining poolside or indoors in the artsy dining hall; meals are served with a local spin on traditional Moroccan cuisine.

Dar Kamar

Kasbah Taourirt; tel. 0524/888 733; www.darkamar.com; 800Dh

With its central location in the old kasbah and stellar service, there is a lot to like about this up-and-coming boutique hotel. Even better, the hotel itself is a piece of real history. This was once the courthouse of the infamous Pasha Glaoui. The property, dating from the 17th century, features a traditional on-site hammam. There have been a number of upgrades, including air-conditioning throughout, something of a must in this oft-sweltering region. There are two suites, both recommended, as they are an excellent value at this level and will give you something of the feeling of a pasha. Breakfast, Wi-Fi, and air-conditioning are all included. Dinners and lunches are available (200Dh).

Information and Services

POST OFFICES AND COURIER SERVICES

Post Office

Ave. Mohammed V; Mon.-Fri. 8am-4:15pm and Sat. 8am-11:45am

The main post office, along the main road to Marrakesh, at the corner of the Rue de la Poste, has Western Union services. At higher-end hotels it is also possible to ask for postal service.

MONEY

Most banks are around the Place Al-Mouhadine. Attijariwafa Bank and Banque Populaire both have branches with 24-hour ATMs and exchange services (Pl. Al-Mouhadine, Mon.-Fri. 8:15am-3:45pm). There is another Banque Populaire (Ave. Moulay Rachid, Mon.-Fri. 8:15am-3:45pm) across from the Hotel La Palmeraie, down the street from the Hotel Le Berbere Palace. It will exchange travelers checks.

HOSPITALS, CLINICS, AND PHARMACIES

The Sidi Hssayne Ben Nacer Hospital (Ave. Bin Sina) is equipped to deal with emergencies, though English is not commonly spoken. Pharmacies are found easily throughout Ouarzazate, especially around the Place Al-Mouhadine. All pharmacies have a list of after-hours and weekend pharmacies posted on their front door. For service outside of regular business hours, keep an eye out for "Le Pharmacie de Garde" posted on all pharmacy doors, with information in Arabic and French. Pharmacy l'Aeroport (151 Cité Al-Wahda, Mon.-Fri. 8:30am-noon and 3pm-7pm, Sat. 8:30am-12:30pm) and Pharmacy Ouarzazate (Mohammed V, just across from Pl. Al-Mouhadine, Mon.-Fri. 8:30am-noon and 3pm-7pm) are two of the more convenient pharmacies around.

Transportation

GETTING THERE

BY PLANE

Ouarzazate Airport

north end of Ave. Mohammed VI,
tel. 0524/887 340

Most visitors will arrive by bus or car, though the Ouarzazate Airport does have regular direct flights connecting with Marrakesh via Royal Air Maroc (www.royalairmaroc.com). The airport is attached to the north end of the city, and taxis are the only option into town (15-20Dh), though if you're traveling light, you can consider walking the 2 kilometers (about a mile) into town through a residential neighborhood.

BY GRAND TAXI AND BUS

The *gare routière* is just off Avenue Moulay Abdellah and is the primary hub for *grands taxis* and buses. *Grands taxis* regularly head to Marrakesh (4hr, 200km/124mi, 100Dh).

Supratours (tel. 0524/888 566 or 0524/885 632, www.oncf.ma) is the bus line that extends the rail network. There are no trains in this region, but the Supratours bus does connect directly with Marrakesh (5hr, 1 daily, 75Dh). There is a handy Supratours office (Ave. Mohammed V, Mon.-Fri. 9am-5pm) in the Tassoumaât neighborhood in the roundabout with the *Movie* monument.

The reliable CTM bus (tel. 0800/0900 30, www.ctm.ma) connects directly with Marrakesh (5hr, 4 daily, 80Dh). The CTM station is at the corner of Avenue Mohammed V and Rue de la Poste.

BY CAR

If you are brave enough to drive in Morocco, be wary of the Tizi n'Tishka pass along the N9 while coming from Marrakesh (4hr, 200km/124mi). Though an extraordinarily beautiful drive, this is also an extraordinarily dangerous one, with hairpin turns, blind corners, steep cliffs, and drivers rambling through without a sense of fear or safety. The pass should be avoided in winter, as the road will ice over, and after heavy rains, when landslides are a real threat.

GETTING AROUND

BY PETIT TAXI

Yellow *petits taxis* can shuttle you around the city for around 10Dh. Taxis here don't use counters, but anything over 20Dh is likely exorbitant. Most drivers are friendly and know most major hotels and restaurants. It's always a good idea to have a map downloaded or well-marked for a driver to refer to, just in case.

BY BUS

Green Lux Transport buses (5Dh) also crisscross the city. Bus 4 conveniently runs along Avenue Mohammed V to Place Al-Mouhadine and the Taourirt Kasbah, usually every 30 minutes from sunrise to until midnight or so, though schedules are sporadic. Buses 1 and 2 pick up directly across from the CTM station (corner of Ave. Mohammed V and Rue de la Poste).

OVERNIGHT IN THE SAHARA

Existential wonder. There are no two better words to describe the experience of spending a night beneath the stars in the great expanse of the Sahara Desert. If you came all the way to Marrakesh and didn't get to dip your toes in the ocher sands of the Sahara and gaze up at the vast delight of the Milky Way, you would be depriving yourself of an unforgettable experience. Before we get away from ourselves, though, let's make one thing clear: if you're going to get out to the middle of nowhere, you're in for a long drive.

There are two great *ergs,* or dunes, to choose

HIGHLIGHTS

✪ **CAMEL RIDES:** No trip to the Sahara is complete without climbing on the back of a mountainous dromedary (page 231).

✪ **GNAWA MUSIC:** You might just fall into a trance listening to this ancient, rhythmic traditional Moroccan music (page 232).

✪ **DESERT CAMPING:** Is there anything more wondrous than curling up beneath a blanket of stars (page 233 and page 238)?

from: Erg Chebbi and Erg Chigaga. Each *erg* offers its own charm, though both are at least a solid half day of driving from Marrakesh. Whichever choice you make, you will cross through the desert capital of Ouarzazate. From Ouarzazate, you can continue northeast, along the famed "Road of 1,000 Kasbahs" on to the desert at Merzouga to venture into the Sahara and climb the dunes of the ever-popular Erg Chebbi.

Another possibility from Ouarzazate is to continue southeast along the N9 through the largest palm grove in all of Morocco, the South Draa Valley. This palm grove hosts over two million palm trees and stretches from the relatively nondescript drive-through town of Agdz; through the oasis town of Zagora, formerly the start of the Caravan Route to Timbuktu; and on to the literal end of the road, M'hamid. From M'hamid, the paved road ends and the real adventure begins. Traverse the desert—by foot, camel, or four-wheel drive—to the distant Erg Chigaga, where you can stargaze beneath the clear desert sky and watch as the sun rises over the golden Saharan sands.

Moroccans and foreigners alike come to Erg Chebbi and Erg Chigaga to take in the great expanse of the Sahara and experience the warm hospitality that this region is known for. They both give travelers the feeling of calm that comes with living life at the edge of the great Sahara.

If you want to explore more of Morocco's desert regions, I suggest you pick up the latest edition of the *Moon Morocco* country guidebook. In this guidebook, I delve much more into these desert regions, from the different palm groves to the mountain gorges you pass on your way to the Sahara. For the purposes of this book, the information presented here is much more limited, but will make it possible for you to spend a night in the desert while you're in Marrakesh.

ORIENTATION

The Southern Oases and Sahara Desert stretch northeast to southwest along the Algerian border that runs alongside Morocco's eastern border. For the purposes of this chapter, I've divided this region into two sections coupling the desert region with its closest town: Merzouga and Erg Chebbi, and M'hamid and Erg Chigaga.

Erg Chebbi and Erg Chigaga are the two largest formations of sand dunes in Morocco. Erg Chebbi towers over

Overnight in the Sahara

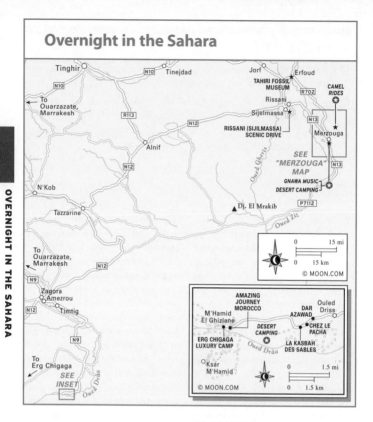

Tinghir ○ N10 ○ Tinejdad

Jorf ● Erfoud
TAHIRI FOSSIL MUSEUM
R702
CAMEL RIDES

To Ouarzazate, Marrakesh N10

Rissani ●

R113

Sijelmassa ★

RISSANI (SIJILMASSA) SCENIC DRIVE

N12

N13

Merzouga

Alnif ○

SEE "MERZOUGA" MAP
N13

N12

GNAWA MUSIC DESERT CAMPING ○

N'Kob ○

Dj. El Mrakib ▲
Oued Ziz
P7112

Tazzarine ○

Oued Gheris

To Ouarzazate, Marrakesh N12

0   15 mi

N9

0   15 km

Zagora ○ Amezrou

© MOON.COM

N12 ○ Timtig

N9

To Erg Chigaga

SEE INSET

Oued Drâa

AMAZING JOURNEY MOROCCO

Ouled Driss

DAR AZAWAD ●

M'Hamid El Ghizlane

DESERT CAMPING ○

● CHEZ LE PACHA

ERG CHIGAGA LUXURY CAMP

Oued Drâa

LA KASBAH DES SABLES

○ Ksar M'Hamid

0   1.5 mi

0   1.5 km

© MOON.COM

the touristic town of Merzouga, 561 kilometers (349mi) from Marrakesh, while the more distant Erg Chigaga is only accessible via 4x4 (or camel) from M'hamid, 452 kilometers (281mi) from Marrakesh. From M'hamid, Erg Chigaga is a two-hour ride via 4x4. Merzouga and Erg Chebbi are the northernmost of the Sahara region in this chapter, easily reached by car and the more popular of the two desert regions. The decidedly less-touristed town of M'hamid, with its neighboring sand dune, Erg Chigaga, marks the southernmost area.

Most travelers will likely enter this region via the mountain pass connecting Marrakesh with Ouarzazate, the largest city in the region.

PLANNING YOUR TIME

Though it is possible to overnight from Marrakesh in the Sahara, it's best to plan at least three days. For both Erg Chebbi and Erg Chigaga, you'll need to budget about 12 hours of drive time to and from Marrakesh. With three days, you'll be able to break up the drive and take your time to experience more of the desert culture. It makes really good travel sense to tuck in after the long drive from Marrakesh in one of the stellar kasbahs in the region that surround the *ergs*. This way, you can rest up for a full-day adventure in the desert. The route to both *ergs* to and from Marrakesh passes through Ouarzazate (see the

TIPS FOR OVERNIGHTING IN THE DESERT

Bonfires in the desert are a time to share stories and make new friends.

By far the easiest way to spend the night in the Sahara is to book one of the **luxury camps** that have popped up across the great desert *ergs*. Not only is this the most comfortable way to spend a night, but for many travelers it is the most practical, and worth the splurge. The better camps will not only ensure a memorable **camel ride** and **great meal,** but will also have **4x4s** around in case of any emergencies.

WHAT TO PACK
If you are going it by yourself or with friends, be sure to pack a **sturdy tent** and **weigh it down.** The winds often pick up in the evenings, and many a tale has been told of campers losing their tents to the stiff breeze that whips over the dunes. Solo travelers can easily become lost in the desert as the sands shift with the winds. You'll want to make sure you have a good functioning **GPS** to help you.

Beyond these considerations, there are no pharmacies out in the desert, so make sure to pack plenty of **sunscreen** and whatever **medications** you might need.

SAFETY
Scorpions are not a big threat, but they do exist. Make sure you shake out your shoes before putting them on. Most scorpion stings are not deadly. You'll want to clean with mild soap and water before using a cold pack to stop the venom from spreading. Take an ibuprofen if needed to alleviate the pain.

Aside from scorpions and losing your way, the only other real danger of this part of the Sahara is a lack of sleep! You'll likely stay up late listening to **music** or **star gazing** and then wake up early to catch the **sun rise.** If you can, limit your driving to no more than a few hours the day after your desert adventure. Morocco is not a place to be drowsy while driving.

Ouarzazate chapter), so an overnight in Ouarzazate on the return can nicely break up your trip.

The roads out here are generally a bit slower and not as well maintained in some places. From Marrakesh, you most likely will come via the N9 through Ouarzazate. It's best to drive this region with a **map,** as roads are often unmarked and sometimes marked only in Arabic. Before setting out, it's best to have an idea of the roads you will take and possible circuits you might do. Roads are all two lanes, which means that **traffic** can sometimes get backed up because of farm equipment and herding animals, adding to drive times. Buckle up for some long drives.

You'll want to avoid the desert in July and August. It's sweltering hot, with temperatures soaring well over 45°C (110°F). In the winters, the days are often warm, generally 25°C (77°F), though night temperatures can dip well below freezing. By far the best times to visit are in the spring and fall. The Milky Way is visible from early March through early November, provided you have clear skies, making this period a real prime stargazing experience.

sand storms come strong and without warning

DO-IT-YOURSELF

For those interested in a solo outing to the desert, without guides or camps, it is possible. The biggest concern with trekking into the desert by yourself is getting lost. You will want to make sure to bring a GPS-enabled device and a sturdy tent. Take care to wear light, long garments that protect your head, arms, and legs from the heat. A rule of thumb if you do get lost is to find some shade and stay where you are. Even though the desert looks devoid of life, the chances are very good that a desert guide or nomad will pass by where you are and be able to help you out. It goes without saying that you should pack plenty of water. Energy bars or loose nuts for quick energy are a good idea as well.

WHEN TO GO

The Sahara Desert is generally much too hot for most people during the summer. The spring and fall are generally the best times to visit, though temperatures can be still be hot during the day and cool at night. Winter can be an excellent time to visit, though rainstorms and flooding can be a concern, and at night temperatures will dip

below freezing in some parts. Without a guide, it would be best to overnight in the desert in either spring or fall. You will also want to take a look at the calendar for Ramadan, which will fall during the spring months for the life of this guide. During Ramadan, many eateries and even some accommodations will be closed.

TRANSPORTATION AND ROAD CONDITIONS

There are no trains in this region, so you will be traveling by bus, grand taxi, or car. The roads are generally passable, and much work is being done to improve the infrastructure, though heavy rains (typically during winter months and early spring) can sometimes wash roads out and make some areas unreachable. For most major destinations, the road is paved and perfectly drivable, though for off-piste roads, such as the roads past Merzouga or M'hamid into the more remote regions, you will need four-wheel drive. If you are not renting a car or have not arranged a driver, then the buses are your best option.

Four-Wheel-Drive Rentals

In Merzouga, you can rent quads, buggies, or 4x4s at Garage Ben Omar (next to Chez Jordi & Naima at the

a seasonal lake at Erg Chebbi

Whichever of Morocco's great desert sand dunes you visit, you will be assured of one thing: an unforgettable adventure. With their relative distance from Marrakesh more or less the same, the question of which *erg* to visit comes down to just a couple of factors. First, which *erg* makes the most travel sense for you? Second, what sort of experience do you want to have?

ERG CHEBBI
When setting out from Marrakesh, particularly if you have rented a car or hired a driver, you might consider making a circle into the northern part of Morocco to visit **Fez.** If so, then you'll want to visit Erg Chebbi (and you might want to pick up *Moon Morocco* as well). Erg Chebbi isn't far off the primary national road that connects the desert region with distant Fez, across Morocco's **Middle Atlas Mountains.** The other reason Erg Chebbi can make a lot of sense is because it is **easily reachable by car or bus.** The road literally ends right at the foot of Erg Chebbi. However, because it is easier to reach and on the way to Fez, this means that Erg Chebbi does get quite a few **more travelers** than Erg Chigaga.

ERG CHIGAGA
In contrast to Erg Chebbi, Erg Chigaga is very **difficult to reach** on your own, requiring skill driving a **4x4,** a solid understanding of driving over desert tundra, and a great **GPS.** Because of this, Erg Chigaga is best for those who don't mind booking with a **tour company** or **guide** and having a more curated experience. The payoff is that the camps of Erg Chigaga are much **more remote** and really give you the isolation and solitude you would expect from an excursion into the vast nothing of the Sahara.

---

entrance of town, tel. 0671/564 956). The garage also has a mechanic on site, which can be handy if your car breaks down. Otherwise, if you want to drive yourself, it is best to rent a **four-wheel-drive** vehicle in Marrakesh. If you're interested in having a driver, a four-wheel-drive rental typically costs 300-500Dh a day with the driver's rate included. Renting with a driver can be beneficial, as the driver generally knows the area quite well and the risks of being lost in the desert are lessened.

ORGANIZED TOURS FROM MARRAKESH
Amazing Journey Morocco
tel. 0665/952 465;
www.amazing-morocco.com; 700Dh

Amazing Journey Morocco has

friendly, English-speaking tour guides with four-wheel-drive vehicles who know the area very well. Not only can they do tours around the desert and Erg Chigaga, but they also lead treks by foot and camel through the stunning Draa Oasis to the Erg Lehoudi at the edge of the desert. Their campsite in Erg Chigaga has rustic Bedouin-style tents complete with bathrooms and a restaurant worthy of Scheherazade.

Journey Beyond Travel
tel. 0610/414 573, U.S. toll-free
tel. 855/687-6676;
www.journeybeyondtravel.com
For those looking for a customized tour that delves deeply into local culture, the team at Journey Beyond Travel creates custom packages and tours while working to maintain an eco-friendly, socially sustainable business model. They are one of Morocco's real leaders in offsetting their carbon footprint. In particular, their tours that touch the areas around Merzouga and Erg Chebbi do a spectacular job of engaging with the local culture. Over the years, they have done a lot of nonprofit work in the area, and their warm connection with the locals here truly shines. The accommodations, drivers, and guides they use are all top-notch.

Merzouga and Erg Chebbi

مرزوكة، عرق الشبي

Snug against the beginning of the vast Sahara desert, **Merzouga** was little more than a collection of a few Bedouin tents a few short years ago. The undeniable draw of the desert has proven irresistible for tourists, as evidenced by the number of new hotels and specialty *riads* that have recently sprung up, as well as the new paved road from Rissani and new boulevard. Merzouga exists largely for tourism, though this hasn't taken away from its seemingly magical pull.

For most travelers, Merzouga is the end of the road. With a four-wheel-drive you can brave the unpacked, sand-strewn route to **Al-Taous**, though this is largely an area exploited for its phosphorous mines. There are a few faded petroglyphs in the area, though the majority are knock-offs carved by industrious locals. Birders will want to look out for the lake, **Dayet Srji**—known as Dayet Tifert by the locals—that usually forms to the west of Merzouga, toward the mountains in the midst of the black-rock desert. During the winter, several migratory birds make their way here, including the greater flamingo.

SIGHTS
ERG CHEBBI

From a great distance, the ocher brilliance of **Erg Chebbi** rises high above Merzouga. Though not as big as some of the great sand seas of the Algerian or Libyan Sahara, it is beautiful nonetheless and a stunning reminder of the sheer awesomeness of the Sahara. Throughout the day, the sands shift in shades of red and pink, making for breathtaking pictures and ever-changing scenery. As the French

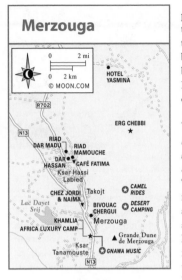

Merzouga

0 — 2 mi
0 — 2 km
© MOON.COM

HOTEL YASMINA

R702

ERG CHEBBI ★

N13

RIAD DAR MADU
RIAD MAMOUCHE
DAR HASSAN
CAFÉ FATIMA
Ksar Hassi Labied

Takojt

CHEZ JORDI & NAIMA
CAMEL RIDES
Laˆc Dayet Srij
BIVOUAC CHERGUI
DESERT CAMPING
KHAMLIA
Merzouga
AFRICA LUXURY CAMP
Ksar Tanamouste
▲ Grande Dune de Merzouga
◉ GNAWA MUSIC

N13

writer Antoine de Saint-Exupéry once wrote: "One sits down on a desert sand dune, sees nothing, hears nothing. Yet through the silence something throbs, and gleams."

A vast *hamada* (barren, rocky plateau) separates this piece of the Sahara from the rest of the desert, making it something of a curious sight in this otherwise rocky region. The dunes rise to heights of nearly 150 meters (500ft) and spread out over an area of over 500 square kilometers (200 square miles). Though more touristed than the other great sand sea, Erg Chigaga outside of M'hamid, this *erg* is much easier to reach, and even with the increase of tourism, a quiet night beneath the stars with the hush of the desert is still very much a possibility.

There are several ways to tour Erg Chebbi. The easiest is to walk, though trekking through the dunes is tough work. Still, many people make it out on foot to the tallest sand dune to take in a sunset. Quads (or ATVs) are another possibility, but the noise and the

pollution they create make this practice something highly discouraged in this region. Not only are quads noisy, but they only serve to really ruin the beauty of this delicate sand formation. For traveling into the desert, there are, of course, more natural solutions. . . .

TAHIRI FOSSIL MUSEUM
Ksar Kssir Siffa outside of Erfoud on the road to Rissani; tel. 0535/576 874; daily 8am-7pm; free

This hard-to-miss museum (just look for the giant fake dinosaur skeletons alongside the road), despite outward appearances, is full of friendly staff, like Brahim, who are passionate about fossils and the region. They'll be happy to show you around the facilities, highlighting some of the more impressive fossils, such as their resident tyrannosaurus. You'll also be able to see how they painstakingly clean fossils for exhibition in museums around the world. There is a large gift shop with many interesting trilobites and other fossils for sale.

SPORTS AND RECREATION
LOCAL GUIDES
The region is best explored with a guide for those who don't have much time but want to be able to experience a glimpse into the desert culture and are looking for something a bit more than just a night in the Sahara.

◉ Morocco Geo Travel
tel. 0661/503 500;
www.moroccogeotravel.com
If you're interested in rocks and stars, this is the outfit to contact. For your trouble, you will get a superb lesson in desert astronomy as well as the geology of the area, which are, surprising for some (like me), intimately linked.

While attending a short lecture, you'll learn how the Little Dipper is known throughout the Sahara as "the baby camel," while the Big Dipper is known as the "mama camel." Excursions are available into the outlying region to discover the geology of the region and some of the different fossils to be found, many of them remnants of when Morocco was buried in the last Ice Age. For families and young archeologists in the making, this is a must-do bit of desert erudition.

Guide Abdelkarim Tata welcomes his guests to the desert.

Abdelkarim Tata

tel. 0662/294 386; www.tataziztrekking.com; email: abdelkarim.tata@gmail.com

The most dependable, honest guide in the region is Abdelkarim Tata. Tata can arrange for day trips in the region, including the nearby Ziz Valley, four-wheel-drives into the desert, overnight trips into reputable Bedouin nomad camps, and meals with a nomad locally famous for *madfouna,* a local specialty of ground camel, chicken, or beef and onion seasoned, spiced, and folded into the unleavened dough, slow cooked beneath hot desert sands (a nontraditional but equally delicious vegetarian option is available).

Merzouga, where the end of the road meets Erg Chebbi

On the road to Merzouga from Marrakesh, Sijilmassa was once a great city—the northern terminus of the trans-Sahara trading route. The abundant dates and water supply made conditions temperate and ensured food and water for the region. The wealth of the city grew, and by AD 771, it divided from the Abbasid caliphate, making itself the first independent kingdom in the region.

Several famous travelers, including Ibn Battuta in the 14th century and Leo the African in the 16th century, passed through Sijilmassa on their tours through the region and recounted the size and beauty of the city, elevating its legend to a near mythic status. Today, Sijilmassa lies on the outskirts of Rissani, mostly destroyed, though a few kasbahs and *ksour* still stand in the midst of the palm grove, slowly crumbling into ruin. Though this area is protected by the World Monuments Fund as an endangered site and preserved by the Moroccan Ministry of Culture, little has been done in recent years to preserve the ancient city.

There is a picturesque drive marked by a "Cirque Touristique" sign approaching Rissani from Erfoud near Merzouga. This 8-kilometer drive takes you through the ruins of Sijilmassa as well as several interesting kasbahs, many of them still lived in. **Ksar Charfat Bahaj** at Oulad Tineghras is interesting to stop at and tour. However, the most interesting kasbah to visit, **Ksar Ouled Abd el Halim**, toward the end of the circuit, is currently under restoration work; it features updated adobe work as well as several ruined palatial *riads* with original layouts, *zellij* work, and Arabic inscriptions, exuding a sense of what it must have felt like to live in this oasis at the end of the great Sahara.

M'Hammed "Hamid" Sergoui

tel. 0621/218 521;

www.moroccodesertstargazing.com;

email: contactastrohamid@gmail.com

Hamid has studied geology and astronomy for over 20 years and has done a number of lectures in the U.S., Europe, and even Japan. He is a veritable wealth of information about Bedouin and Touareg culture in the region. Hamid can arrange an excursion into the desert where you will be able to collect your own fossil to take home as a truly one-of-a-kind souvenir.

✪ CAMEL RIDES

Numerous guides with their camels—sorry, *dromedaries*—hang out right at the base of Erg Chebbi. In the off-season, some deals can be had if you bargain hard. The typical going rates are 100Dh for a ride out to enjoy the sunset, 200-500Dh for an overnight stay with dinner and breakfast in a Bedouin tent, or 700-1,000Dh for a "luxury stay" overnight complete with en suite toilets. You've come all this way . . . it would be a shame not to ride that camel, or rather, dromedary, out into that wonderful Saharan sand and experience a bit of life in the desert.

As a rule of thumb, those looking for a quieter night beneath the stars should stick to the camel rides leaving directly from Merzouga right at the base of Erg Chebbi. Typically, these tours head south of Erg Chebbi into the quieter parts of the dunes. For those wanting a bit of luxury, this is the place to be as all of the luxury Bedouin tent camps are here.

a camel heading out to the desert

For those that don't mind the buzz of quads and dirt bikes, or those looking to save a few dirhams, head to Ksar Hassi Labied just 3 kilometers north of Merzouga. The tours here veer toward the northern half of Erg Chebbi and are usually around 100Dh less expensive.

a sand boarder hits the hot desert slopes

SANDBOARDING

One of the new rages is to surf the sand. This is done with old snowboards, for rent at numerous spots throughout the village of Merzouga for anywhere from 50Dh to 100Dh for a full day. Rental includes boots, board, and bindings. Most camps now have their own set of "sandboards," and if you're spending the night at one of the desert camps, you'll have use of these for no extra change. These are all recycled, tossed-off snowboards that have been used and abused, though they are perfectly good for shredding some sand. Keep in mind that there are no "sand lifts" here, so you'll have to do the trekking up the dunes yourself. This is a fun diversion

in the desert, though seasoned surfers, skiers, and snowboarders will likely get quickly bored from the lack of speed. Still, it makes for some good photo ops, and when is the next time you're going to be able to surf a part of the Sahara?

⭐ GNAWA MUSIC
Khamlia

The ever-rhythmic Gnawa music is popular in these parts, with many Gnawa musicians entertaining around the different hotels and even in the far-out villages. The music itself has a much more spiritual feel, and the most renowned musicians often fall into a trance as they communicate with the spiritual world through this ancient music. The village of Khamlia is home to an incredibly popular Gnawa musician group. Trips out to Khamlia to listen to the musicians, sip tea, and eat lunch can be arranged with any of the tour guides or through your accommodations. Khamlia is 7 kilometers (4mi) beyond Merzouga on the route to Taouz. For those without a car, it's sometimes easier to catch a taxi from Rissani (40min, 48km/30mi, 40Dh); although taxis can be had in Merzouga (20min, 7km/4mi, 20Dh), you'll likely have to pay the entire taxi fare.

FOOD

Besides the hotel restaurants, there are few options for dining around Merzouga. In addition to the restaurants in this section, you can contact any of the accommodations listed below a day in advance to reserve lunch or dinner. Typically, these meals will range from 150-250Dh with full table service and are a step above any of the food available on the streets.

Chez Jordi & Naima

N13 Merzouga; tel. 0661/631 591;
daily early-late (hours vary); 50Dh

Just off the main road at the entrance into town, this is the best of the small snack stands and cafés. They serve cold beer, which can be a welcome reprieve after a hot day. Otherwise, the snacks in town offer the same fare (salads, meatballs, chicken tajines) without much variation.

Café Fatima

R702 Hassilabied; daily, hours vary,
generally 10am-9pm; 50Dh

You will also find Café Fatima, a non-smoking café that is also a great hub if you are interested in renting snowboards or skis (100Dh), bicycles to tour the town (from 50Dh), and even quad rentals (from 300Dh). If you're feeling hungry, try the Berber omelet (35dh), deliciously spiced and cooked in a tajine.

✪ DESERT CAMPING

This is what you came all the way out here for, right? A night—or maybe a weekend—in the desert. There are many ways to spend the night in the desert, some more comfortable than others. Any of the local hotels or guides at the edge of the *erg* will be able to arrange an overnight camping trip, usually including a tajine dinner, water, and tea as well as a light breakfast. Overnights typically range from 200-500Dh per person. At that range, there is little that distinguishes the camps. Bargain hard.

Africa Luxury Camp

Merzouga; tel. 0671/079 134 or 0677/766
857; https://africaluxurycamps.com/en;
900Dh per person

Located on the edges of the dunes, this is a good bargain for a luxury

Gnawa musicians performing in Khamlia

experience, with kind guides and on-site staff who will see to your every need. However, the one real nice perk at this camp are the lounging spaces, including the swinging hammock chair. This is desert luxury done right. The only downside to this camp is that when you get to the tops of some of the local dunes, you can really see into some of the other camps closer to Merzouga, which takes away a bit from the desert experience. Still, this is one of the better-run luxury camps in the region, complete with en suite bathrooms for each of their rooms. Price includes breakfast and dinner.

a Bedouin Tent for shelter in the desert

✪ Bivouac Chergui

Merzouga; tel. 0535/578 504; http://bivouac.chergui.com; 1000Dh per person

For the absolute best in luxury desert glamping, you'll want to book with this outfit. The spacious camps and desert rooms fit for a sultan include everything you would expect, from dependable running water and walk-in showers to air-conditioning, which can be a real life-saver in the hotter months. To my knowledge, this is the only outfit in all of Erg Chebbi that has dared to install air-conditioning units in their tents. For families with young children or those sensitive to the heat, this site would be recommended for this thoughtful inclusion alone. However, with its more distant location, the tent camp here really gives you the feeling of isolation and solitude you might expect from a desert adventure. Prices include breakfast, dinner, and the nightly music and warm festivities that only happen in the Sahara.

ACCOMMODATIONS

Just outside of Merzouga, the old village of Ksar Hassi Labied has developed over the last 20 years, adding to the number of boutique hotels and serving the popularity of desert excursion. Several smaller *riads* and hotels nestle at the foot of the dunes. Ksar Hassi Labied is a bit quieter than Merzouga, with fewer hotels and auberges, making this a better spot to get a good night of sleep cozied up to the Saharan dunes. The easiest route into Ksar Hassi Labied is to take a left as you come into Merzouga on the asphalt road that makes a T-intersection with the main road right at the post office and Al Barid Bank.

Riad Mamouche

Ksar Hassi Labied; tel. 0666/662 110; www.riadmamouche.com; 400Dh d

A good option for families because of the large rooms that can fit up to five people very comfortably, Riad Mamouche spreads out, circling around a small swimming pool, the perfect spot for a little tanning while the kids play in the water. There is a second courtyard, an Andalusian-style garden where birds happily chirp throughout the day, adding to the Alhambra-esque allure of this *riad*. Alcohol is served in the restaurant, making this a popular stop. Air-conditioning, Wi-Fi, and a bountiful breakfast buffet are all included, and the rooms are all nonsmoking. Camel rides directly from the hotel can be arranged (350Dh per person) and include comfy lodgings, as well as campfire, music, and a tajine dinner for a slightly livelier night in the desert.

Hotel Yasmina

Merzouga; tel. 0535/576 783; http:// hotelyasminamerzouga.com; 700Dh d

Hotel Yasmina was one of the very first hotels in Merzouga. It started over 20 years ago as a series of Bedouin tents on the edge of the desert and has expanded to include standard rooms in a traditional mudbrick kasbah that sits on the edge of the desert lake. They are far enough away from the cluttered hotels and *riads* at the end of the paved road that, though not quite the experience of the Bedouin tents in the desert, spending the night here still gives the feeling of isolation expected from the great Sahara. Rooms are comfortable, with wonderfully hot showers, and breakfast and dinner are included. Bedouin tents, just next to the hotel, are also available (200Dh) and include breakfast. This is a fantastic option for those on a tighter budget.

✪ Dar Hassan

Ksar Hassi Labied; tel. 0535/576 274 or 0677/743 298; https://darhassan.com; 700Dh d

Opened in 2018, this midrange option does everything right, from the friendly service to the comfy, clean rooms. The interior pool is refreshing, particularly in the warm months, and dinner is delightful, with a full range of traditional Moroccan plates on offer. The breakfast buffet is a bit more international than you might expect. Served in the common rooms, these meals are a great time to meet fellow travelers. Hassan, the owner and manager, is usually close by, so if

you do have any questions or issues, he'll be able to help you out. For drivers, the attached covered parking is a thoughtful touch.

✪ Riad Dar Madu

Ksar Hassi Labied; tel. 0535/578 740 or 0661/352 895; www.madu-events.com; 800Dh-1,100Dh d

For one of the most luxurious nights in the desert, reserve with Riad Dar Madu. Operated by the owners of the hotel by the same name, the tents are second-to-none. The Bedouin tents are solar-powered and feature a Moroccan restaurant worthy of *1,001 Nights*. Keep in mind that prices are per person and, like everything else in Morocco, are negotiable. If you were to have just one night in the desert in your life, you would want it to be here. The *riad* also has a hotel in Merzouga constructed of eco-friendly mudbrick, romantically lit with hand-worked metal lamps resting beneath bamboo ceilings. For the cold nights, a crackling fireplace makes it a cozy spot to curl up with that vacation read you've been ignoring. The swimming pool looks out into the nearby Sahara. A scrumptious breakfast is included, and the restaurant (well worth checking out) uses only the freshest ingredients sourced daily from the nearby markets.

INFORMATION AND SERVICES

There is a **post office** with a **cash machine** right at the beginning of town at the T-intersection with the road for Ksar Hassi Labied. Several cash machines, a post office branch, and a seldom-open **tourist office** are found at the end of the road, near the edge of the dunes along the main commercial strip of Merzouga. Many hotels and nearly all tour operators accept only cash, so you will likely have to make liberal use of the cash machines. Keep in mind that the maximum amount most cash machines let you take in one transaction is 2,000Dh, which means you might have to do several transactions if you are paying for a larger group.

TRANSPORTATION

GETTING THERE

Getting to the edge of nowhere can be a little tricky without a car, and even with a car you will likely want to rent a four-wheel-drive vehicle to further explore this edge of the Sahara.

By Car

From Marrakesh, you'll take the N9 to Ouarzazate before turning northeast on the N10 following the signs to Errachidia and then Merzouga (9.5hr, 561km/349mi). You'll likely run into some traffic and want to stop a couple of times, so give yourself around 12 total hours for the drive out. Once in Merzouga, there is convenient free parking at the end of the main road where the pavement meets the desert at the base of the Erg Chebbi sand dunes.

By Bus

The Supratours bus (tel. 0524/888 566 or 0524/885 632, www.oncf.ma) runs all the way to Merzouga from Marrakesh (12hr, 1 daily, 175Dh). Buy tickets a few days in advance to guarantee seating. It is a morning bus that passes through the nearby towns of Rissani and Errachidia.

GETTING AROUND

From Merzouga, you can continue into the Sahara on foot or negotiate with the numerous camel drivers for a tour or overnight trip into the desert. The going rates are 100Dh for a ride out to enjoy the sunset, and 200-500Dh for an overnight stay with dinner and breakfast in a Bedouin tent, but all prices are negotiable, so work on your bargaining skills. To get around Merzouga, you'll be walking, so just be aware of the typically hot afternoon sun.

M'hamid and Erg Chigaga

محاميدالغزلان ,عرق الشجاج

M'hamid (short for M'hamid al-Ghizlan) is at the literal end of the road. Historically, this was a settlement for Hassani-speaking nomads. It now serves as a tourist staging point for desert excursions, with a few cafés and snack restaurants. Some travelers might spend the night here or in the nearby village of Bounou before or after heading out into the desert.

Beyond M'hamid, the great Erg Chigaga rises, the largest sand formation in this part of the desert. Amid epic sand dunes, bivouac tents have been established near deep-water wells. Here you can spend nights beneath the stars, with constellations seen free from the light pollution of major cities, bringing the intricacy and immensity of the night sky alive. Erg Chigaga is five days round-trip

looking up at the Orion constellation from the dark desert

by dromedary and four hours by car. Erg Lehoudi (Jewish Dunes) is an easier-to-manage day-trip from M'hamid, though far more cluttered with tourists and trash and far less interesting. A relatively easy-to-drive road takes you north from M'hamid (8km/5mi) to Erg Lehoudi and can be driven without four-wheel drive.

Just before M'hamid lie the twin villages of Bounou and Oued Driss. While Bounou hosts a number of great options for accommodations, Oued Driss is the more interesting locale. This is a 400-year-old traditional village that hasn't changed. Shadowed corridors covered by palm fronds keep the passageways protected from the searing desert sun. Rays of light pierce through, alighting the mudbrick adobe walls magically, making for a wonderful exploration and to catch a glimpse of how day-to-day life has been lived out here for hundreds of years.

While in Oued Driss, make a quick stop by the Oued Driss Museum (20Dh for entry, 30Dh for guided tour of museum, kasbah, and tea). Though you'll find artifacts of Arab, Berber, and Jewish life from the region, the real treat is the 400-year-old house itself with its incredibly well-preserved Arab-Berber construction. Ibrahim, the owner and operator of the museum, is university educated and speaks English well enough for a quick tour (30min-1hr).

Most desert wildlife tends to be nocturnal, but keep on the lookout for sand fish (also known as the Berber skink), sand lizards, desert sparrows, the black-and-white *tamanghar* (a small bird said to bring the *baraka*, or "blessing"), the elusive fennec fox, and the endangered dorcas gazelle. Animals are generally found near water and their food source. Look for evidence of their passing by in the early mornings near your camp.

The souk of M'hamid is on Monday, making this a good day to stock up on fruits, vegetables, and supplies for those planning longer treks in the area.

SPORTS AND RECREATION

CAMEL RIDES

The wonderful thing about the desert is that a camel ride is something of a quotidian affair, and is seen as fun for international travelers as well as locals. You can find rides in any of the towns, with prices ranging from just a few dirhams for a couple of minutes to 200Dh for a 30min-1hr ride into the desert. You'll be able to find camels in M'hamid, though you'll likely only want to ride for a few minutes. For longer rides, head into Erg Chigaga. Let the proprietor know ahead of time that you're interested in a sunset camel ride to make sure that you'll have a dromedary waiting for you on arrival.

QUADS

You'll find several places willing to rent you a quad for 400Dh (or more!) an hour. However, the best and safest way to ride quads in this region is as part of a half-day excursion. You'll not only be assured of a well-running quad, but you'll also have safety instruction as well as a helmet and gloves. The trips run by **Desert Bivouac** (www.desertbivouac.com) are top-notch and include transfer from your hotel or desert camp, as well as interaction with some of the locals in the smaller, seminomadic villages that dot this region. If you are going to ride a quad, this is the best area for environmental purposes.

SANDBOARDING

Unlike in Merzouga, there are no sandboards for rent in M'hamid. The only way to do some sandboarding is to join one of the camps out in Erg Chigaga. Most camps now have at least a couple of boards to use with the necessary bindings. If you're going to spend a night out at one of the camps, just let them know ahead of time that you might be interested in sandboarding, and they should be able to get the equipment for you at no extra charge.

TOP EXPERIENCE

✪ DESERT CAMPING

A quintessential trip through Morocco includes at least one night in the desert. Though it's possible, and generally easier, to check this off the "must-do" list in Merzouga at Erg Chebbi, it is infinitely more interesting and somehow conceptually closer to the idea of a night in the desert to do this at **Erg Chigaga.** The desert camps are more spread out and the trip out takes much longer, especially if done by dromedary, adding to the sense of being really disconnected and off the

the rocky desert to distant Erg Chigaga

grid. Though it is possible to drive out to Erg Chigaga with your own four-wheel-drive, it is not really recommended. The desert shifts, often imperceptibly, and drivers have been known to get lost. For this reason, it is best to go with a guide.

Erg Chigaga Luxury Camp

Erg Chigaga; tel. 0654/398 520 or 0656/563 385; www.desertcampmorocco. com; 2,500Dh per person

The owners, Nick and Bobo, have been running this camp since 2011. They have the service down to an art, with their quick staff able to help with nearly everything imaginable. The tents are spacious, allowing for plenty of air flow, with king-size beds, en suite bathrooms, hand-carved furniture, percale cotton sheets, and fluffy duck down duvets for those cold desert nights. For couples and honeymooners, or those just seeking more solitude, splurge for the private nomadic camp. Located about a 2-3 hour hike away (or 30 minutes by 4x4), it's an incredible desert experience and something you will remember for a lifetime. Price includes all 4x4 transport out to the camp, breakfast, dinner, camel rides, guided walks, and their informal nightly entertainment. This outfit can also organize trips to and from Marrakesh for you, taking a lot of the stress out of planning an overnight trip to the desert.

Al Koutban

Erg Chigaga; tel. 0655/778 173 or 0679/006 221; wildmorocco.com; 900Dh

Owned by Wild Morocco, a British-Berber-owned tour company, this is stellar desert camp in Erg Chigaga, 95 kilometers (60mi) from the nearest road, and at a great price. The camp offers some plush tents with fluffy carpets and king-size beds. There are no en suite bathrooms, but there is a separate facility for toilets and showers in the camp. The camp itself hugs the bottom of the largest of the sand dunes, making a trip to the top to catch the sunset something of a must. All meals and guided camel walks are included with the price. This is perhaps the best value proposition around. Like most other camps, they will be able to arrange travel to and from Marrakesh for you.

Medfouna is something like the pizza of the desert.

FOOD AND ACCOMMODATIONS

The small Amazigh village of Ait Ghanima nearby can provide some food and supplies. Besides desert camping, there are a few kasbah-styled lodgings along the road to M'hamid from Zagora. The village of Bounou (8km/5mi from M'hamid) is now basically a concentration of small hotels and provides the best lodgings in the area.

✪ La Kasbah des Sables

Bounou; tel. 0662/403 115; 250Dh d

One of the absolute best values in the region is La Kasbah des Sables, a wonderfully authentic guesthouse in the middle of the oasis. Palm trees cast shade from the hot Sahara sun and the swimming pool is cool and inviting. The barbecue is open for anyone to use, so it's possible to throw your own desert-front barbecue with food bought at the local souk. Wi-Fi is available, as are meals (on request). The staff is friendly and will be happy to find you a guide for the treks out in the desert and other more interesting, often out-of-the-way, gems that encompass the diverse nature of the region.

✪ Dar Azawad

Bounou; tel. 0524/848 730;
www.darazawad.com; 800Dh d

Dar Azawad was featured as one of the top 10 most far-flung romantic getaways by traveller.com in 2016, and it's easy to see why. While some might be drawn to the on-site hammam (130Dh for a basic spa; a massage will set you back 400Dh with a full spa service including exfoliation), nearly everyone will dig the traditional Draa-style architecture with lots of touches from the desert and the local tribes, including wood doors, carpets, and traditional palm wood and reed ceilings. The property has an on-site bar, a pool, and Wi-Fi throughout. The rooms all have air-conditioning and en suite bathrooms. For a real treat, and if the budget allows, take the Sultan's Suite (2,500Dh). It will make you feel like a real pasha. The private terrace looks out into the palm groves and Sahara for a perfect night of private stargazing with your partner. Make sure to treat yourself to one of Salah's special juices while you're there. I'm partial to his homemade lemonade, a refreshing break from mint tea. A three-course dinner can be included with demi-pension for 180Dh per person.

Chez Le Pacha

Bounou; tel. 0524/848 696 or 0524/848 207; www.chezlepacha.com; 800Dh d

Chez Le Pacha is the local five-star, a sprawling complex featuring numerous restaurants and a lavish pool. The spacious rooms are romantically set around a beautiful flower garden, making this a veritable oasis beyond the oasis. Larger rooms are available. An on-site hammam offers full-body massages, perfect after a couple of days in the desert or a few days of trekking. Service is friendly, food is outstanding, and rooms have air-conditioning, which is practically a necessity. The hotel can arrange for trips to several different campsites in Erg Chigaga and the Sahara. The restaurant (Mon.-Fri. 8:30am-12:30pm and 2:30pm-6pm, Sat. 8:30am-1pm, 100Dh) requires reservations, though typically you can call just an hour or so before arrival

a spacious suite at Dar Azawad

the long, dusty roads of the Sahara

and they should be able to have something prepared for you.

TRANSPORTATION

GETTING THERE

Getting to M'hamid from Marrakesh (9hr, 452km/281mi) is easy; just follow the N9 east until the end of the pavement. It's possible to reach M'hamid in one day, though a more casual pace will have you stopping at Ouarzazate (5hr, 261km/162mi), Agdz (3.5hr, 190km/118mi), or Zagora (2hr, 100km/62mi) overnight either on the way there or on the way back.

Travelers without their own vehicles will likely take the CTM bus (tel. 0800/0900 30, www.ctm.ma). The bus leaves Marrakesh (1 daily, 10hr, 185Dh) at 11:15am every day, arriving in M'hamid at 9:15pm, often later. The same bus stops in Ouarzazate (5hr, 1 daily, 80Dh) at 4:15pm. (Note that the CTM website uses an alternative spelling of M'hamid. It's listed there as "Lamhamid Ghozlane.")

To continue on to Erg Chigaga from M'hamid, you need either a dromedary or a four-wheel-drive.

GETTING AROUND

M'hamid is little more than a desert village, while the great Erg Chigaga is a complex system of sand dunes. For either one, you'll want to pack a good pair of walking shoes.

ESSENTIALS

Transportation

GETTING THERE

The **Mohammed V International Airport** in Casablanca is the primary international airport in Morocco, though it is small by international standards, with only a couple of terminals servicing flights in and out of the country. After arriving, you will be asked to fill out a customs form and likely have to wait for about an hour to make

it through customs and sometimes even longer to retrieve your luggage. You may be asked to pass your luggage through a scanner for additional security measures.

There are money exchange offices and ATMs just beyond the customs area. It's a good idea to exchange for some local currency before heading out of the airport. There are taxis and an airport train that connect with Casablanca.

FROM NORTH AMERICA

Most flights from North America connect with European travel hubs, with many of the least expensive flights connecting in Spain at either Madrid or Barcelona for a short layover via **Iberia** (www.iberia.com). Direct flights to and from North America are available only via **Royal Air Maroc** (tel. 0522/489 751, www.royalairmaroc.com), which provides nonstop service via Boston, Miami, Montreal, and New York City to Casablanca. For budget travelers and those looking to break up their trip in Europe, it's sometimes worth booking a less expensive round-trip ticket to and from Europe, like in Madrid, and then purchasing a separate ticket via one of the low-cost carriers directly into one of the other destinations in Morocco, such as Marrakesh.

FROM THE UK AND EUROPE

Europeans have a few modes of transport available to them beyond airplanes, though Morocco is extremely well connected with nearly all major airports in Europe.

By Plane

Most European cities are 2-4 hours away. Agadir, Casablanca, Essaouira, Marrakesh, and Ouarzazate all have direct connections with European transport hubs, often via low-cost airlines such as **Air Arabia** (www.airarabia.com), **Ryan Air** (www.ryanair.com), and **Transavia** (www.transavia.com). If you can, try not to arrive in/depart from Casablanca. Other airports in the country, such as Marrakesh, generally involve a lot less waiting time with customs, check-in, and luggage retrieval, and are generally a better travel experience.

By Bus

The **CTM** (www.ctm.ma) runs international bus lines that use the ferries between Morocco and Spain. Buses stop in major cities in Spain, France, and Italy. Tickets generally cost the same as a plane ticket and are sometimes more expensive. Buses leave from most major cities, as well as numerous small ones, generally once a week or more, and travel through Morocco via Tangier to Casablanca, generally making a stop in Rabat on the way south.

By Car or Camper Van

Ferries run services back and forth to Morocco, making it easy for people with their own vehicle in Europe to road-trip through Morocco. Drivers might be asked to provide proof of ownership and insurance that will cover any potential accidents while in Morocco. Check with your insurance company to purchase international driving insurance for the duration of your stay. If you are traveling in a car that is not your own, you must have a certified, stamped letter from the vehicle's owner. At the border, in Tangier, Ceuta, or Melilla, if you do not have international insurance, you will be able to purchase it from **Assurance Frontière** (59 Blvd. Bordeaux,

Casablanca, tel. 0522/484 156) for 950Dh. This will cover driver and vehicle for one month. It is possible to renew this insurance at the headquarters in Casablanca. An International Driver's License is not a requirement for driving in Morocco, nor will you be asked for it. Your license from your home country will suffice.

By Boat

From Spain it's possible to take ferries over the Strait of Gibraltar into Morocco. Cars, camper vans, and walk-ons are all served by numerous ferry companies shuttling back and forth throughout the day. By far, the most effective crossing is between Tarifa, Spain, and Tangier, Morocco. This is the quickest ferry crossing at 35 minutes and will drop you off directly at the bottom of Tangier's old medina. However, this passage is occasionally closed if the seas are particularly stormy. FRS (www.frs.es), one of the longer-running ferry services, and the new Intershipping (www.intershipping.es) ferry service both have the same runs, alternating departure times across the strait. A typical four-door sedan with one passenger costs around 2,500Dh round-trip. It is not possible to cross the strait with a rented car.

Ferries also service Tangier across the strait from Algeciras and Gibraltar. These ferries take much longer to cross the strait and to load passengers and cargo. Additionally, they make port at the Tangier Med station (not Tangier Ville) about a 45-minute drive from Tangier. This port is also used by freight trucks and construction equipment, slowing the entire boarding process. The crossing from either Algeciras or Gibraltar will take an entire day with loading and unloading the ferry, customs, and additional drive times in Morocco. Prices are much the same as the crossing at Tarifa.

The Spanish exclaves of Ceuta (Sebta) and Melilla in the north of Morocco are also serviced by ferries from mainland Spain with prices and services more or less the same as the ferry service between Tarifa and Tangier, though with longer travel times.

You do cross an international border when arriving or departing Morocco via ferry and will be asked to fill out a customs form. When arriving, you will show this form along with your passport to a customs officer aboard the ferry. To avoid waiting in a long line, it's best to arrive immediately to the customs officer and present your passport and form. If a line has already formed by the time you enter the ferry, relax, enjoy the trip, and wait until the ferry has almost arrived to have your papers checked. There's no reason to spend the entire ferry ride waiting in a customs line.

From Tangier, Marrakesh is about a six-hour drive to the south mostly on the A1 and A7, following the Atlantic Coast and passing Rabat and Casablanca before turning inland toward the Red City.

FROM AUSTRALIA AND NEW ZEALAND

Unsurprisingly, there are no direct flights to Morocco available from the other side of the planet. Most flights will connect you with a travel hub, such as Doha or Dubai. Many travelers coming from Australia and New Zealand bookend their trips to Morocco with long stays in Europe.

THE MARRAKESH EXPRESS

The "Marrakesh Express" was the nickname for the train ride between Casablanca and Marrakesh used by travelers to Morocco in the 1960s and 1970s. It was popularized by the Crosby, Stills & Nash song of the same name. Today's Marrakesh Express still runs between Casablanca and Marrakesh, but with a newer train and fewer hippies—though there are generally still a few lingering around, "traveling the train through clear Moroccan skies," just as the band sang 50 years ago. Plans are afoot to extend the high-speed train that runs from Tangier to Casablanca all the way to Marrakesh by 2025.

From Europe, it's a quick flight and easy to purchase a separate ticket via one of the low-cost carriers directly into Marrakesh, thus bypassing Casablanca. The quickest, most direct, and often least expensive flight into Morocco from Sydney or Auckland is via Qatar airlines with a stopover in Doha. This flight is still over 24 hours long, so be sure to pack a pillow.

FROM SOUTH AFRICA

There are no direct flights into Morocco from South Africa. Because you'll have to have a layover anyway, it's often worth it to book your round-trip ticket directly into one of the other destinations in Morocco, such as Marrakesh, to bypass Casablanca. Common cities for layover include Doha, Istanbul, Paris, and Rome. Like those coming from North America or Australia, it is an inviting proposition to bookend your holiday in Europe or the Middle East.

GETTING AROUND

BY PLANE

There are a few in-country flights worth thinking about to maximize time in Morocco. Direct flights between Fez and Marrakesh, Marrakesh and Ouarzazate, and Tangier and Marrakesh are the most interesting to cut down on some travel time. Flights within Morocco are operated by the state-run Royal Air Maroc (www.royalairmaroc.com).

BY TRAIN

For most travelers, the national train run by ONCF (www.oncf.ma) is the most convenient way to get around Morocco. Though limited, the train does stop in most major cities. There are two primary train lines, which meet at Sidi Kacem, a small town roughly in the middle of Rabat and Fez. One line travels up and down the Atlantic seaboard from Tangier south through Rabat and Casablanca before ending in Marrakesh. This is the train the majority of travelers will take after landing in Casablanca and heading down to Marrakesh. The other line begins in Casablanca and runs northeast through Meknes and Fez and crosses the mountains to distant Oujda.

Trains are inexpensive, and most travelers will want to purchase first-class tickets. These are a relative bargain, generally costing only 20-40Dh more, and ensure air-conditioning and a reserved seat.

During peak travel times, such as popular holidays like Eid al-Adha or school holidays, trains can quickly fill up, and sometimes first-class tickets are not available. If this is the case, be prepared for a long, stuffy ride standing in the side corridor walkway, avoiding the smell of the usually open and rarely cleaned toilet in second class.

Train stations are often unannounced. If you're unsure of what station you are at, ask around. Chances are that someone knows and will be willing to tell you when you've reached your station. Outside of the stations, be prepared to fight off taxi drivers and faux guides who will try to lure you into overpriced taxis or, even worse, overpriced lodgings. Simply walk out of the station and wait along the nearest busy street to hail a passing taxi.

The new Al-Boraq **high-speed train** makes getting to and from Tangier very quick, though requiring passengers from Fez and Meknes to change trains at Kenitra. From Kenitra to Tangier is now a short 45 minutes on the Al-Boraq, and Casablanca to Tangier is about 2.5 hours. It's best to purchase tickets on the ONCF website a day or two ahead of your travel for the Al-Boraq, or in-person at the station.

BY BUS

The network of privately run buses is a great alternative to riding the rails and is a safe, comfortable way to travel to destinations that are not serviced by the train. If traveling in the heat of the day, to avoid overheating make sure to sit on the side of the bus that will be the most shaded. Buses on trips of more than two hours make 15- to 30-minute rest stops at roadside cafés catering to the bus crowd.

CTM (www.ctm.ma) runs buses that crisscross the country. Most of their buses are comfortable, and there are even premier bus tickets available on buses with slightly more legroom and Wi-Fi—indispensable for some digitally tethered travelers. In larger cities, the CTM buses have their own stations, though in smaller cities they will be found at the main bus station or *gare routière*. During the busy travel seasons it is best to buy tickets a day

ahead of time whenever possible, if not two or three days ahead of time, as these buses often fill up, making seats a scarce commodity.

The other recommended bus company is **Supratours** (www.oncf.ma), which has teamed with the ONCF train company. These buses pick up where the rails give out. The buses are comfortable, safe, and reliable, though, like the CTM buses, they will fill during peak travel times, so it is best to book ahead. When traveling by either CTM or Supratours, you will be asked to store any larger bags beneath the bus for a fee of 5-10Dh.

Other local companies also operate buses. These buses are generally less comfortable, less expensive, less punctual, and less safe. Buyer beware. The night services, though cooler, are subject to far more accidents, particularly in the mountain passes and along National Road 8 (N8) from Marrakesh to Agadir.

BY *GRAND TAXI*

The *grands taxis* relay passengers between cities and towns. Taxis are regulated by the local government, which sets the prices. Prices sometimes need to be negotiated (refer to relevant locations in this guide for average prices) with less-than-honest drivers, and the cost generally goes up by 50 percent after nightfall. Prices are per seat. Sometimes, *grands taxis* will ask one of the travelers for a passport to register travel outside of their normal jurisdiction with the local authorities.

It seems like almost every story of a traveler to Morocco involves some sort of a harrowing trip in one of these *grands taxis*. The seat belts often don't function and drivers are often exceedingly aggressive. However, many of the taxis now in service have been purchased since 2015, offering an infinitely more comfortable ride than their predecessors. By all means, when traveling by *grand taxi*, make sure you get one of the newer cars for your own story of a harrowing taxi ride.

BY *PETIT TAXI*

Petits taxis run in all cities and most midsized towns. Typically they use a counter in the cities and charge double rates after nightfall, though in some smaller towns a flat rate is common. Throughout Morocco, it is illegal for a *petit taxi* to travel outside of its city or town or to have more than three passengers at one time.

BY CAR

Driving in Morocco, though a bit more dangerous than in Australia, New Zealand, North America, or the UK, is perfectly doable for drivers who practice good defensive driving techniques. The roads are, for the most part, well paved, and road-tripping through Morocco can be a wonderful way to get off the beaten path and find pieces of this stunning country that are less explored. Those who have driven in other parts of North Africa, India, or even around the Mediterranean will be right at home driving in Morocco.

Moroccan drivers, by and large, are some of the worst drivers in the world. The legal driving age is 21, and driving school, a comprehensive written test, and a performance test are all required by the government to earn a driving license. However, most Moroccan drivers have simply paid a small bribe to have their license issued, bypassing the school and test. Therefore, most drivers are unaware or care little for the basic traffic laws. Drivers sometimes pass on blind turns, run red lights, and will straddle two lanes on the paid autoroute. In the cities, the aggression is compounded, and streets are unmarked, adding to the confusion.

Driving at night should be avoided, as there are few street lights. Often, herders with camels, sheep, goats, and cows try crossing streets after dark, particularly in the countryside, making the possibility of hitting livestock a real concern. Keep in mind that the signage, generally in Arabic and French (though occasionally only in one or the other language) is not usually lit, making following turn-offs and other directions that much more difficult. Wherever possible, we've included the Arabic script for the names of the cities and towns appearing in this guide. Even if you can't read Arabic, you can match the script in this guide to the script on the signage. This could double as a fun road-trip game in the car for the kids.

However, daytime driving is perfectly fine. The speed limit on the autoroutes is typically 120 kilometers (75mi) per hour. Beware of speed traps and police who walk out onto the road, even the autoroutes, to stop speeding traffic. Keep your passport and driver's license on you at all times. A typical driving infraction will set you back 400Dh. You will be given a receipt for this and are expected to pay the fine on the spot. If you are unable to pay the fine, your ID may be confiscated and taken to the local court for you to pay the fine there.

Gasoline isn't exactly cheap in Morocco (12Dh a liter, around 25Dh a gallon), though it is subsidized by the government. Consider renting a newer, fuel-efficient diesel car. Diesel is slightly cheaper (less than 9Dh a liter, around 20Dh a gallon), and a new diesel engine can fetch nearly double the mileage of unleaded engines. Always fill your car up to the maximum whenever stopping at a station, particularly in the rural areas, as sometimes stations can be far apart.

Car Rentals

If you're renting a car in Morocco, to get the best deal and a wider variety of cars to choose from, it's best to arrange it before arrival. Be sure to request an automatic transmission if you need one, because the majority of rental cars are manual.

Rental insurance is required, and it comes included with car rentals. Check with your insurance provider at home to see if rentals are covered overseas. Some credit cards offer rental insurance if you use their card to rent a car. If your home auto insurance or credit card covers the rental insurance, you might be able to get the insurance that is included with the rental waived—it's worth inquiring. Spending a little extra on travel insurance is always a good idea.

Typical prices in Morocco for rentals with unlimited mileage range from 300Dh per day for a standard four-door sedan to 600Dh per day for four-wheel drive, with large discounts often available for weekly rentals. It's possible to find rentals for as little as 100Dh per day if you plan a bit in advance.

Hertz (www.hertz.com) and Avis (www.avis.com) have locations at Mohammed V Airport in Casablanca as well as airports in Agadir and Marrakesh. Large groups or families might consider the large vans available for rent through GM2 Tours (www.gm2tours.ma).

BY BICYCLE

Bicyclists share the road with the drivers and can be seen training throughout the Middle Atlas and High Atlas regions through the fall and spring seasons. Mountain biking has grown increasingly popular with European and North American travelers. It's a pleasant way to get around to otherwise inaccessible areas, and the roads are generally quieter than those found back at home. Biking is safe enough when sharing the road with vehicles, as long as bicyclists stick to the shoulder, though a helmet and lamp are highly recommended. However, biking is not regulated by Moroccan law, and in cities bikers are often seen without helmets. Bikes are welcomed on most buses for 10Dh.

Visas and Officialdom

PASSPORTS AND VISAS

Morocco is a tourist-friendly destination that doesn't require entry visas for visitors from most countries. Travelers from the UK, Europe, North America, Australia, and New Zealand are exempt from any form of visa and granted automatic 90-day entry. However, your passport should be valid for at least six months from the date of entry. On a customs form you will be asked to mark your profession. Journalists should consider writing in another profession, as customs officers have been wary of letting journalists into the country without extensive documentation.

South Africans do have to apply for visas, which they can do in their country of residency through the nearest Moroccan embassy. Otherwise, to extend your stay in Morocco, it is possible to exit to Morocco for a stamp via Ceuta or Melilla and reenter, sometimes on the same day, for another 90 days. However, some customs officers will ask you to travel to mainland Spain and spend at least one night there before returning for a 90-day extension.

CUSTOMS

Customs regulations are fairly lenient in Morocco. Hand luggage is rarely checked upon arrival, and while traveling across the borders between Ceuta, Melilla, and Morocco, customs officers almost never ask foreigners what they are taking with them. However, legally there are limits to what can be taken into the country. The limits are as follows: one liter of spirits (hard alcohol) or two liters of wine; 200 cigarettes, 50 cigars, or 400 grams (14 ounces) of tobacco; 150 milliliters (5 fluid ounces) of perfume or 250 milliliters (8 fluid ounces) of *eau de toilette*; one camera and one laptop for personal use; and gifts totaling no more than 2,000Dh.

Border controls are particularly wary of the smuggling of hashish. It and other controlled substances are forbidden. If you are traveling with many books or if you have a book that is controversial, prepare to be questioned. If the customs officers consider the text to be "immoral" or "liable to cause a breach of peace," it may be confiscated. Generally speaking, books condemning Islam, questioning the king, or questioning Morocco's right to the Western Sahara are banned throughout the country.

EMBASSIES AND CONSULATES

The Canadian Embassy (66 Ave. Mehdi Ben Barka, tel. 0537/544 949, www.canadainternational.gc.ca) in Rabat is generally open Monday-Thursday 8am-4:30pm and Friday 8am-1:30pm. It is closed for Canadian and Moroccan holidays. Australians traveling in Morocco who need assistance can be helped at the Canadian Embassy. For emergencies, Canadian and Australian citizens can call collect to reach the Emergency Watch and Response Centre (Canada tel. 613/996-8885).

New Zealanders will have to travel to Madrid, Spain, for consular services (7 Calle del Pinar, tel. +34 915 230 226, email: madrid@embajadanuevazelanda.com).

The UK Embassy (28 Ave. S.A.R. Sidi Mohammed, Souissi, tel. 0537/633 333) in Rabat deals largely with political interests. It keeps consulate offices in Casablanca (Villa Les Sallurges, 36 Rue de la Loire, Polo, tel. 0522/857 400, Mon.-Thurs. 8am-4:15pm, Fri. 8am-1pm), Marrakesh (Borj Menara 2, Immeuble B, 5th fl., Ave. Abdelkrim El Khattabi, tel. 0537/633 333, appointment only), and Agadir (no address, tel. 0537/633 333, Mon.-Thurs. 8am-4:15pm, Fri. 8am-1pm, appointment only). For emergencies, UK citizens should call tel. 0537/633 333.

The US Consulate (8, Bd Moulay Youssef) in Casablanca is available for US citizens who need consular services or assistance, such as in the case of a lost or stolen passport. The consulate is closed on observed US and Moroccan holidays. For emergencies, contact the American Citizen Services hotline (tel. 0522/642 099 Mon.-Fri. 8am-5pm, tel. 0661/131 939 after hours). The US Embassy

(Km5.7, Ave. Mohammed VI, Souissi, tel. 0537/637 200) in Rabat is strictly diplomatic without services for citizens.

The **South African Embassy** (34 Rue des Saadiens, Quartier Hassan) in Rabat has services for their citizens. It is best to call ahead for an appointment on one of the following numbers: 0537/689 159, 0537/700 874, or 0537/689 163, or you can email: safricamissionrabat@gmail.com.

Food

Moroccan cuisine is widely considered one of the best cuisines in the world. While you can find good Moroccan food at restaurants, the best is made at home. This is largely because Morocco is not a dining-out country. Most of the meals happen at home, generally cooked by the wife or mother, and, as most Moroccans will tell you, made even more delicious upon the arrival of a guest.

MOROCCAN CUISINE

A typical **breakfast** in Morocco consists of different breads (such as *harsha*, a semolina flatbread), Moroccan pancakes (*m'smmen* or *mil\oui*), goat cheese, olives, freshly squeezed orange juice, and a hard-boiled or fried egg. Often, breakfast is served with a salad, just like lunch and dinner.

There are numerous Moroccan **salads,** nearly all of them involving steamed and cooked vegetables. Some of the better-known salads include eggplant, beetroot, roasted peppers, onions, and tomatoes. These are served sometimes before, after, or with the **soup,** traditionally a *harira* (a tomato-based soup, often with chickpeas, lentils, or pasta noodles) or lentil soup, though sometimes *bissara* (a soup made of fava beans or split peas). In fact, in most Moroccan medinas and along the seaports you'll find sellers with vats of thick *bissara*. It is filling, inexpensive, and said to have properties that are great for the lungs. For vegan travelers, it often becomes a staple while wandering through the complex medinas.

The **tajine** is a main staple of Moroccan cuisine. Tajines are served in conical clay dishes (also called tajines), traditionally cooked over an open flame, and are something like a slow-cooked stew. Tajines generally involve some sort of meat. Some of the more common preparations include chicken, lemon, and olive; spiced meatballs and eggs; beef with honey, dates, and prunes; lamb with prunes and olives; and spiced sardine meatballs. Vegetarian tajines are available, though invariably these lack many of the spices and are typically more bland than meat tajines.

Traditionally, families would gather around for **couscous** lunch on Friday after the imam gave his afternoon sermon. A lot of them still do, and to honor this tradition and make time for families, many businesses have shortened afternoon hours—many of the old medinas are closed for the entire day. Couscous, as it is known in Morocco, is quite different from its bastardized cousin in the West that comes in a box and is ready in less than five minutes. Couscous

For some delicious, inexpensive treats, the seemingly infinite number of snack carts you'll find in most medinas are a wonderful way to interact with locals and taste some fast food, Moroccan style. Street food generally ranges from 1-10Dh. This is a taste of true local flavor.

- One of the more common street foods is a snail soup known as **babboosh** in most of Morocco. Steaming bowls of this brothy treat are for the escargot lover. The snails are typically seasoned with a warm mix of spices, such as licorice, cinnamon, bay leaves, and the spice blend *ras el hanoot*.

- Another chickpea treat is **hoomus.** This steamed chickpea snack is seasoned with generous amounts of salt and cumin. It's a bit like popcorn and made to be eaten on the go.

- A more filling treat is **bissara,** generally made with fava beans, though sometimes with split peas as well. This is a thick, hearty soup, popular with sailors for its rumored qualities to help rheumatism. Usually this sailor staple is served with a half loaf of Morocco round bread and plenty of olive oil and chili pepper.

- Popular barbecues sell **brochettes** of seasoned chicken and beef, and other vendors sell **tropical fruits** by the slice. For some energy on the go, consider the local nut roaster who'll be selling a variety of **nuts**—such as walnuts, almonds, and cashews—that can be had for peanuts, bad pun fully intended.

takes many, many hours to make. The small grains of pasta are hand rolled and steamed over the meat and vegetables in a special couscous maker. A traditional couscous is shared with the family from one large dish, with the meat, usually chicken, beef, or lamb, arranged in the middle of the plate. If you're eating with a Moroccan family, the portion in front of you on the plate is yours, and you will often be eating with your hands. Keep in mind that it is rude to eat with your left hand. This is considered the "dirty" hand as it should be used for performing your toiletries. Eat with your right hand only. You can either form balls of couscous and vegetables with your hand or use bread to scoop up the little grains and sauce.

Undoubtedly, you will have had enough mint tea by the end of your stay. Often jokingly called "Berber whisky" or "whisky Moroccan," mint tea is a customary ritual and something hosts offer to their guests. You will likely be offered mint tea at the many shops and bazaars in the medina, particularly at carpet sellers, where some time must be spent haggling over a price, as well as at most smaller hotels, guesthouses, and family homes. The tea is generally sweetened with copious amounts of sugar, making it a syrupy mint affair. It's okay to ask for only a little bit of sugar or no sugar at all.

VEGANS, VEGETARIANS, AND GLUTEN-FREE

Veganism and vegetarianism are somewhat novel concepts in Morocco. Outside of major cities and high-end restaurants and *riads,* explanations about not eating meat or meat products are often met with confusion. Meat is a staple of the Moroccan diet. If invited to a Moroccan family's home for a meal, meat will invariably be the central feature. It is considered somewhat rude not to offer a guest meat and equally rude not to partake. Dishes generally served when a guest arrives are either tajine or couscous, each usually with some vegetables, though cooked or served with the meat. This leads to some true moral and ethical decisions for hardcore vegans and vegetarians. Is it okay to try to explain that you don't eat meat and pick at the vegetables around the dish or to refuse the dish altogether, thus insulting the host? In practice, it is best to pick at some vegetables, do your best to explain, and repent later.

While eating out, you will typically find seven-vegetable couscous (usually written in French: *couscous de sept legumes*) and vegetarian tajines and pizzas. Sometimes meat broth may be used for flavor, though, so beware. If asking for a dish without meat, you may be served something with fish, chicken, or turkey unless you are very clear, as these are often not considered meat dishes; the Moroccan concept of meat is generally confined to beef, goat, and sheep.

Good staples for vegans and vegetarians include Moroccan salads, generally vegan, as well as *bissara,* a kind of fava bean or split pea soup that is usually served with bread and plenty of olive oil and chili pepper. Plenty of shops in the medinas sell roasted nuts. Supplements, such as B12, iodine, iron, and calcium, should be packed with you, as you will likely not find them in Morocco.

The good news is that there are plenty of delicious fresh fruits and vegetables. Though the use of pesticides and herbicides has grown and includes crop-dusting over some of the larger farms around Rabat and Casablanca, the vast majority of farmers are simply too poor to purchase these and rely on eco-friendly methods of growing their fruits and veggies. Fruits and vegetables should be washed thoroughly and be allowed to soak in vinegar for five minutes to kill unwanted bacteria.

Eating gluten-free is easy enough, though don't expect your waiter to understand what it means. Only the high-end restaurants and *riads* understand what a gluten-free food is. Couscous is decidedly not gluten-free and should be avoided, but rice and potatoes are plentiful in Morocco and make for easy substitutes.

BEER, WINE, AND HARD ALCOHOL

Though Morocco produces some fine wines (and has for over a thousand years) and now even produces beers, drinking alcohol is considered forbidden by Islam and is often an underground affair. In more liberal homes, wine might be served with dinner, but by and large this is a rarity. Drinking is not allowed within view of a mosque. In upscale restaurants, comprehensive beer, wine, and alcohol menus are available. Most local bars cater to men, and women seen drinking or smoking in these establishments will likely be considered prostitutes. Upmarket bars frequented by European and North American expats are generally okay, while nightclubs offer another type of scene, though again prostitution is often rampant and drinks are outrageously expensive.

In some medinas, such as in Tangier, alcohol sales are entirely banned. Before and after religious holidays, stores selling alcohol are required to close completely. During these holidays, nearly the only places to find alcohol are tourist-specific enclaves, such as big chain hotels.

Accommodations

Accommodations in Morocco are wide ranging—from the dingiest, dirtiest fleabag hostels to the exquisitely luxurious seaside resorts found up and down the Atlantic Coast to nights in the Sahara wrapped snug in a Bedouin tent under the stars. Though it is perfectly possible to travel throughout most of the country using chain hotels and resorts, the more interesting options are generally found in the old medinas of Morocco. You will find traditional 18th- and 19th-century homes, known as *dars* and *riads,* renovated and converted into modern-day B&Bs replete with curvy stucco work, ornately carved woodwork, and imaginative tile work only found in Morocco. Because the homes are crammed into the medina, literally side by side, there is little (if any) attention paid to the exterior. Thus, rotting doors and rusty locks often give way to the welcome surprise of luxurious lodgings.

DARS, RIADS, AND MAISONS D'HÔTES

A *dar* is a traditional Moroccan home featuring a central patio and a series of surrounding rooms. The patio opens to the sky, allowing in fresh air. These homes were historically used by smaller families. Downstairs were the main living quarters, featuring a kitchen and one or two salons. Terraces were used primarily to wash and dry clothes, though they were also places for the children to play and for women to chat across rooftops.

Riads are much like *dars,* though considerably larger. The central patio often has a garden and almost always a fountain. Downstairs was traditionally the public space, with the quarters upstairs reserved for family and the terraces again used for laundry, play, and conversation. Some *riads* included a private hammam, a considerable luxury.

The French term *maison d'hôte,* meaning guesthouse, is used liberally throughout Morocco to refer to *dars, riads,* and new constructions outside of the medinas to house travelers. These are typically a bit less expensive than *riads,* as *riads* are considerably trendier. Many *dars, riads,* and *maisons d'hôtes* are foreign-owned or owned by Moroccans who have usually lived in Europe for some time.

In practice, *dars, riads,* and *maisons d'hôtes* are the best accommodations in the country, with locations generally near major tourist destinations and comfort often exceeding the best hotels in town. However, because the majority of these are remodeled homes from the 18th and 19th centuries, many have steep stairways that are not suitable for young children or mobility-impaired travelers. Because the market for B&Bs is loosely monitored, it is also worth taking a tour of the property, examining the beds, sheets, and bathrooms, before agreeing to stay at a property not recommended in this guide.

HOSTELS

The network of hostels throughout Morocco is quite good, particularly along the Atlantic Coast and at most of the major destinations. A typical bed will cost 40-100Dh a night, depending on availability, location, and season. Most Moroccan hostels are plugged into the Hostel World (www.hostelworld.com) network. It is best to book hostel rooms ahead of time, particularly around European holidays, as hostels will often be full of backpacking students.

GÎTES D'ÉTAPE AND REFUGES

Along popular hiking trails through the mountains of the Rif, Atlas, and Anti-Atlas, there are *gîtes d'étape* and refuges to keep you warm, dry, and safe from the elements. Refuges are generally little more than a rickety wood shack, though are occasionally something more of a low-end hotel, complete with a small café or restaurant. Bedding is of the bunkbed/army cot type. The *gîtes d'étape* sprinkled through many of the smaller mountain towns of Morocco are family homes where they welcome guests. Sometimes there are beds, but often you sleep like the family, on layers of wool carpets directly on the floor. Prices range from 100-300Dh a night, and often food is included.

Conduct and Customs

By and large, Moroccans are some of the friendliest, most genuinely helpful people you can meet. Morocco is always ranked in the top 10 "friendliest countries in the world." Of course, a few bad apples may try to use this to their advantage and request something that seems unfair, such as an exceedingly high price for an item or service. But for the most part, people are friendly, curious about where you came from, and, if you've taken the time to master a few phrases in Moroccan Arabic, likely to invite you over for tea or dinner. That said, customs are different in Morocco than in many Western countries. Greetings are more elaborate. The importance of the family is heightened. The roles of men and women are more defined, in some cases rigidly. In many regions, even the clothing is significantly different. With this said, women have experienced harassment, typically in the form of persistent catcalls or, on rare occasion, being touched inappropriately. For the most part, tourists are left alone as they are an important part of the economy, though aggression does occasionally happen.

GREETINGS

Greetings in Morocco vary from region to region, though they are all elaborate. A typical greeting inquires about your health and the health of your family (often each individual member), and then finishes with "so everything is well, then?" before a conversation can be started. When women are meeting for the first time, it is generally customary to kiss once on each cheek, *á la française*. This is the case in most cities, though in some rural regions women kiss each other on the hands, arms, or foreheads as well. Men generally meet with a handshake, though often this handshake will be soft, even limp. Greetings between men and women are a bit more complex. For female travelers, it is best to stick with shaking hands with men, as some men might make the wrong assumption about your intention if you try to hug them or give them a friendly peck on the cheek. For male travelers, it is best to let the woman take the lead. Some Moroccan women kiss on the cheek, some shake hands, and some cannot be touched and will give you a deferential nod of the head, sometimes without even eye contact.

If traveling as a couple, you will likely be asked many times how many kids you have or, if you're younger, when you are expecting to have children. If you are older, you will be expected to have children, the more the better, and even grandchildren. You will be asked about your children—what they do, what they study, where they live, if they are married and have children. This is considered polite conversation. It's a great idea to have a few pictures of your family to share with people you meet along the way, even if just on your phone.

When invited for dinner or tea to a person's home, it is customary to take off your shoes at the entryway. Single women should be wary of any invitation to a man's house. If you are offered food and refuse, this is seen as very insulting. Vegetarians and vegans, in particular, are put in an awkward situation because nearly anything offered will contain some sort of meat product. Most Moroccans do not understand the concept of vegetarianism, let alone veganism or gluten allergies, and the host will feel bad, often for days and weeks on end, because he or she was not a good enough host. I find it best to swallow your morals in this rare instance in

the name of cultural diplomacy. If you can't, then tell them you have an allergy. Your host will still feel bad, but less so.

Many friendly encounters happen in the context of public transportation. If you can't, then tell them you have an allergy. Your host will still feel bad, but less so.

Many friendly encounters happen in the context of public transportation. In this case, it is customary to share food. If being offered food, it is polite to take what is offered. Another semi-elaborate ritual between Moroccans involves offering and accepting food. A person should offer food three times. The first two times the food is offered, it should be declined out of politeness. The third time it is offered, this time more persuasively, the person being offered the food is then free to take it or refuse it.

BEGGARS

You will likely encounter quite a few people asking you for money. Keep in mind that as a foreigner visiting Morocco, you are considered wealthy. The country teems with poverty and there is no real social security. People, particularly the elderly, are entirely reliant on their families for support. Generally speaking, you will find older beggars outside of mosques and at gates into the old cities. A few dirhams will be appreciated, and you can expect some form of blessing for you and your family in return. If you do not have any dirhams to spare, master the phrase, *"Allah yejeeb tisseer,"* meaning "May God make it easy on you." This is a polite blessing for beggars to be used in lieu of giving them any cash.

If a beggar is being persistent, particularly younger beggars who are obviously able-bodied, it is best to ignore them. When possible, duck into the nearest shop or, if you're working on your Moroccan Arabic, tell them

MOROCCO: A TIMELINE

250,000 BC	Earliest known hominid in the world (discovered near Salé in 1971)
12,000 BC (possibly earlier)	First known human inhabitants of Morocco: the Amazigh
1,200 BC	Phoenicians control the Moroccan coast, using Essaouira to produce Tyrian Purple dye derived from the shell of the Murex sea-snail. After the fall of the Phoenician Empire, the Carthaginians take control.
CE 40-285	Rome officially annexes the lands of Morocco into the Roman empire, establishing Volubilis as the regional capital. Eventually, the Amazigh overtake Volubilis, signaling an end to the Roman empire in Morocco.
711	Tariq ibn Ziyad crosses the Strait of Gibralter (named after him) with a large army, overtaking the Visigoths in Spain and helping to establish the Umayyad Empire.
788	Fleeing for his life, Idriss I, the great-great-great-grandson of the Prophet Mohammed, ends up in Volubilis and establishes the modern Moroccan state as the Idrisid dynasty, the first ruling dynasty of Morocco. The Idrisid dynasty ends around 200 years later and for many years, Morocco is under the power of the Umayyad dynasty.
1040	Almoravid Empire begins, establishing Marrakesh as the capital, expanding the Moroccan empire into Spain and south to Mauritania. Under the Almoravids, Fez was united and expanded.
1124	The Almohad Caliphate begins, taking over the former Almoravid lands. The landmarks of the Koutoubia Mosque in Marrakesh, the Giralda of Sevilla, and the Hassan Tower of Rabat are testaments to their art and architecture.
1244	The Marinid dynasty begins. They make Fez their capital city, expanding out into Fez Jdid (New Fez), thus making the entirety of the old Fez medina as we know it today. The Marinid rule marks Fez's Golden Age.

"mandeesh whalloh, saafi, baraka." This means, "I don't have anything. That's enough, really enough." If the beggar is being more persistent, you have permission to tell them, *"bahd mehni"*—literally, "get off my back," meaning "get lost."

Sadly, you will likely see quite a few children, sometimes begging and sometimes selling tissues near bus stations, train stations, and at busy intersections. It is best to never give children money. Better to give them pens, pencils, paper, or even candy. Gangs of street kids are known to use their money to buy glue and gasoline to huff. This is a very sad reality of contemporary Morocco.

CLOTHING

Generally speaking, the urban areas are Westernized, with jeans, T-shirts, tank tops, shorts, and skirts all being the norm. In the more popular beach-fronts, such as Taghazoute and its environs, walking around in swimwear and flip-flops is generally acceptable. Otherwise, keep in mind that Morocco is generally more conservative. Men are expected to cover their chests, upper arms, and legs past the knees. Women are expected to be covered from the ankle to the wrist. It is best to wear loose-fitting clothes with natural fibers that allow your body to breathe. When traveling in the places in Morocco where the sun is stronger,

1549	The short-lived Saadian dynasty begins, leaving some ornate art and architecture behind, including the recently discovered Saadian Tombs in Marrakesh.
1666	The Alaouite dynasty begins. This is the current ruling family of Morocco and the world's second-oldest continuous hereditary dynasty in the world just after the Yamoto dynasty of Japan.
1777	The Sultanate of Morocco, under Mohammed ben Abdallah, is the first nation to recognize the United States as an independent nation.
1912	The Treaty of Fez is signed, establishing much of Morocco as a French Protectorate. A separate agreement between France and Spain later in the year grants Spain protectorate rights in the north and south of Morocco.
1920-1927	The Rif War rages, pitting the local Moroccans, largely Riffian, against the Spanish, directly after WWI. The fierce Riffian warrior and judge, Abd el-Krim, establishes short-lived Republic of the Rif.
1956	The French and Spanish protectorate era come to an end under the stewardship of Sultan Mohammed V, transforming Morocco into what it is today: a constitutional monarchy.
1975	The Green March occurs, allowing Morocco to seize the Western Sahara, something still at debate in international politics today and something of an ongoing dispute between Spain, Algeria, and Morocco.
1999	Mohammed VI, the current king of Morocco, ascends to the throne following his father's death. Under Mohammed VI, large gains have been made in the realm of human rights, gender equality, tourism, and business, though there is still much work to be done.
2011	The February 20 Movement, inspired by the larger Arab Spring, saw peaceful protests around Morocco. This led directly to constitutional and political reform.

such as the mountains and desert, you will be thankful for the extra covering.

Depending on what kind of beach, pool, or mountainside waterfall you're at, Morocco can be either conservative or very, very liberal with swimwear. Largely, this does depend on your comfort level as a traveler to this country. As a general rule of thumb, private beaches and swimming pools are much like Europe, North America, or Australia with two-pieces being the norm (though rarely, if ever, would a woman go topless). However, on public beaches, one-piece bathing suits for women are more the norm. It's a good idea to take a look around, see what other people are wearing, and dress accordingly within your comfort zone.

MUSLIM ETIQUETTE

Religion is taken quite seriously in Morocco, and it is illegal to mock, deride, or otherwise insult Islam, the Prophet Mohammed, or the king, who is the religious leader, or "Commander of the Faithful," of Morocco. The mosque is a sacred space, and as disappointing as it might be for non-Muslim travelers, mosques, *zawiyas,* and other religious buildings are largely off-limits for nonbelievers. The exceptions are the guided tours at the Hassan II Mosque in Casablanca, the courtyards of some of the *zawiyas,* and a couple of the mosques that remain unused, such as the Tin Mal Mosque in the High Atlas. Muslims dressed in western fashion will often be questioned at the doors of the mosque and, in some instances, be asked to prove that they are indeed believers through reciting the *shahada* (Islamic creed), particularly in the more superstitious *zawiyas*.

RAMADAN

The holy month of Ramadan is one of the spiritual pillars of Islam, marking the first revelation of the Quran to the Prophet Mohammed. It is the ninth month of the Islamic calendar, a lunar-based calendar, so its dates according to the Gregorian calendar shift each year. Unlike other Muslim countries, Morocco does not use astronomic calculations to dictate the particular months of the lunar calendar and instead uses observation by authorities with the naked eye.

Ramadan is a period of abstention. Believers are required to fast from sunrise to sunset. Nothing is allowed to pass through the lips, including food, water, cigarettes, or even gum. Believers are also expected to abstain from sex and impure thought. It is illegal to disrespect Ramadan, as it is a pillar of Islam, and a few Moroccans are jailed each year, usually for eating or smoking in public during the daylight hours of Ramadan.

Non-Muslims are not required to fast, though they'll often be encouraged to, with Muslims telling them how good it can be for their health, both spiritual and physical. Pregnant women, women menstruating, children, the elderly, those sick or disabled, and nonbelievers are all exempt from fasting. However, those not fasting should be as respectful as possible, which includes eating, drinking, and smoking in private, away from crowds and off the streets.

Ramadan can be a beautiful time to travel the region. Because it is a period of heightened religious awareness, there are some unexpected benefits for single women travelers, who will rarely, if ever, be harassed, and throughout the daytime, because smoking is not permitted, cafés, restaurants, trains, and other public areas have improved air quality. Moroccans are often more convivial and are more likely to invite guests to *ftoor*, the breaking of the fast, which happens at sundown. In most cities, towns, and villages there is a particular signal to mark the end of the day's fast—often the sound of a siren, firing of a cannon, or lighting of a lamp atop a minaret.

A fast is traditionally broken with a glass of water, dates, and a bowl of *harira* (a soup typically made with lentils, chickpeas, and sometimes meat). The giving of alms, or *zakat*, is also a pillar of Islam, and during religious periods it is thought that the spiritual value of any *zakat* given doubles in value. Thus, much almsgiving to beggars happens during this period, particularly just after breaking the fast.

After sundown the party starts, with cities bursting into liveliness every night, particularly on the Jemaa el-Fnaa. Families will be out with children in tow, cafés and restaurants will open, and a seemingly endless promenade happens in the busy boulevards and medina streets, such as Casablanca and Tangier, while in the countryside, many of the smaller villages break into religious song and dance.

Travelers will find many cafés and restaurants serving primarily Moroccan clientele closed for the month, and most businesses, including banks, post offices, and government offices, keep shorter hours. Restaurants geared toward tourists, particularly in heavily touristed areas in Marrakesh, Agadir, and Essaouira, remain open during normal operating hours. Trains, buses, and other modes of public transportation are often delayed, and the entire pace of the country seems to slow to a crawl.

OTHER ISLAMIC HOLIDAYS

Besides Ramadan, the dates of other key Muslim holidays change on the Gregorian calendar each year. **Eid al-Fitr**, often called Eid es-Seghir or "the little holiday," marks the end of Ramadan. It is a period of festivity when things swing back to normal. Trains, buses, and *grands taxis* are often crowded just before and after this holiday. Eid al-Fitr will be in the month of May in 2020, 2021, and 2022, though days change according to the Islamic calendar.

The most important holiday during the Muslim year is **Eid al-Adha**, also known as Eid al-Kabir or "the big holiday." In French-speaking circles, this is also known as *la fête de mouton,* or "sheep festival." Eid al-Adha takes place two lunar months after the end of Ramadan, and it marks Abraham's willingness to sacrifice his son Ismael to God (similar to the Old Testament, though in the Old Testament it is Isaac who is offered as sacrifice). This is something like a multi-day Thanksgiving feast. In 2020, 2021, and 2022, Eid al-Fitr will be in the month of July, though days change according to the Islamic calendar.

Just before the feast, you will likely see sheep being transported around the country and tethered to rooftops and balconies. Occasionally, kids take their new sheep out to play with them in the front yard.

The first day of the holiday is marked by the slaughter of a sheep—thus the French reference to the holiday. Outside, streets are generally barren, with people inside with their families, except for the butchers who go door-to-door, slaughtering each family's sheep. Meanwhile, it is customary to burn the heads of the sheep in cauldrons. These are found on the corners in most neighborhoods, with young men looking after this task. Generally speaking, these holidays are a time of great joy in Morocco, with many families reunited after the long year and friends coming together again, though some Moroccans are beginning to regret the commercialization of the holiday.

Even more so than during Eid al-Fitr, expect all modes of transportation to be congested and traffic to be at a standstill just before and just after the holiday, as families move back and forth across the country visiting relatives or returning home. During the holiday itself nearly everything is shut down, including most city buses, and taxi drivers are a scarce commodity. It is not advisable to schedule travel over this time, unless you are staying with a family in the country or sticking to metropolitan cities such as Casablanca or Marrakesh.

Other Moroccan holidays include **Ashoura,** a festival occurring one lunar month after Eid al-Adha. During Ashoura children will often ask for presents, which has given rise, with the help of Western influence, to the character of Baba Ashoura, or Father Ashoura, a Moroccan take on Father Christmas. Traditionally, children are given small toys, particularly little drums, during this smaller festival. **Moharem,** the Islamic New Year, happens two lunar months after Eid al-Adha. The **Mouloud,** which is the celebration of the birth of the Prophet Mohammed, is also observed in Morocco.

OPENING HOURS

The opening and closing hours of many businesses and restaurants is fluid, to say the least. Don't be surprised to find a museum or restaurant opening half an hour or later after a stated opening time. National holidays and religious holidays will also affect opening and closing times for most local businesses.

PUBLIC HOLIDAYS

In addition to the observed Islamic holidays, some national holidays are fixed to the Gregorian calendar. Many of these holidays are observed by government institutions and banks, though otherwise it is business as usual. The dates and corresponding holidays are as follows:

- **January 1:** New Year's Day
- **January 11:** Proclamation of Independence (1944 declaration of independence from France)
- **May 1:** Labor Day
- **July 30:** Throne Day (King Mohammed VI ascends to throne)
- **August 20:** Revolution of the King and the People (King Mohammed V returns from exile in 1955)
- **August 21:** Youth Day and King's Birthday (King Mohammed VI's birthday)
- **November 6:** Green March (1975 demonstration that annexed Western Sahara into Morocco)
- **November 18:** Independence Day (independence from France in 1956)

RESTROOMS

For the most part you'll find sitting toilets, though squatting toilets are common—particularly in poorer areas, less-expensive hostels, and in bathrooms at roadside cafés. Public restrooms are fairly easy to find, though often untidy (if not downright filthy), despite having an attendant. Tip attendants, particularly if the bathroom is fairly clean; 2Dh-5Dh is standard.

When traveling, it is a very good idea to bring your own roll of toilet paper. Many public restrooms in Morocco lack this basic necessity. It is customary for Moroccans to use water when cleaning in lieu of paper.

Health and Safety

COMMON HEALTH PROBLEMS

Beyond the effects of jet lag for those crossing the Atlantic, there are few health problems to be worried about in Morocco.

ALTITUDE SICKNESS

For those hiking the mountains, particularly the High Atlas, and particularly those peak bagging, altitude sickness can be a concern. It's best to wait until your body adjusts to being in Morocco before beginning any ascent. Altitude sickness generally occurs after 2,400 meters (about 8,000ft). There are quite a few peaks in the High Atlas well over this, including Toubkal at 4,167 meters (13,671ft), Immouzzer at 4,010 meters (13,156ft), and Timesquida at 4,089 meters (13,415ft). However, even the passes through the High Atlas climb well above the commonly accepted threshold for altitude sickness, reaching heights near 3,000 meters (about 10,000ft). Common symptoms of altitude sickness include headache, fatigue, stomach pains, dizziness, and an inability to sleep. Usually, effects subside in 1-2 days, though if they persist, you should descend. Avoid drinking alcohol, particularly when your body is first adjusting to the higher altitudes, as this can exacerbate symptoms and effects.

TAP WATER

By and large tap water is okay to drink. In fact, many seasoned travelers suggest that drinking the local water helps to acclimate your body to the local bacteria normally found in the water that is used to clean fruits and vegetables, and can be an effective way to avoid upset stomachs and diarrhea. However, in the older medinas you should stick to bottled water, available everywhere. It's also possible to carry a refillable bottle and use the numerous local fountains.

TRAVELER'S DIARRHEA

By far the most common health complaint of visitors to Morocco is traveler's diarrhea. This is contracted through eating foods that have not been properly washed or cooked or water that has been contaminated with unfamiliar bacteria. This bacteria

enters the body and acts like a mild food poisoning. Symptoms include a low-grade fever, stomach pains, loose stool movements, nausea, and sometimes vomiting. Usually within 1-3 days symptoms will go away. Eat only well-cooked and well-washed foods. Drink bottled water to stay hydrated. Locals recommend liberal doses of cumin coupled with a hot oregano infusion, as these both have antibacterial properties and help to flush unwanted bacteria from your system. Others recommend Coca-Cola. You could also pack loperamide (Imodium A-D).

HEALTH MAINTENANCE

Of course, you should travel with **medical insurance.** Check with your insurance agency to see about coverage in Morocco. Often major credit card companies offer travel insurance automatically or for a small additional fee when you use their credit card to book your plane ticket. Be sure to read the small print and contact your credit card company if you have any questions. Travel insurance generally covers any medical expenses, as well as theft, canceled or delayed flights, lost luggage, and any other manner of mishap, though extreme sports, such as kayaking, surfing, and rock-climbing, will only be covered if you pay a premium.

Of the hazards you may face in Morocco, **snakes** and **scorpions** are of a little concern. The Sahara is host to a few poisonous types of snakes, and scorpions are fairly common. It is best to wear thick-soled shoes (not flip-flops), walk with care through heavy brush, beware of turning over loose stones when in the desert, and be sure to shake out your shoes as a precautionary measure before putting them on. If bitten or stung, treat it as a medical emergency as it can be deadly if left untreated. **Dogs and monkeys,** though more of a nuisance, can be rabid. There are many wild dogs, particularly in the mountains, and they are pests to many hikers. Carry a few rocks in your pocket while hiking. You can slowly back away from the wild dogs' territory while threatening to throw a rock or, if they get too close, throwing it at their feet. If bitten, a rabies vaccination is required.

Sunstroke, heat exhaustion, and **dehydration** can be major concerns, even in the cooler mountains. Morocco's sun is strong, and the heat can be intense. Always travel with a light sunhat, drink plenty of fluids, and wear high SPF sunscreen. These are particularly important precautions for young travelers, who are more susceptible to the effects of the Moroccan sun. Symptoms of heatstroke include high body temperature, dizziness, and nausea. This is potentially fatal. Attempt to lower the body temperature through cool baths or showers before seeking help. Dehydration is always a potential problem. Make sure to drink plenty of fluids, especially if symptoms, such as headaches or lack of urination, are apparent.

MEDICAL SERVICES

For major medical emergencies, contact your consulate. Though all large cities in Morocco have public hospitals, often private clinics provide better, more hygienic service. If at all possible, make for Rabat, host to the best public hospitals and private clinics. Every major city and town will also have pharmacies, including the local *pharmacies de garde,* which are the all-night and off-hour pharmacies. You'll find a list of these posted at every pharmacy in the city. Pharmacists can often recommend local doctors. The **US Consulate** keeps a page of **recommended doctors and physicians** (http://morocco.usembassy.gov), including those who speak English.

EMERGENCY NUMBERS

For **police** in urban areas, dial 19. Outside of urban areas, dial 177 for the **Gendarmerie Royal.** For **firefighters** or **medical emergencies,** dial 15. For **roadside assistance,** dial 5050. For the **operator,** dial 160. Though sometimes you will find someone that speaks English, generally it is good to have someone who can speak French or Arabic call.

If you have a health, safety, or legal emergency, consider contacting the following numbers:

Australian and Canadian citizens can call collect to reach the **Emergency Watch and Response Centre** (Canada tel. 613/996-8885).

New Zealanders will need to call their consulate in Spain during working hours (tel. +34 915 230 226).

UK citizens should call their consulate emergency number (tel. 0537/633 333).

US citizens should dial the **American Citizen Services hotline** (tel. 0522/642 099 Mon.-Fri. 8am-5pm, tel. 0661/131 939 after hours).

South African citizens should contact their embassy (tel. 0537/689 159, 0537/700 874, or 0537/689 163).

CRIME

The crime rate in Morocco is quite low and violent crimes are a rarity. As anywhere else, tourists are marks for thieves and pickpockets. Muggings are uncommon, even in the dark, twisting paths of the medina. Stealth is more likely, with pickpockets slipping hands into the purses of distracted pedestrians or perhaps breaking into hotel rooms, particularly in Agadir. Travelers have been known to have phones or laptops snatched from café tables, as well. Police are hesitant to file any paperwork for stolen goods or money, though they will always give you a form for a stolen ID or passport.

HARASSMENT

Sexual harassment is often a problem experienced by women travelers, who are targeted by aggressive males. It is best to act confident, let it be known that you do not appreciate the lewd comments or suggestions, and if touched, grabbed, or fondled, feel free to yell at the offending man in public. A simple *"hashooma!"* (meaning "shame on you!"), said loudly, clearly, and confidently in a public space should be enough to attract unwanted attention to the man and cow him into submission.

Women might consider dressing so as to show as little skin as possible and avoid tight-fitting clothes. Baggy pants, long skirts, and long-sleeved shirts that cover as much skin as possible can deter much unwanted attention. Some women enjoy traveling with a loose scarf that can be shawled around the head and even the face, when they feel the stares are becoming too much. Though this might deter some men, the fact is sexual harassment is a real issue in Morocco.

Another form of harassment comes from street vendors and children. They can be sticky, to say the least. Street vendors generally won't leave their storefronts, so you won't have to worry about them following

you, though faux guides and young children have made trailing tourists something of a bothersome art form in some of the medinas. Often when walking through the medina you may find yourself with a small group of children, usually young boys, asking for money or to guide you through the medina. You may have to repeat *"la"* (Moroccan for "no") many, many, many times before the boys get the hint. If they become aggressive or if you are particularly worn out, usually saying *"la, baraka, saafi"* (meaning "no, that's enough, really enough") is enough to deter them from bothering you anymore. The same goes for faux guides, many times found at the major entrances of the medinas.

DRUGS

Hashish, kif, and majoun, all derivatives from marijuana, are by far the most seen, smelled, and used drugs in Morocco. Smoking marijuana is illegal, though tolerated almost everywhere in Morocco. Among the affluent, particularly nightclubbers and partygoers, cocaine and ecstasy are also commonly seen and used. Penalties for these drugs are severe. Tourists should beware of scams involving the police and bribery, particularly in the Rif. If arrested, contact your consulate. They cannot provide legal service, though they can recommend a lawyer.

Under no circumstances should you attempt exporting any amount of any drug to Spain or the rest of Europe. Border controls are tight and the penalties severe.

SMOKING

Smoking is widely permitted in restaurants and hotels. There are occasionally nonsmoking areas, though the ventilation is often inadequate to make them truly smoke-free.

Women smoke in Morocco, more often in the cities, but there is still a cultural taboo against it.

During the holy month of Ramadan, Muslims are required to abstain from many things, including smoking. It would be very rude to smoke in the open during the daytime over the course of this month. If you need a cigarette, try to keep it to your accommodation, where the staff are trained to be much more tolerant toward those not abstaining.

Travel Tips

MONEY

CURRENCY

The unit of currency of Morocco is the Moroccan dirham, listed throughout this guide as "Dh" and written on official exchanges as MAD. Banknotes come in denominations of 20, 50, 100, and 200 dirhams. Coins are in denominations of 1, 2, 5, and 10 dirhams. There are smaller coins called *centimes* that are divisions of 1 dirham; these come in denominations of 1, 2, 5, 10, and 20 centimes.

In Morocco, cash is king. Many venues and services do not accept credit or debit cards as payment. If possible, order Moroccan dirhams from your bank, perhaps 500-1,000Dh, before traveling to take care of taxis and emergencies. It's also a good idea to keep smaller bills (20s and 50s) and change on you at all times, as it can be hard to find someone to break larger notes. Euros, and sometimes US dollars, will be accepted in lieu of local currency, though at a less-than-desirable exchange rate.

EXCHANGE RATES

The Moroccan dirham is tied with the Euro and fluctuates accordingly. Check the exchange before your departure and keep in mind the difference between "buying" and "selling" a currency. Historically, exchange rates typically hover around 10Dh equal roughly to the following: 0.9 EUR, 0.8 GBP, 1 USD, 1.4 CAD, 14.5 ZAR, 1.5 AUD, or 1.5 NZD.

ATMS

Thankfully, ATMs are seemingly everywhere. You can find them at major banks throughout the *villes nouvelles* and near major transportation hubs, such as the airports and bus stations. ATMs all take credit and debit cards from around the world, though you should notify your bank that you are traveling. If you are unable to take money out of a machine, it is most likely because your bank or credit card company has issued a stop on your card. You will have to contact them to reactivate your card.

Most ATMs have options for instructions in English. North Americans should keep in mind that "current account" means "checking account." Most ATMs have a daily withdrawal limit of 5,000Dh, though you will only be allowed to withdraw a maximum of 2,000Dh at a time. This can make expensive purchases sometimes a hassle if the seller does not accept credit or debit cards because of the multiple trips required to the cash machine. Most Moroccan ATMs charge a small fee for the transaction—generally around 20Dh. If given the option to do your transaction in Moroccan dirhams or another currency, choose Moroccan dirhams, as this will be less expensive and save unnecessary currency exchange fees.

CREDIT AND DEBIT CARDS

The use of credit and debit cards is something new in Morocco. Many shops, particularly smaller bazaars, accept only cash. It is always best to check ahead of time, but most accommodations take plastic, except for budget lodgings, which often take only cash.

Make sure to notify your bank at home of your travel plans so that your debit and credit cards will not be blocked. It can be a hassle to attempt to call outside of Morocco to unblock cards. Cards without a chip will not work at some sellers. Generally, for purchases you will not sign but will enter your PIN. It is a good idea to keep a separate card listing emergency numbers in your home country, including emergency bank contact numbers, in case of a blocked card. Keep this information separate from your wallet or purse.

In Morocco, there is sometimes a surcharge of 2-5 percent added to credit or debit card purchases. Often, credit card companies and banks also charge per usage and add a fee for currency conversion. Check with your company to see about exact charges and, as always, read the fine print to avoid unforeseen charges when returning home.

TIPPING

Tipping is quickly becoming something of a norm in Morocco. For a quick coffee or tea, you can leave a couple of dirhams. For a meal, you can expect to tip 5Dh, though in upscale restaurants a typical tip is 5-10 percent of the bill. You will also be expected to give change to the parking attendant, gas attendants, and porters (5-10Dh). Otherwise, tipping is at your discretion.

BUDGETING

Morocco is a country for almost any budget. True shoe-string budget travelers can find lodging for as little as 50Dh per night, if not free, in some limited cases. True five-star lodgings can be found littered throughout the country, catering to Hollywood types, oil barons, and shipping magnates. Most travelers will want to be sure to spend at least a few nights in a restored *riad* in the old cities of Morocco. These can be had for as little as 200Dh per night, or as much as 800-1,000Dh per night.

Moroccans eat extremely well for very little. Travelers wanting to cook their own meals will find that they can pretty easily feed a family of four on 200-300Dh for an entire week by shopping at the local markets. Most fruits and legumes are sold by the kilo. Root vegetables are generally 2-5Dh a kilo (about 2.2 pounds), while most fruits are 5-20Dh a kilo. Small berries are usually sold in 150-gram (one-third of a pound) baskets for 8-22Dh.

There are a number of street vendors that sell kebabs and traditional Moroccan street food for pocket change, while a night out at a very nice restaurant in Marrakesh costs about the same as a bistro in Paris (budget 300Dh per person).

Most travelers will enjoy mixing up types of lodgings and dining experiences. Generally speaking, it's a fine strategy to spend a few nights roughing it at some of the nicer hostels in places like Chefchaouen and Essaouira and then splurge on a nice *riad* in Fez or Marrakesh complete with a feast. Most lodgings will include breakfast with your stay.

If you plan ahead, you will save money and get some of the best accommodations. Right now, Morocco is experiencing more tourism than they have room for in some locations, so the best lodgings fill up six months ahead of time. Renting a car is another great way to potentially save some money and will allow you freedom to explore.

There is no "one size fits all" budget. You'll need an absolute minimum of 100Dh a day to survive, though 500Dh a day will give you some more freedom to experience some of the attractions and history and take advantage of a few nice meals and better lodgings, particularly if you're traveling with a friend on the same budget. Travelers looking to have the best possible experience with the least amount of hassle should consider a substantially larger budget of 3,500Dh a day, which will allow for a hired driver the entire time you're in the country, some fantastic lodgings, incredible meals, guided treks, cooking classes, Sahara desert glamping, and more. Still other travelers will budget even more for royal suites at every property they enjoy, Moroccan spa treatments, private yoga lessons, surf classes, and hot-air balloon rides over Marrakesh.

COMMUNICATIONS
PHONES AND CELL PHONES

Phone numbers in Morocco are 10 digits beginning with 05 for landlines followed by a two-digit city code. For example, the city code for Rabat and the area is 37. Thus, most phone numbers in Rabat begin with 0537. When in Morocco, it is generally not necessary to dial the 0 before numbers, though if your call does not work the first time, try it with the 0 prior to the number. Cellphones in Morocco start with 06 or 07.

To dial a phone number in Morocco:

From Australia, first dial 0011 (or + if using your cell phone), and then dial Morocco's country code (212), followed by the Moroccan phone number, omitting the 0 at the beginning.

From Canada or the US, first dial 011 (or + if using your cell phone), and then dial Morocco's country code (212), followed by the Moroccan phone number, omitting the 0 at the beginning.

From Europe, New Zealand, the UK, or South Africa, first dial 00 (or + if using your cell phone), and then dial Morocco's country code (212), followed by the Moroccan phone number, omitting the 0 at the beginning.

If you have an unblocked cell phone, it's worth purchasing a SIM card in-country for your travel to use for your phone. For about 20Dh you will have a local number with limited talk time and texts. For 200Dh, you will likely get enough Internet credit to use for a week or two on local 3G or 4G networks, which is sometimes faster than what you might find in London. Maroc Telecom (www.iam.ma), Orange (www.orange.ma), and Inwi (www.inwi.ma) are the major service providers in Morocco, with networks that operate around the country. Maroc Telecom features the widest network, though Orange has better download speeds in most metropolitan areas. You will find outlets for these providers along the main boulevards in the *villes nouvelles* of all the cities and in the Mohammed V Airport in Casablanca.

Having a smartphone can come in handy for all the usual tasks, and the GPS function can be a lifesaver when attempting to navigate unfamiliar city streets, follow winding medina paths, drive around the country, or look for a restaurant.

INTERNET

Internet access is widely available throughout the country. For some websites, the use of a VPN may be preferable. Wi-Fi is found at most accommodations, though sometimes only available in the public spaces, while Internet cafés can easily be found in all major cities and larger towns.

SHIPPING AND POSTAL SERVICE

One of the most common issues for shoppers is how to get all the special handwoven rugs and hand-spun pottery back home. In practice, nearly every shop in the medina can ship your items home for you. Even your new breakable will be expertly wrapped; shop owners are accustomed to providing this service. You will be informed of the cost of the shipping, though you will have to take care of customs if applicable in your home country.

Post offices are easily found around Morocco, often on the edges of the old cities and near tourist hubs, making sending letters and postcards easy and inexpensive. Visit the national post office website for more information: www.poste.ma.

WEIGHTS AND MEASURES

Morocco follows the metric system. Grams, liters, and kilometers are the primary units of measurement you'll be using on your trip. The country operates on the continental European 220-volt system, with electronics having two round plugs.

ACCESS FOR TRAVELERS WITH DISABILITIES

Though many people in Morocco have disabilities, public assistance is scarce and they are reliant on their families and the generosity of strangers for support. Moroccans are quick to help people with disabilities, but the infrastructure to assist those with disabilities, such as wheelchair ramps and signs in Braille, is basically nonexistent. Even in the new cities, you cannot expect to find sidewalk ramps. Most of the *villes nouvelles,* found in Agadir, Casablanca, and Marrakesh, and even the older medinas found in Marrakesh and Rabat, should be easy enough to navigate with assistance.

Buses and trains are comfortable enough, though boarding may prove difficult. The steep stairs and crush of people generally coming on and off will be worthy obstacles, to say the least. In this instance, *grands taxis* are generally a better idea. You can pay for two seats, having the entire front seat to yourself, and in the case you need help getting in or out or need any help with luggage, the driver and other passengers would normally be more than happy to help. Another option is to hire a driver for the course of your trip (200-300Dh a day) who can conveniently also double as a translator and guide through the country. Contact one of the tour companies if you're interested in hiring a driver. It may also be worth it to think about a packaged tour and put a company familiar with Morocco and its various challenges in charge of your travel in-country.

For the most part, remember that Morocco is predominantly a walking country, inside and outside. Outside, the old medinas generally have lots of slopes and narrow, often rocky, passageways, making the going tough for those with limited mobility. Most kasbahs, restored *riads,* and *dars* have oddly placed, often steep stairs, though some do offer lodgings on the ground floor, making stays possible. Some of the high-end lodgings, particularly in Agadir, Casablanca, and Marrakesh, have made changes to cater to mobility-impaired travelers, including accessible rooms and toilets, wheelchair ramps throughout, spacious elevators, and even special vans to assist those who might require the use of one for their stay. Of course, this luxury comes at a cost.

TRAVELING WITH CHILDREN

Morocco is a child's dream come true. There are many fascinating sights and sounds, and the people are very indulgent to children. Children are kissed, hugged, caressed, and often blessed by total strangers. For children not used to this sort of attention, it can be disconcerting at first, though usually after a day or two, they've gotten the swing of it and are happy to meet all these smiling strangers. For parents, this unwanted and unasked-for attention might come as a shock, but it is meant to entertain the children as much as to compliment the parents. It is part of the social fabric of the culture and should be embraced.

As paramount as child safety can be, you'll see many children playing in the streets, often late at night, without a parent in sight. In many ways, this is akin to the time in Europe or North America when children were turned loose in the streets to run around until they were tired. Other than the occasional fight between kids, there are no real dangers. The only potential dangers children face while traveling in Morocco are the many, many feral cats in the streets and the wild dogs in the more rural areas. Rabies, though rare, can be a concern. If a child is bitten, then precautions should be taken and a vaccination gotten immediately. Otherwise, the chaotic traffic, particularly in the cities, is something to be aware of.

Children under four generally travel and are lodged for free. Notify your accommodations ahead of arrival if you will be needing extra beds in your room. Higher-end hotel chains and resorts often have children's playgrounds and even baby-sitting services. There are parks and other entertainments geared especially for children.

Babies will often be coddled, and as a parent you will be complimented on the beauty of your child more times than you will be able to count. However, traveling with a baby does pose certain challenges. Breastfeeding can be awkward. Outside of the airports, there are no changing stations. It is best to breastfeed as discreetly as possible. Some women are comfortable doing this in train cars and on park benches and just use a loose cloth or thin scarf to cover. In Morocco, this is perfectly acceptable.

You can find supplies, including disposable diapers and baby food, at local stores and at the larger grocery store chains, such as Carrefour and Marjane, both usually located on the outskirts of town. Outside of major cities, however, supplies can be more difficult to find, so stock up. If you need hot water or milk for formula, any restaurant or café will be able to help, and more than likely you'll find assistance a notch kinder than in North America or Europe.

The sun in Morocco can be particularly strong. Children are prone to sunstroke. It is best to keep children out of the hot afternoon sun, layered with high-SPF sunscreen (available at any pharmacy in Morocco), and hydrated with plenty of water. Kids can also be more sensitive than adults to the stressful effects that travel has on our bodies. This may manifest itself in a longer-than-normal period of jet lag, upset stomach, or cold-like symptoms. Because of this, light food and plenty of rest are recommended for the first 2-3 days in-country.

WOMEN TRAVELING ALONE

Overall, Morocco is a perfectly safe destination for women travelers. Adventurous single women travelers often make new friends, are invited to family homes, and bring back stories to share, along with a few souvenirs. That said, sexual harassment is a real issue in Morocco, though this is felt in some places more than others. In the cities, particularly Agadir, Casablanca, Essaouira, and Marrakesh, women traveling alone are rarely bothered more than other tourists or foreigners. Women alone or in pairs can expect catcalls as well as more vulgar comments, though if you don't understand Moroccan Arabic, this will probably go unnoticed. Older men will sometimes flirt, though this is generally not meant to be taken seriously, while young men can be not only vulgar, but persistent. This is particularly the case in more rundown parts of cities and in less-affluent areas. Be firm, though not aggressive; make it clear that you want nothing to do with them, and find a populated area or duck into a shop. Consider finding a pack of like-minded people, whether as part of a guided tour or at the local hostel, to accompany you through the medinas. Some ability in French or Arabic is recommended, and, as always, confidence is a must.

While in rural areas, keep in mind that a woman traveling alone, without the company of her husband, father, brother, or cousin, or even with a group of her friends, is viewed suspiciously. If you drink, smoke, or walk around remote towns at night, most people will think you are looking for companionship. At the very least, you will be seen as something *zeen*—that is, encouraging sinful behavior. Most Moroccan women appear diffident, if not snobbish, in public. This is for good reason. If you are seen as smiling easily in the company of men, too friendly, or too physical—that is, if you touch their arms or hands, hug them or kiss them on the cheeks when greeting—these are all seen as cues to the men that you are coming on to them.

Agadir and the beaches around it are the most touristed by Europeans and showing skin is the norm, though elsewhere in Morocco, particularly away from the beaches, it is discouraged. As a rule of thumb, the less skin you show, the better, which will also protect you from the sun. For visiting any religious monument, such as

NAVIGATING THE MEDIEVAL MEDINAS OF MOROCCO

Most Moroccan cities have an older neighborhood dubbed the *medina*. Literally, *medina* means "city" in Arabic, though in this context, it is meant to mean "the old city." Most medinas are smaller, usually only a handful of city blocks across, and are a fun distraction for a morning. However, the older, expansive, sprawling, labyrinthine medina Marrakesh is a veritable maze filled with sights and smells that can disorient even the most travel-hardened. Here are some tips for exploring the medina:

- Be sure to be well rested and wear a suitable pair of **walking shoes.**

- Have some small **Moroccan money** on you—5Dh and 10Dh coins will be invaluable for snacks or help along the way.

- Having a **map,** whether in this guide or downloaded on your phone, is also a good idea. Mark your starting point.

- Remember that people don't know **street names** in Morocco. It's better to know the name of your **accommodation** and a **local landmark** you can return to.

- You will likely encounter **fake guides** and young boys along the way who will ask you if you are looking for something in particular, like the tanneries. A firm and persistent "no" is your only defense against these hustlers.

- **Store owners** can also be sticky, sometimes holding you by the elbow or arm to get you to visit their shop, sip a tea, and hopefully spend your money.

- To find your way out of the medina when you're lost, it's often a good strategy to **follow a main thoroughfare** until you find something you recognize or a door out of the old city, where you can find a taxi to take you somewhere you might be more familiar with, such as the Jemaa el-Fnaa in Marrakesh.

If all else fails, feel free to enlist the help of one of those pesky hustlers asking you where you want to go; 10Dh is usually enough, though they will always ask for more.

---

the Hassan II Mosque in Casablanca, you will need to cover your shoulders and have your legs covered beyond the knee. Some women feel most comfortable carrying a light scarf that can be used to cover their head to blend in with local women, though this is not necessary.

SENIOR TRAVELERS

Morocco is a country that still has a profound respect for its elders. This carries over to visitors from other countries, as well. Well-traveled, adventurous tourists of a certain age will feel right at home in Morocco. If you take medication or supplements, be sure to bring enough for the length of your stay. It can also be helpful to know the French equivalent of the generic medicine (unbranded) before you arrive so that you can likely track it down at a local pharmacy or notify a doctor if need be. You should also talk to your doctor at home about your trip and any dietary restrictions you should be aware of. For instance, if you're taking an ACE inhibitor, you will want to stay away from bananas. Travelers diarrhea is a real concern in Morocco. It helps to stick to fully cooked foods. You might want to consider packing some loperamide (Imodium A-D).

Keep in mind that Morocco is not a wheelchair-friendly country and lacks much of the infrastructure required for the mobility impaired. In larger cities, you may be more of a target for pickpockets and purse snatchers, so take care to keep your important documents on your body. It's a neat trick to leave the sign on the door of your hotel turned to "do not disturb." This can ward off potential intruders in your hotel room.

Otherwise, take care to protect yourself from the hot sun, apply liberal doses of sunscreen, pack your best pair of walking shoes, and stay hydrated. Morocco is very much a country to experience on your two feet, whether it's trekking through the High Atlas or wandering the medieval medina of Marrakesh.

LGBTQ TRAVELERS

For many years Morocco was a haven for the LBGTQ community in Europe. Cities like Marrakesh developed a reputation for being liberated places that, despite the local culture, tolerated and even accepted practices that were derided, lampooned, and prosecuted in Europe. Today, the culture has swung more current conservative, and unfortunately Morocco is no longer quite the safe haven it once was. However, Marrakesh and other major destinations like Essaouira and Agadir are still popular with much of the European LGBTQ crowd. In general, LGBTQ travelers will feel most welcomed in the higher-end accommodations and should keep discrete in the public sphere.

Homosexual travelers, particularly men, should understand that engaging in homosexual behavior (such as kissing on the lips) is illegal in Morocco and punishable by a fine and/or jail time. (Same-sex friends kissing on the cheeks and holding hands is not uncommon, though holding hands is falling out of fashion among men.)

For the most part foreigners are generally not bothered unless officials believe it to be possible that prostitution is happening. This is particularly the case if older foreigners are seen in the company of young Moroccans. Gay men should also be cautious if out on the town or using online dating sites. Moroccan men have been known to seduce foreign men to try to scam money from them. A common scam is to offer to go back home with you, only to steal stuff from your hotel room. When at nightclubs and bars, keep one eye on your drink and refuse drinks from strangers.

Around Marrakesh and in high-end hotels and *riads* around the country, particularly foreign-owned ones, same-sex couples shouldn't worry about sharing a bed. However, in budget and midrange accommodations or accommodations owned by Moroccans, caution should be taken and discretion is advised.

TRAVELERS OF COLOR

Morocco is an incredibly diverse country, and Moroccans are used to travelers visiting the country from all over the world. However, physical traits can be a subject of comment. Black travelers might be asked if they are a popular public figure (like Barack Obama, Beyoncé, or Oprah) or somehow related. There may even be a request for a selfie; feel free to politely decline. This is all meant in good humor and not intended to offend. It's primarily a hustle to sell an item or service.

As wonderful as Morocco can be, there is some racism, though most Moroccans will not easily admit this. With the rise of immigration from Sub-Saharan Africa, tensions have risen between Moroccans and other African countries. If a store owner or taxi driver thinks you might be from somewhere south of Morocco, you might find yourself being entirely ignored, particularly in newer parts of Casablanca, where immigration is most prevalent.

Tourist Information

TOURIST OFFICES

Tourist offices can be notoriously difficult to find and are generally not in the most touristed parts of town. I've included the addresses and hours of operation for the offices in major destinations. If you're interested in festivals and events, the local tourist offices will invariably have the most up-to-date information and nearly always have at least one person who speaks good English.

MAPS

For most travelers, the maps in this guide should be sufficient to navigate the twisting and often confusing medinas and to get around the country without much trouble. In Morocco, maps can be difficult to find. Occasionally, bookstores, newsstands, or tourist information booths carry some sort of map, generally a free small map of the city and occasionally a road map. For the most part, it's better to purchase your maps outside of Morocco. Guidebooks and country maps that do not include the Western Sahara as part of Morocco are banned and liable to be confiscated upon arrival. This is something to remember when shopping for maps.

Drivers and cyclists should consider picking up the **Michelin road map** (1:4,000,000 with sectors of 1:600,000) or the waterproof **National Geographic Morocco map** (1:1,000,000). These maps include smaller roads between cities and towns and are essential for exploring some of Morocco's harder-to-reach places by car or bike.

Good topographical maps are essential for trekkers. The **Toubkal Trekking Map** (1:50,000) made by Cordee is the best topographical map. It's waterproof and should be the number one choice for hiking around Toubkal. The reverse side features a great map of Marrakesh. The second highest and arguably prettier range, M'Goun Massif, is highlighted in the **Central High Atlas Map** (1:100,000) produced by West Col.

Visit your local map specialist, travel bookstore, or independent bookstore, or browse maps and shop online with **Omni Map** (www.omnimap.com) for a great selection of Moroccan-specific maps and guides to help you on your journey.

If you're using your tablet or phone while traveling, be sure to download maps via the app Maps.me. Having a map of all the Moroccan cities you'll be exploring stashed in your pocket is a great idea.

Phrasebook

There are few countries as linguistically complex as Morocco. The official languages, Classical Arabic and Tamazight, are not used nearly as often as Moroccan Arabic, otherwise known as Darija, a creole-type language that people from most other Arabic-speaking countries have a hard time understanding. Darija is not standardized, so even in different regions of the country people use different words for things and sometimes misunderstand each other. So don't feel too bad if you have a hard time understanding or speaking Darija! However, learning a few words of Darija will go a long way in making your stay in Morocco that much more enjoyable and, especially outside the major metropolitan areas, a little smoother.

If you know some French, Spanish, Italian, or German, you might find these languages useful as well. English is often spoken around heavily touristed areas, but French is more common. For those traveling in the north, Spanish is much more commonly used and can come in handy as well. Keep in mind that like many European languages, such as French, Darija is also a gendered language with rules for "masculine" and "feminine" words and adjectives. Following basic convention, there are "masculine" and "feminine" translations below for the Darija and French when appropriate.

If you are really linguistically adventurous, you can try your hand at learning a few phrases in Tamazight, the language of the Amazigh, spoken mostly in rural areas. Of course, even this won't be easy, as the language has multiple regional dialects. Most Tamazight speakers also speak some Darija, if not other languages.

PRONUNCIATION

Some sounds in Darija (and Tamazight) do not have equivalents in English. They can only be explained phonetically or by finding the closest sound.

aa like the "ah" in "blah"

d an emphatic "d"; the closest pronunciation in English is "d" as in "dark"

gh close to the French "r" as in "Paris"

h a pharyngeal "h"; think of this as a "whispered h" sound, as no similar sound exists in English

j like the "s" in "illusion"

kh like the Spanish *jota* ("j") or the Scottish "ch" as in "loch"

q an emphatic uvular sound that doesn't exist in English; the closest pronunciation in English is "k" as in "key"

s an emphatic "s"; the closest pronunciation in English is "s" as in "massage"

t an emphatic "t"; the closest pronunciation in English is "t" as in "star"

y a stressed consonant "y"; sort of like the Chinese "y" in "Ying"

The **apostrophe** refers to a sound that does not exist in English called a pharyngealized glottal stop. In phonology, it is referred to as a creaky-voiced sound. Since the sound may be hard to pronounce, you can just skip the apostrophe sound and pronounce the vowel following it.

DARIJA AND FRENCH
BASIC AND COURTEOUS EXPRESSIONS

English	Darija (pronunciation)	French
Hello	assalaam 'alaykoom	Salut / Bonjour
Hello (response)	wa 'alaykoom assalaam	Salut / Bonjour
Good morning	sbaah el kheer	Bonjour
Good evening	msa el kheer	Bonsoir
Good night	tesbah 'alaa kheer	Bonne nuit
Thank you.	shokran	Merci.
Thank you very much.	shokran bezzaf	Merci beaucoup.
You're welcome.	laa shokran 'alaa waajib / marhba / al 'afoow	De rien / Je vous en prie.
Good-bye	beslama	Au revoir
please	'aafak	S'il vous plaît.
yes	yeh / na'am	oui
no	laa	non
Where are the restrooms?	Fin les toilettes?	Où sont les toilettes?
I don't know.	ma'arafetsh	Je ne sais pas.
Excuse me, please (when you're trying to get attention)	smahli, 'aafak	Excusez-moi, s'il vous plaît.
Excuse me / I'm sorry (when you've made a mistake)	smahli	Désolé (m.) / Désolée (f.)
enough	baraka / saafi	assez / ça suffit
How do you say ... in Darija?	keefash katqolo le ... b darija?	Comment dites-vous ... en Darija?
Do you speak English?	katehdar b lingliziya?	Parlez-vous anglais?
I don't speak Darija well.	ana makanehdarsh b darija mezyaan	Je ne parle pas bien darija.
Please speak more slowly.	'aafak hdar b tqala	Parlez plus lentement, s'il vous plaît.
I don't understand.	mafhametsh	Je ne comprends pas.
What is your name?	shenoo smitek?	Quel est votre nom? / Comment vous appelez-vous?
My name is ...	(ana) ismi / (ana) smitee ...	Je m'appelle ...
I am from ...	ana men ...	Je viens de(s) ...
I am American / Canadian / British / Australian / from New Zealand / South African.	ana men... america / kanada / ostralia / nyoozilanda / janoob ifriqia	Je viens... des Etats-Unis / du Canada / de l'Australie / de la Nouvelle-Zélande / de l'Afrique du Sud

English	Darija (pronunciation)	French
Pleased to meet you.	metsharfeen	Enchanté (m.) / Enchantée (f.)

TERMS OF ADDRESS

English	Darija (pronunciation)	French
Mr.; sir	sidi	Monsieur
Mrs.; Madam	lalla	Madame
Miss; young lady	lalla	Mademoiselle
woman	mra	femme
wife	zawja / mra	épouse / femme
man	rajel	homme
husband	zawj / rajel	époux / mari
friend	sadeeq (m.) / sadeeqa (f.)	ami (m.) / amie (f.)
girlfriend; boyfriend	sahebtee; sahbee	petite amie; petit ami
daughter; son	bent; weld	fille; fils
sister; brother	okht; akh	soeur; frère
mother; father	oom / walida; abb / walid	mère; père
grandmother; grandfather	jedda; jedd	grand-mère; grand-père

TRANSPORTATION

English	Darija (pronunciation)	French
Where is ...?	feen ...?	Où est ...? / Où se trouve ...?
How far is it to ...?	sh-haal ba'eed ...?	A quelle distance est ...?
from ... to ...	men ... le ...	de ... à ...
(intercity) bus station	mahaTa dial keeraan / mahaTa Toorooqiyya	gare routière
(city) bus station	mahaTa dial Tobiss	station d'autobus
taxi station	mahaTa dial Taxiyaat	station de taxis
Where is this (intercity) bus going?	feen ghadi had l-kar?	Où va ce bus?
Where is this (city) bus going?	feen ghadi had Tobiss?	Où va ce bus?
boat	babor / baaTo	bateau
airport	maTaar	aéroport
I'd like a ticket to ...	bghit wahed biyyé le ...	Je voudrais un billet pour ...

English	Darija (pronunciation)	French
reservation	rezervasion / hajez	réservation
baggage	bagaj	baggages
next flight	l-vol lli men ba'ad	vol prochain
Stop here, please.	weqaf hena, 'aafak	Arrêtez-vous ici, s'il vous plaît.
entrance	dakhla	entrée
exit	kharja	sortie
right	limeen	droite
left	lisaar / shmaal	gauche
straight ahead	neeshan	tout droit
in front	qebalt	en face de; devant
beside	hda / qeddam	à côté de
behind	mor	derrière
north; south	shamaal; janoob	nord; sud
east; west	sharq; gharb	est; ouest

ACCOMMODATIONS

English	Darija (pronunciation)	French
hotel	oTel	hôtel
Is there a room available?	kayen shi beet khaawee?	Avez-vous une chambre disponible?
May I (may we) see it?	moomkin nshoofoo (nshoofooh)?	Pourrais-je (pourrions-nous) la voir?
room	beet	chambre
single room	beet dial wahed	chambre simple
double room	beet doobl	chambre double
double bed	fraash doobl	lit double
single bed	fraash dial wahed	lit simple
with private bath	feeh hammaam	avec salle de bain
television	telfaza	télévision
window	sherjem	fenêtre
view	menDar	vue
hot water	l-ma s'khoon	de l'eau chaude
shower	doosh / doocha (Northern)	douche
towel	fooTa	serviette
soap	Saboon	savon
toilet paper	papié twalet	papier toilette

English	Darija (pronunciation)	French
pillow	m-khadda	oreiller
blanket	beTTaniyya	couverture
sheets	gh-Ta / sabana (Northern)	drap
air-conditioning	kleem	climatiseur / clim
fan	ferfaara	ventilateur
Turkish (or Moorish or Roman) bath	hammaam	bain turque
swimming pool	piseen	piscine
gym	jym	gym
bike	beshkliTa	bicyclette
key	saroot / meftah	clé
lock	qfel	serrure
safe	kofr for	coffre-fort
manager	mes-ool / moodeer	gérant
maid	moonaDifa	femme de ménage

FOOD

English	Darija (pronunciation)	French
I'm hungry.	fiyya joo'e	J'ai faim.
I'm thirsty.	fiyya le'Tesh	J'ai soif.
Table for two, please.	Tabla le jooj de nass, 'aafak (rarely used in budget restaurants; in mid-scale or fine-dining restaurants, use French)	Une table pour deux, s'il vous plaît.
food	makla	nourriture
menu	menoo	menu
order	Talab	commande
glass of ...	kaas dial ...	verre de / d' ...
fork	forsheTa	fourchette
knife	moos	knife
spoon	me'elqa	cuillère
napkin	zeef / mendeel	serviette
soft drink	monada	boisson non alcoolisée
coffee	qahwa	café
coffee with milk	qahwa nuss nuss / qahwa bel hleeb	café au lait
tea	atay	thé

English	Darija (pronunciation)	French
drinking water	l-ma dial shorb	eau potable
bottle (of)	qar'a (dial)	bouteille (de / d')
bottled carbonated water	qar'a dial l-ma ghaazi (or use "… dial walmas," after a brand name, Oulmès, turned generic)	eau gazéifiée en bouteille
bottled uncarbonated water	qar'a dial l-ma 'aadi	eau non gazeuse en bouteille
tap water	l-ma dial robiné	eau du robinet
beer	birra / servisa (Northern)	bière
wine	vin (French) / vino (Spanish/Northern)	vin
red wine	vin rouge	vin rouge
white wine	vin blanc	vin blanc
milk	hleeb	lait
juice	'aSeer	jus
cream	crem	crème
sugar	sookkar	sucre
breakfast	fToor	petit déjeuner
lunch	gh-da	déjeuner
dinner	'esha	dîner
Do you have vegetarian options?	'andek makla nabaatiyya? / 'andek makla bla l-ham?	Avez-vous des plats végétariens?
I'm vegetarian.	ana nabaati	Je suis végétarien.
I don't eat …	makanakoolsh …	Je ne mange pas …
Does it have …?	feeh (m.) …? / feeha (f.) …?	Il y a …?
without meat	bla l-ham	sans viande
without cheese	bla jben	sans fromage
Check, please.	lehsaab, 'aafak	L'addition, s'il vous plaît.
tip	poorbwar / propina (Northern)	pourpoire
Is the service included?	wash poorbwar dakhel?	Est-ce que le service est inclus?

SHOPPING

English	Darija (pronunciation)	French
money	floos	argent
cash	kash	espèces
change	Sarf	monnaie

English	Darija (pronunciation)	French
credit card	la karT (dial kredi)	carte de crédit
debit card	la karT	carte de débit
money exchange office	mahal dial Sarf	bureau de change
Do you accept credit cards?	kateqbel lé karT?	Acceptez-vous les cartes de crédit?
How much does this cost?	be sh-haal hada (m.)? / be sh-haal hadi (f.)?	Combien ça coûte?
Is there something cheaper?	kayen shi haja r-khas?	Y at-il quelque chose de moins cher?
value added tax	Tax	taxe sur la valeur ajoutée
discount	sold / takhfeeD / rebakha (Northern)	réduction / soldes
small grocery store	hanoot	épicerie
large grocery store	soopermarshi	supermarché

HEALTH

English	Darija (pronunciation)	French
Help me, please.	'aawenni, 'aafak	Aidez-moi, s'il vous plaît.
I am ill.	ana mreeD (m.) / ana mreeDa (f.)	Je suis malade.
Call a doctor	'ayyeT le Tbeeb	Appelez un docteur
hospital	SbiTaar	hôpital
clinic	klinik	clinique
drugstore	farmasya / Saydaliyya	pharmacie
pain; cramp	hreeq	douleur; crampe
burn (with fire)	horqa (bel 'afya)	brûlure
fever	s-khaana	fièvre
headache	hreeq raas	mal de tête
stomach ache	hreeq fe l-ma'eeda	mal d'estomac
nausea	dookha	nausée
vomit (verb)	t-qiyya	vomir
medicine	dwa	médicament
antibiotic	antibiotik	antibiotique
pill	keena / pastiyya (Northern)	pilule
aspirin	aspirin	aspirine
ointment; cream	pomada; krema	pommade; crème
bandage (big/small)	binda (kbeera/segheera)	bandage (grande/petite)
Band-Aid	sparadra	sparadrap

English	Darija (pronunciation)	French
cotton	q-Ton	cotton
sanitary napkin	serviet ijyenik / Always (in Darija, the brand name "Always" refers generically to a sanitary napkin)	serviette hygiènique
birth control pills	hooboob man'e el haml	pilules contraceptives
condoms	prezervatif	préservatifs
toothbrush	sheeta dial snaan	brosse à dents
dental floss	kheyT dial snaan	fil dentaire
toothpaste	dontifris	dentifrice
dentist	Tbeeb dial snaan	dentiste
toothache	hreeq fe snaan	mal aux dents
vaccination	jelba / talqeeh	vaccin

AT THE GAS STATION

English	Darija (pronunciation)	French
gas station	bomba / sTasion dial leSanS	station d'essence
gasoline	leSanS	essence
unleaded	son plom	sans plomb
diesel	mazoT	diesel
full, please	l-plen, 'aafak	Le plein, s'il vous plaît.
tire	rweeDa	pneu
air	le-hwaa (differentiate between /h/ and /h/ in this word to avoid confusing with the word for "fornication")	l'air
water	l-ma	l'eau
oil (change)	(beddel) zeet	vidange
car	Tomobeel	voiture
RV	karavan	caravane
motorbike	moTor	moto
4x4	kaTkaT	katkat (colloquial)
battery	batri	batterie
repair shop	mikanik	mécanicien
Can you clean my window, please?	msahli jaaj, 'aafak?	Pouvez-vous nettoyer ma fenêtre, s'il vous plaît?
My ... doesn't work.	... diali makhaddamsh	Mon ... ne marche pas.

NUMBERS

English	Darija (pronunciation)	French
zero	Sefer	zéro
one	wahed	un
two	jooj	deux
three	tlaata	trois
four	arb'aa	quatre
five	khamsa	cinq
six	setta	six
seven	seb'a	sept
eight	tmenya	huit
nine	tes'ood	neuf
10	'ashra	dix
11	hedaash	onze
12	Tenaash	douze
13	tleTaash	treize
14	rba'aTaash	quatorze
15	khamesTaash	quinze
16	seTaash	seize
17	sba'eTaash	dix-sept
18	tmenTaash	dix-huit
19	tse'eTaash	dix-neuf
20	'oshreen	vingt
21	wahed oo 'oshreen	vingt et un
22	tenayen oo 'oshreen	vingt-deux
23	tlaata oo 'oshreen	vingt-trois
30	tlateen	trente
31	wahed oo tlateen	trente et un
32	tenayen oo tlateen	trente-deux
33	tlaata oo tlateen	trente-trois
40	arb'een	quarante
50	khamseen	cinquante
60	setteen	soixante
70	seb'een	soixante-dix
80	tmaaneen	quatre-vingts
90	tes'een	quatre-vingt-dix
100	meya	cent

English	Darija (pronunciation)	French
101	meya oo wahed	cent un
200	meyateyn	deux cents
500	khamsemeya	cinq cents
800	temnemya	huit cents
1,000	alf	mille
10,000	'ashralaf	dix mille
100,000	meyat alf	cent mille
1,000,000	melyoon	un million
one half	noss	un demi
one third	tooloot	un tiers
one fourth	reba'e / raab'a	un quart

TIME

English	Darija (pronunciation)	French
What time is it?	sh-haal fe sa'a?	Quelle heure est-il?
It's one o'clock.	hadi lwehda	Il est une heure.
It's three in the afternoon.	hadi tlata dial le'shiya	Il est trois heures de l'après-midi.
It's three in the morning.	hadi tlata dial sbaah	Il est trois heures du matin.
six-thirty	setta oo noss	six heures et demi
quarter to eleven	hedash la roob'e	onze heures moins quart
quarter past five	khamsa oo rba'e	cinq heures et quart
minute	dqeeqa	minute
hour	sa'a	heure
late	me'aTal	tard
early	bekri	tôt
today	lyoom	aujourd'hui
tomorrow	ghadda	demain
yesterday	l-baarah	hier
morning	sbaah	matin
afternoon	le'shiya	après-midi
night	leel	soir
day before yesterday	wel baarah	avant-hier
day after tomorrow	ba'ad ghadda	après-demain
in an hour	men daba wahed sa'a	dans une heure
day	yoom	jour

English	Darija (pronunciation)	French
week	simana	semaine
month	sh-har	mois
after	ba'ad	après
before	q-bel	avant
holiday	'oTla	vacances

DAYS

English	Darija (pronunciation)	French
Monday	letneen	lundi
Tuesday	tlaata	mardi
Wednesday	larbaa'e	mercredi
Thursday	lekhmees	jeudi
Friday	joom'aa	vendredi
Saturday	sebt	samedi
Sunday	l-hadd	dimanche

MONTHS

Morocco follows both the Western (or Gregorian) calendar and the Muslim lunar calendar. The first is the one most used. The second is used mainly for religious holidays. Moroccans will generally use the name of the months in French, and in a few instances in classical Arabic, but don't be surprised if some refer to months by numbers ("Sh-har wahed" or Month 1 for January, "Sh-har jooj" or Month 2 for February, and so on). Be prepared to practice your numbers here, too.

English	Darija (pronunciation)	French
January	yenayer	janvier
February	febrayer	février
March	mars	mars
April	abril	avril
May	may	mai
June	yoonyoo	juin
July	yoolyooz	juillet
August	ghosht	août
September	september	septembre
October	october	octobre
November	nuvember	novembre
December	disamber	décembre

GOD-INVOKING EXPRESSIONS

English	Darija (pronunciation)
In the name of God	bismillah (used when you're about to start an action, such as eating, drinking, driving, or pouring tea)
May God save you from (that) evil	allah ya'afoo 'aleek
Thanks be to God/Praise be to God	alhamdulillah
May God help you	allah ye'awen (can be used to mean "good-bye," especially to service providers or people going to work)
If God wills / God willing	inshaa allah
God's blessings be upon you	tbarkellah 'aleek (used to compliment someone for effort or accomplishment)
May God bless you	allah ybaarek feek / baraka allaho feek (used in response to "tbarkellah 'aleek"; can be used to mean "thank you")
May God make it easy for you	allah ysahal / allah yejeeb tisseer (to a beggar if you don't have anything to give them)
May God have mercy on your parents	allah yerham waldeek (used to thank someone or to ask them for help)
Please; May God protect you	allah ykhalleek
May God help with recovery	allah yeshaafi
God forgives	allah ysameh (in response to an apology)
Condolences / May God greaten the good deeds	allah ye'aDem l-ajar
To your health	beSaha (to someone who has just taken a bath, had a haircut, bought something new, or had a nice time somewhere)

TAMAZIGHT

The language of the Amazigh is complex, heavily regionalized, and can be different from village to village. Knowing a few words in Tamazight is particularly helpful in the rural areas in the mountains and desert. Some of the more common phrases have been adopted from Darija.

English	Tamazight
Hello	la bas dereek (to a man) / la bas dareem (to a woman)
How are you?	iz tna ghrog (to a man)? / iz tna gh-rum (to a woman)?
I am good.	tnaa tia lman
Please	lyrham waladeen
Thank you.	barakaaloufeek

English	Tamazight
Do you speak English?	iz teewilt lingliziya?
What is your name?	msm minum?
My name is …	… ishm (m.) / … ishmini (f.)
I like (that).	tehbouh
Yes	eh / ayaa
No	la
How much (is that)?	sh-haal ooya
That's too much!	ighrla bezzaf
OK (agreement)	magheeden (literally "why not?")
hello	azoul
What is your name?	matgit sism?
My name is _____	ism inu _____
What is this?	maynna?
Can you help me?	is imkn ayyi taahwnt?
Delicious!	izel
How much (is this)?	mnashk atteskr?
good-bye	akkiahawn rabbi

Index

List of Maps

Acknowledgments

For a little over 10 years now, I've been taking the Marrakesh Express south into what is probably Morocco's most vibrant city. I've been lucky in my friends over these years, who are willing to lend me their time and, more importantly, restaurant suggestions! Seriously, though, they help me uncover the best addresses and most adventurous outings in their neighborhoods. Thanks to each and every one you for helping me put this guide together.

To Kamal Abdelfadil, Lahsen Alkouch, Abdelghani Bouimzgane, Driss el-Khoukhi, Brahim Jarrou, Hamid Jarrou, Naim Souhel, and Mohamed Tabalquit, thank you all so much for showing me around and taking the wheel when I was too tired to do otherwise. Omar Jellah, shokran khoya. You make the High Atlas magic. I wouldn't want to do a hike there without you. Amanda Ponzio-Mouttaki, your food tour (and blog!) are amazing! Keep doing great work and thanks for the scrumptious bites. Abdelkarim Tata, I couldn't do the Sahara without you. And thanks for the dates! Ilias el-Mejdoub, my man from Tetouan who is becoming more and more Casaoui each day, thank you so much for showing me your Casablanca and eating Indian with me. Last but not least, the shopping addresses found here would be so much less cool without my ever-stylish friend's input. Brigitte Grillon, *merci mille et une fois*.

A giant thanks for your hospitality and great food to the teams at Domaine Malika and Douar Samra in the High Atlas; Hotel Point du Jour in Casablanca; Kammy Hostel, Riad Boussa, Riad Chergui, and l'Hotel in Marrakesh; La Rose du Desert in Erfoud; Le Petit Riad in Ouarzazate; and the Chill Art Hostel and Riad Chbanate in Essaouira.

Megan, Hannah, Lucie, and Albert, my awesome team at Moon (Hachette), thanks for putting up with me. This book couldn't happen without you. Megan and Hannah, you take my writing to the next level. Lucie, you were wonderful working with me for the photos on this edition. *Chapeau*. And Albert, these maps are great! Thank you so much!

A giant *shokran bezzaf* to my family in Morocco for all of their patience with my Arabic, French, and Spanish, not to mention the authentic cultural insights that just wouldn't be possible otherwise: Souad Abbad, Nabiha Abbad, Mohktar Abbad, Lina Alouche, Celina Nana, and Mohcine Regragui. And another big thank you to my family and friends spread across the US, Europe, and the rest of the world for their unwavering support, especially Jill and Bob Stone; Dev, Nate, and Nicholas Prouty; Sylvain, Laura, and Miles Gasser; Mike, Zhueng and Mina Miello; Thomas Hollowell; Gregory Hubbs; Fazia Farrook; and Tahir Shah (who convinced me to quit the 9-5). You all make travel special.

Amina Lahbabi, my incredible Tangerina wife, took many of the photos that appear in these pages, has traveled Marrakesh and much of the south with me, as well as lent her translator's expertise to this phrasebook. *Hbiba*, your patience is without peer. I do not know how you put up with me when I'm stressing out about deadlines and travel logistics. I literally could not do this without you.

Photo Credits

MAP SYMBOLS

═══════ Expressway	○	City/Town	ⓘ	Information Center	♣	Park
═══════ Primary Road	◉	State Capital	₱	Parking Area	⛳	Golf Course
∿∿∿∿∿ Secondary Road	◉	National Capital	⛪	Church	✛	Unique Feature
⌐ ⌐ ⌐ Unpaved Road	◎	Highlight	🍷	Winery	🐟	Waterfall
---------- Trail	★	Point of Interest	🚩	Trailhead	△	Camping
·········· Ferry	•	Accommodation	🚉	Train Station	▲	Mountain
·━·━·━ Railroad	▼	Restaurant/Bar	✈	Airport	⛷	Ski Area
═══════ Pedestrian Walkway	■	Other Location	✗	Airfield	〰	Glacier
⋈⋈⋈⋈ Stairs						

CONVERSION TABLES

°C = (°F − 32) / 1.8
°F = (°C x 1.8) + 32
1 inch = 2.54 centimeters (cm)
1 foot = 0.304 meters (m)
1 yard = 0.914 meters
1 mile = 1.6093 kilometers (km)
1 km = 0.6214 miles
1 fathom = 1.8288 m
1 chain = 20.1168 m
1 furlong = 201.168 m
1 acre = 0.4047 hectares
1 sq km = 100 hectares
1 sq mile = 2.59 square km
1 ounce = 28.35 grams
1 pound = 0.4536 kilograms
1 short ton = 0.90718 metric ton
1 short ton = 2,000 pounds
1 long ton = 1.016 metric tons
1 long ton = 2,240 pounds
1 metric ton = 1,000 kilograms
1 quart = 0.94635 liters
1 US gallon = 3.7854 liters
1 Imperial gallon = 4.5459 liters
1 nautical mile = 1.852 km

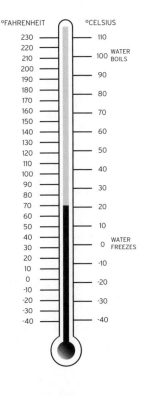

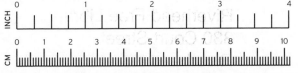

MOON MARRAKESH & BEYOND
Avalon Travel
Hachette Book Group
1700 Fourth Street
Berkeley, CA 94710, USA
www.moon.com

Editor: Megan Anderluh
Graphics and Production Coordinator: Lucie Ericksen
Cover Design: Faceout Studios / Derek Thornton
Interior Design: Megan Jones Design
Moon Logo: Tim McGrath
Map Editor: Albert Angulo
Cartographers: John Culp, Brian Shotwell, and Albert Angulo
Proofreader: Lina Carmona
Indexer: Gina Guilinger

ISBN-13: 978-1-64049-794-8

Printing History
1st Edition — February 2020
5 4 3 2 1

Text © 2020 by Lucas Peters.
Maps © 2020 by Avalon Travel.

Front cover photo: shopping in the Marrakesh Medina © Andy Smith / Sime / eStock Photo
Back cover photo: Moroccan *gimbri* is used to play traditional *Gnawa* music © Lucas Peters
Inside cover photo: a cat at the Hassan II Mosque in Casablanca © Lucas Peters

Printed in China by RR Donnelley